1982
—
1

Pears Encyclopaedia

of

Myths and Legends

Pears Encyclopaedia
of
Myths and Legends

The Ancient Near and Middle East
BY SHEILA SAVILL

Classical Greece and Rome
BY ELIZABETH LOCKE AND SHEILA SAVILL

GENERAL EDITORS: MARY BARKER AND CHRISTOPHER COOK

PELHAM BOOKS

Acknowledgments

We wish to express our warm gratitude to Professor Geoffrey Parrinder for so kindly reading this book and for his generous foreword. We are also grateful to Philippa Lewis, who sought out the illustrations; to Donald Shewan, Department of Cartography, Queen Mary College, London, who drew the map; and last, but by no means least, to Eric Marriott of Pelham Books, our long-suffering publisher.

In any work of this type, it is possible for errors and omissions to occur. Both the authors and editors would be most grateful if any such errata could be brought to their notice.

CI JUL. 31 1979

First published in Great Britain by
Pelham Books Ltd, 52 Bedford Square,
London, WC1 1976

© 1976 by Sheila Savill, Elizabeth Locke,
Mary Barker and Christopher Cook

ISBN 0 7207 0834 6

Filmset and printed in Great Britain by
BAS Printers Limited, Wallop, Hampshire

Contents

Illustrations

Nut and Geb are separated. To the left a ram symbolises Osiris; a goose, Geb as the Great Cackler. Papyrus of Tameniu, XXI Dynasty. British Museum. (*Photo: Michael Holford.*) p. 63

Bronze head of Ra, *c.* 850 B.C., probably from the prow of a solar barque. It originally bore a solar disc and *uraeus* of which only the *uraeus'* tail remains. British Museum. (*Photo Michael Holford.*) p. 65

Bas-relief of the lion-goddess Sekhmet. (*Photo: Mansell Collection.*) p. 66

Nun, god of the primordial waters, raises the boat of day as Khepri pushes forth the dawn sun. Supported by Osiris, Nut receives the solar disc. Papyrus of Anhia, XX Dynasty. British Museum. (*Photo: Photoresources.*) p. 68

Bronze figure of Sebek, Ptolemaic period. British Museum. (*Photo: Michael Holford.*) p. 70

Bronze statuette of Isis suckling Horus. British Museum. (*Photo: Michael Holford.*) p. 72

XXV Dynasty statuette of Neith of Sais wearing the red crown of Lower Egypt. British Museum. (*Photo: Michael Holford.*) p. 75

Lightning symbol of the Assyrian storm-god Adad, from a boundary stone *c.* 1120 B.C. British Museum. (*Photo: Michael Holford.*) p. 77

Ninth-century Phoenician ivory caryatids of Astarte, found at Nimrud in Assyria. British Museum. (*Photo: Mansell Collection.*) p. 79

Papyrus painting of the *ba* hovering over its mummified body. British Museum. (*Photo: Michael Holford.*) p. 80

Bronze figure of Bast with attendant cats, *c.* XXII Dynasty. British Museum. (*Photo: Mansell Collection.*) p. 81

Winged goddess possibly Beltiya or Ishtar from the palace of Ashurbanipal II (883–859 B.C.). British Museum. (*Photo: Mansell Collection.*) p. 83

A Phoenician figure of the Egyptian god Bes. Barracco Museum, Rome. (*Photo: Mansell Collection.)* p. 84

The cow-goddess Hathor, wearing the solar disc and *uraeus*, suckles the (obliterated) Queen Hatshepsut (*c.* 1503–*c.* 1482 B.C.). (*Photo: Ronald Sheridan.*) p. 86

Horus Behdety wearing the white crown of Upper Egypt. Statue from his temple at Edfu. (*Photo: Michael Holford.*) p. 87

Papyrus painting of the Egyptian god Khons wearing the war crown. (*Photo: Michael Holford.*) p. 89

Bronze statuette of the god Min wearing the war crown and solar disc. British Museum. (*Photo: Michael Holford.*) p. 91

Limestone statue of the Assyrian god Nebo from Nimrud, *c.* 800 B.C. British Museum. (*Photo: Mansell Collection.*) p. 92

King Urnashi of Lagash (*c.* 2630 B.C.), attended by his heir Akurgal and retainers, helps to build a temple to the god

Ningirsu and later celebrates its completion. Louvre. (*Photo: Mansell Collection.*) p. 93

Statuette of the Egyptian god Ptah from the tomb of Tutankhamun (*c.* 1361–*c.* 1352 B.C.). (*Photo: Ronald Sheridan.*) p. 95

Seventh-century B.C. clay tablet with outline map of the world, surrounded by the waters of the Persian Gulf. Beyond lie various mysterious regions denoted by the triangles. The text describes the conquests of King Sargon of Agade. British Museum. (*Photo: B. Museum.*) p. 95

The Egyptian goddess Selket protecting the canopic chest of Tutankhamun. (*Photo: Roger Wood*). p. 96

Symbol of the Akkadian moon-god Sin, from a boundary stone, *c.* 1120 B.C. British Museum. (*Photo: Michael Holford.*) p. 97

The Egyptian goddess Tefnut as the lynx, kills the wicked snake Apophis. XIX Dynasty papyrus of Hunefur. British Museum. (*Photo: Photoresources.*) p. 98

The ibis-headed Egyptian god Thoth. Painted relief from the tomb of Amon at Karnak. (*Photo: Roger Wood.*) p. 99

The lion gate of the citadel at Mycenae, thirteenth century B.C., looking towards the plain of Argos. (*Photo: Charisiades, Athens.*) p. 106

Linear B script on a Minoan tablet found in the 'Palace of Nestor' at Pylos. (*Photo: Mansell Collection.*) p. 107

The Titanomachia depicted on a frieze from Delphi, *c.* 525 B.C. (*Photo: Mansell Collection.*) p. 115

Graeco-Etruscan bronze figure of Athene (Minerva) in her aspect as a warrior goddess. British Museum. (*Photo: Mansell Collection.*) p. 120

Greek relief *c.* 460 B.C., possibly once part of an altar, shows two nymphs helping Aphrodite from the sea. Ludovici Boncompagni alle Terme Museum, Rome. (*Photo: Mansell Collection.*) p. 122

Black-figured painting on an amphora shows Leto holding the twins Apollo and Artemis. British Museum. (*Photo: Michael Holford.*) p. 124

Painting from the inside of a fifth-century B.C. cup, shows Apollo pouring a libation, watched by his cult bird, the raven. Delphi Museum. (*Photo: Photoresources.*) p. 126

The ' Diana of Versailles', thought to be a copy of a fourth-century B.C. original, perhaps by Leochares. Louvre. (*Photo: Mansell Collection.*) p. 128

Red-figured Attic vase painting, 490–480 B.C., shows Triptolemus honouring Demeter and Persephone. British Museum. (*Photo: Mansell Collection.*) p. 133

Dionysus in his transformed boat surrounded by the erstwhile pirates, now dolphins. Interior of a black-figured cup by the artist Exekias, *c.* 535 B.C. Staatliche Antikensammlungen, Munich. (*Photo: Mansell Collection.*) p. 134

Colour Plates

Foreword

'And is it true?' asked Belloc after writing a cautionary satire and concluded that it was not, though it struck near the bone. In the nineteenth century a myth was thought to be untrue, opposed to reality, whether it was the creation of Adam or the genealogies in Hesiod. These were regarded as fables or fairy tales whereas, according to Mr Gradgrind, 'facts alone are wanted in life. Plant nothing else, and root out everything else.'

In modern times comparative studies of religion and mythology, strongly supported by psychology, have revealed again the importance of myths. And one 'fact' that confronts us immediately is that myths have universally been thought to express truth, not mere detail of present existence but primordial and eternal reality. The myth is real and sacred, and it serves as an example in providing a pattern for human behaviour and an explanation of its mysteries. These elements can be seen in great modern myths. In Communism, quite apart from economic theory, there is a revival of Jewish and Christian mythical themes in the redemptive role of the innocent, the proletariat, the inevitable struggle of good and evil, and faith in a coming Golden Age. At a lower level the Nazi myths, held recently by millions of intelligent and educated people, propounded the myth of the chosen people, the master-race, and tried to revive Nordic paganism with its doom of the world and destruction in chaos. Other myths, about the Empire on which the Sun never Set, or the American Way of Life, had their potency but were also subject to the weakness of modern mythology in not being sufficiently anchored in age-old symbolism and therefore inadequate to represent lasting reality. But psychology has shown also that the dreams and fantasies of modern men, formerly dismissed by rationalists as nonsensical, often repeat great themes of mythology and produce their effect upon the unconscious and half-conscious behaviour of individuals.

An authoritative and comprehensive collection of myths such as this book provides, therefore, is of absorbing interest and topical significance. It may seem extreme to begin in Mesopotamia, but that was where much of the mythology first emerged which framed the culture of the near eastern and western worlds. The names of the deities are often strange to us but the themes of creation, earthly paradise, division and suffering, are of perennial interest. Myths of floods, god-men or super-men, sun and storm deities, fights with dragons and visits to the underworld, read better than much science-fiction. In Egypt the great stories of Isis and Osiris, among many others, expressed human and eternal motifs of love and grief, death and resurrection.

It has been said that the Greek Olympians were models of a warrior aristocracy, though they were more than this; they ate and drank enormously, made war and love, and never did a stroke of honest work. In this they resembled the gods of the Indian Vedas, who were also aristocratic but more devout. But below both classes there were other potent figures for working people. Demeter, the earth and fertility mother, lost her daughter Persephone or Proserpine to the god of the Underworld till she was brought back to the surface, and having eaten pomegranate seeds the maiden had to return to Hades every year. This was a plain story of the death of vegetation every autumn and rising again in spring, and it was applied to human life. In the Mysteries of Eleusis these myths were enacted in ritual, and when Christianity came it entered into the heritage of the Mysteries with personal and communal faith expressed in ceremonies.

This reveals the ritual purpose of myth. It is not just an explanatory yarn, like a 'just-so story' which might account for the elephant's long nose and would be a true fairy story. But a myth is essentially functional and repeatable; it provides a libretto to ritual action, and it inspires social ceremony. So the myth was acted out or danced out, and its inner truth was realized when the participant was transported into the realm of the sacred and eternal. If the purpose of some myths is now lost, so that they are only narratives for us, many of them remain valid, and particularly so if their central interests have been transmuted or preserved in continuing celebration, at Christmas or Easter, at harvest or children's festival. The themes are constant: beginning and end, birth and death, good and evil, hope and despair, world and eternity.

This volume begins with the setting of the myths, relates them in detail, and provides comprehensive index and bibliography. It is a splendid work, for reading and reference, and enlightened by illustrations. When the four volumes are completed they will be an unrivalled and up-to-date source for knowledge of these age-old mythologies.

GEOFFREY PARRINDER
Professor of the Comparative Study of Religions
King's College, University of London

General Introduction

The standard reference book of world myths, *The Mythology of All Races* (ed.: Louis Herbert Grey and John Arnott MacCulloch), appeared between 1916 and 1932. It comprises thirteen weighty volumes and its price, approaching one hundred pounds, puts it beyond the means of most readers. Moreover, although this great work, which has recently been reissued, contains material of lasting importance and interest, much new knowledge has become available since it was compiled. The researches of the linguist and archaeologist have extended our knowledge and understanding of the myths and legends of the ancient civilisations, such as Sumer, Greece and China. Anthropologists and ethnographers have done the same for those of Africa, and parts of the Americas, Oceania and Australia. A number of books offer information on particular aspects of this new knowledge, but much of it remains tucked away in specialised libraries, the pages of learned journals and academic theses. Here therefore we have aimed to provide an up-to-date yet reasonably compact encyclopaedia for the growing number of readers who share our interest in this perennially fascinating subject.

This volume is the first of a proposed four which the publishers plan to issue. Each volume contains two chapters, each dealing with the myths and legends of a particular region:

Vol. 1
    Chapter 1 The Ancient Near and Middle East
    Chapter 2 Classical Greece and Rome
Vol. 2
    Chapter 3 Northern Europe
    Chapter 4 Southern and Central Africa
Vol. 3
    Chapter 5 Ancient Iran, India and S.E. Asia
    Chapter 6 Northern and Eastern Asia
                (Tibet, China, Korea, Japan)
Vol. 4
    Chapter 7 Oceania and Australia
    Chapter 8 The Americas

Each chapter is divided into four parts. The first gives a brief introduction to the historical, religious and cultural background of the region's myths and legends, the second outlines the chief stories of each area, in so far as these are known, or, as in the case of Africa and India, offers a representative selection from them. The third part of each chapter consists of an index and glossary, referring particularly to the numbered paragraphs of the second part and also including brief details of many other myths and legends of the region. Finally comes a bibliography and guide to further reading. This pattern is based on that devised for the original section on Greek myths and legends, first published in *Pears Cyclopaedia*. Many readers said how helpful they found the scheme, which enables any character or story easily to be pinpointed.

Examples of reference:
  23 refers to paragraph **23** of part 2 of the current chapter;
  4.1 refers to chapter 4, part 1;
  vol. 2: 4.2.**23** refers to volume 2, chapter 4, part 2, paragraph **23**;
  vol. 3: 7.3 refers to volume 3, chapter 7, part 3.

The encyclopaedia as a whole contains many references to Jewish and Christian myths and legends, but for two reasons no specific chapter is devoted to them. The first is that the chief Jewish and Christian myths and legends, which are all we would have had space to include, are already very easily available in that best-selling work *The Bible*. The second is that the thousands of myths and legends concerning patriarchs, rabbis, saints, relics and miracles belong to various regions of the world. Where space allows, and particularly in chapter 3, we will include some information on such stories. Readers seeking a more detailed survey are referred to L. J. Ginsberg: *The Legends of the Jews,* Philadelphia, 7 vols. 1909–46, and G. Everly, *Christian Mythology*, London, 1970.

Information on the myths and legends of Islam, which also cover a wide geographical area, will be found in chapters 4 and 5, on those of Hinduism in chapter 5, of Buddhism in chapters 5 and 6.

The terms *myth* and *legend* are often used rather ambiguously. Here *myth* is taken to denote a particular kind of fictional narrative, *legend* a narrative of a similar kind whose fictitious elements are based, or seem to be based, on a substratum of historical fact.

In speaking of fictions we do not imply that myths and legends offer false images of the world. They have a serious function and express a people's feelings and intuitions about the significance of their lives, the nature of human relationships and human potentialities for good or ill.

Studies of comparatively unsophisticated peoples have clearly shown that not even in primitive societies are myths taken literally, any more than we, remembering Crick and Watson's famous model, imagine that the DNA molecule is made of coiling wires. We find the model a meaningful image because it expresses the scientists' intuitive understanding of DNA's form. Myths have a similar function. They are not literally true but are meaningful images expressing men's understanding of aspects of life's essential nature.

Thus, although in ritual enactments of myths people may, and do, feel that the actors become gods, they are perfectly well aware that they remain human beings, just as we in a performance of, say, *Hamlet* feel that the players become the characters whose rôles they assume. The way in which people identify actors and actresses with the parts in TV and radio soap operas is well known. In each case the willing suspension of disbelief is, it seems, essential to full participation in the life-enhancing drama.

It used to be thought that myths were stories devised to explain or to accompany rituals, but, although the evidence suggests that many did originate in this way, it is now accepted that the theory does not account for the origin of all myths, whose genesis remains a matter of speculation.

In the last century it was popular to think of myths as no more than naïve attempts to explain the existence of natural phenomena. The validity of this approach was wittily undermined by Andrew Lang in a satire offering 'proof incontrovertable' that Mr. Gladstone was no more than an expression of a solar myth. Some myths certainly embody poetic 'explanations' of natural phenomena, but this in itself could not account for the fascination they continue to hold for highly educated minds, fully aware that, for example, the sun does not either sail across the sky in a boat nor ride across it in a chariot drawn by fiery steeds.

Certain mythological paradigms (mythologems) and symbols such as those of the flood, the theft of fire, the monster/dragon in its cave, the ladder from earth to heaven, appear to have a very widespread and potent significance for mankind. This fact was noted by Jung and forms the basis of his influential theory of the Collective Unconscious, which has done much to illuminate our understanding of the world's myths and legends.

More recently, studies of animal behaviour have led to the suggestion that perhaps some of the power of these archetypal images is analogous to that of the stimuli which provoke automatic responses in less highly developed species. A newly hatched chick will immediately cower if it sees a hawk or even an image of hawk shape, though it shows no fear of gulls or similar birds.

Each society gives its own particular form to such 'archetypal images' or stimuli, for myths and legends are expression of communal feelings and intuitions.

During the past century scholars have made us increasingly aware of the important part myths and legends have played in shaping our own culture. The influence of Greek and Roman mythology had long been acknowledged but critical consideration of Jewish and Christian myths and legends was taboo, while very little was known of those earlier stories of the Near and Middle East from which many of our most compelling myths seem to have originated. Nor did we know much of the myths and legends of primitive peoples, or of the geographically remote Chinese and Indians.

The disciplines of archaeology, linguistics, psychology, anthropology, ethnography, sociology, comparative mythology, comparative religion and religious history have all played a part in helping to extend our knowledge and understanding of the world's myths and legends. Some of their discoveries and theses are discussed in the introductions to the various chapters.

It is impossible in a work of this size to incorporate detailed discussion of various theories regarding the provenance and significance of individual myths and legends, but wherever possible we have included brief details, and referred the reader to the appropriate scholarly works.

The following general studies are particularly recommended:

CAMPBELL, Joseph *The Masks of God,* 3 vols. New York: The Viking Press. 1959–65.

DUMÉZIL, Georges *Mythe et epopée.* 3 vols. Paris: Gallimard. 1974.

ELIADE, Mircea *The Sacred and the Profane.* New York: Harcourt Brace

& World Inc. 1959.

——*Myths, Dreams and Mysteries*. Harvill Press. 1960.

——*From Primitives to Zen*. Collins. 1967.

HUXLEY, Francis *The Way of the Sacred*. Aldus/Jupiter Books. 1974.

JUNG, Carl *Psychology of the Unconscious*. Kegan Paul, Trench Trubner & Co. 1919.

——*Symbols of Transformation*. Vol. 5 of *Collected Works*. Routledge & Kegan Paul. 1956.

——*Archetypes and the Collective Unconscious*. Vol. 9, Part 1 of *Collected Works*. Routledge & Kegan Paul. 1959.

JUNG, Carl and FRANZ, M. L. von (eds.) *Man and His Symbols*. George Allen & Unwin. 1964.

LÉVI-STRAUSS, Claude *Mythologies*. 3 vols. Translated as *An Introduction to the Science of Mythology*. Vol. 1 *The Raw and the Cooked,* Vol. 2 *From Honey to Ashes*. Jonathan Cape. 1970–73.

LOMMEL, Andreas *Masks Their Meaning and Function*. Paul Elek Books. 1972.

SCOTT-LITTLETON, C. *The New Comparative Mythology*. Revised ed. New York & London: University of California Press. 1974. (This book outlines the main ideas of Dumézil and critical reactions to them.)

CHAPTER 1

The Ancient Near and Middle East

PART 1

Introduction

MESOPOTAMIA

'History Begins at Sumer,' says Kramer. So, we may add, does mythology, for although it is possible to deduce something of the nature of prehistoric beliefs and cults from the evidence of cave paintings and burial goods, as well as from the attributes of early gods assimilated by later religions, the study of mythology really begins with mankind's earliest written records, those of the Sumerians, who inscribed clay tablets with the strange wedge-shaped script we know as cuneiform.

Early cuneiform writing commemorating the building of a temple at Erech c. 2500 B.C. (*Photo: Mansell Collection.*)

The Ancient Near and Middle East

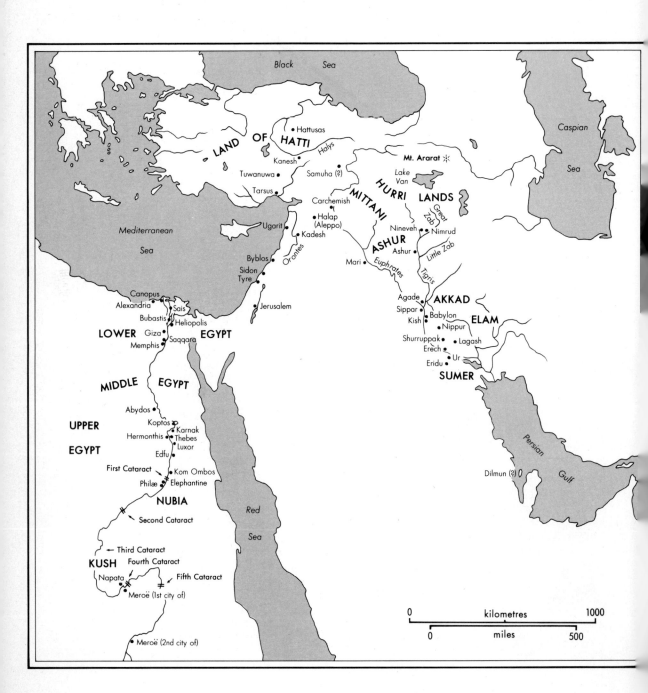

It was probably at some time in the fifth or very early fourth millennium B.C. that the Sumerians entered the Tigris-Euphrates delta, an area of marsh and flood plain already inhabited by farmers and artisans, who were almost certainly of Semitic stock. Where the Sumerians themselves came from is a mystery and their agglutinative language has no relation to any other known. Some scholars believe they originated in Armenia, but the Sumerians themselves claimed to have come from Dilmun. If, as many think likely, Dilmun was modern Bahrein, perhaps the Sumerians originated in Iran or the Indus valley, an area with which by the third millennium they were certainly trading, as they also were with Egypt, Armenia and Anatolia, the Lebanon and Syria, as well as with the nearer settlements of the Persian Gulf.

By the middle of the fourth millennium their delta city-states were flourishing trade centres, each built around the temple complex of its patron deity, a god or goddess who was also worshipped in other Sumerian cities, at least in historical times. The centre of the temple buildings was a ziggurat or step-pyramid, later to be immortalised in the Hebrew story of the Tower of Babel. The splendour of this Sumerian civilisation is vividly conveyed in Kramer's *The Sumerians* and Woolley's *Excavations at Ur* (Woolley's dates are now thought to be too early).

Ruins of the last ziggurat of Ur, built by King Ur-Nammu *c.* 2113–*c.* 2096 B.C. (*Photo: Mansell Collection.*)

21

Throughout its history Sumer was inhabited by Semitic peoples as well as by the Sumerians themselves, and eventually power passed to those Semites who had established themselves farther north, in Babylon. Later, in c. 1115 B.C. the hegemony passed to Assur or Assyria, under the great Tiglath-Pileser I, but eventually the Assyrians too gave way to the Chaldeans, another Semitic people from the west. Finally in 538 B.C. the whole of Mesopotamia became subject to the Persians, followers of the Zoroastrian cult (see vol. 3: 5.1) which now gradually superseded the ancient Mesopotamian religion developed from that of Sumer, whose pantheon had been adopted by the Babylonians and Assyrians.

Our account of Sumerian myths and legends is supplemented with examples of Babylonian and Assyrian stories, many of which developed from Sumerian ones. The later texts are usually called Akkadian, since the Babylonians and Assyrians spoke versions of this Semitic tongue, which became the *lingua franca* of the whole ancient Near and Middle East.

Although the earliest Mesopotamian tablets so far discovered date from c. 2800 B.C. the first narratives come from the middle of the third millennium. However these seem to be copies of much earlier tablets and our knowledge of Sumerian and Akkadian mythology is constantly expanding as tens of thousands of fragments scattered among museums of the Middle East, Europe and America are copied, deciphered and collated. It is all but certain that many more yet lie beneath the Mesopotamian sands.

The study of these myths and legends has more than intrinsic interest for the Sumerians and Akkadians seem to have exerted no small influence on other peoples' beliefs. The Hebrew story of the Flood is of Sumerian origin; ancient Egyptian and Greek creation stories may reflect Sumerian influence; certainly they reveal remarkably similar concepts. Even more extraordinary is the parallel between some Mesopotamian and Egyptian myths and those of Polynesia (vol. 4: 7.2.**23**–**55**) to which they may gradually have been carried via India.

ANATOLIA AND NORTHERN SYRIA

A second group of ancient myths and legends comes from the Anatolian plateau and the north Syrian plains. The original inhabitants of Anatolia were probably those Hattian peoples who were assimilated by Indo-European Hittites, immigrants from Armenia. By the early second millennium B.C. the Hittite kingdom was well established and, just as the Akkadian-speaking peoples of Mesopotamia had absorbed Sumerian beliefs, so, it seems, the Hittites assimilated those of the Hattians.

A second influence on Hittite religion and mythology came from the Hurrians, who had migrated from the Lake Van area and established themselves as far west as northern Syria. During the period c. 1525–1380 B.C. they also dominated Anatolia. The influence of their beliefs continued throughout the later Hittite empire, whose founder, Suppiluliumas (c. 1380–

13th-century B.C. bas-relief from Yazilikaya depicting a procession of Hittite warrior-gods. (*Photo: Sonia Halliday.*)

*c.*1350 B.C.), may have been of Hurrian stock. Consorts of later emperors were certainly Hurrian ladies, most notably the queen Puduhipa, wife of the great Hattusilis III (1289–*c.*1270 B.C.).

Carvings from the rock galleries of Yazilikaya suggest that by *c.*1300 B.C. all the chief gods of the Hurrian pantheon had been adopted by the Hittites and scholars believe it was probably due to Hurrian influence that the Hittite sun-goddess, consort of the Storm God, came to be regarded as his equal or even his superior.

The Hurrians themselves had been much affected by Mesopotamian ideas and beliefs and both Hittite and Hurrian scribes commonly used Akkadian symbols as a shorthand for a number of their own words. For this reason the Hittite and Hurrian names of some deities are unknown.

Texts of Hattic, Hittite and Hurrian myths and legends have been found at only one place, near the modern Turkish village of Bogazköy, among the ruins of the ancient Hittite capital, Hattusas. Epigraphs and other texts have been discovered in Syria and northern Iraq, but no narratives have yet come to light in these areas.

The Hittite empire included a number of other peoples, among them the Luwians, who lived in the south or south-west coastal region. Their language, very closely related to Hittite, possibly a dialect of it, later developed into Lycian and Neo-Hittite or Hieroglyphic Hittite, the tongue of those peoples who moved into the south-east of the empire after the central government had collapsed under pressure from invading Phrygians.

Unlike the earlier Hittites and Hurrians these Neo-Hittites used a hieroglyphic script. Very little is known of their beliefs or those of their Luwian forebears, while the Hittites of the Old Testament have never been traced at all. Readers interested in this mystery are referred to Gurney's classic *The Hittites*.

UGARIT

Although no traces of the Biblical Hittites of ancient Canaan have yet been discovered, in 1929 tablets found at Ras Shamra—the ancient city-state of Ugarit—on the Syrian coast, threw vivid light upon the beliefs and religious practices of other early Canaanite peoples, hitherto known only from Hebrew fulminations and a few Classical references. Texts from Egyptian Amarna, Luxor and Saqqara have provided further information, but these contain no narratives, so that at present Canaanite myths and legends are known to us only in the versions from Ugarit, which date from the middle of the fourteenth century B.C.

Bronze statue of a god, possibly Baal, from Ugarit fifteenth–fourteenth century B.C., now in the Louvre. (*Photo: Mansell Collection.*)

PHOENICIA AND THE PHILISTINES

Of the myths and legends of the Phoenicians and their Punic cousins, as of the Philistines or 'sea people', whose cultures succeeded those of Ugarit on the Canaanite coast, we have scanty information. Notes on their deities are included in Part 3, but no connected narratives have yet been found. Even the late Hellenised version of the Adonis cult of Byblos, written by the Greek Philo (fl. A.D. 160) has survived only in Eusebius' even later second-hand account.

ANCIENT EGYPT

Finally this initial chapter concerns itself with the myths and legends of Ancient Egypt, whose history stretches back to the late fourth millennium, when the small riverside communities united, first into the Two Kingdoms of Upper and Lower Egypt, and then, in c. 3000 B.C., under a single monarch, Menes. A parallel cultural advance was greatly stimulated by Sumerian ideas, most obviously in art, architecture and writing. Religious concepts also seem to have become more sophisticated.

In early times the Hamitic peoples of Egypt had worshipped animal gods, though not, it is thought, animals themselves. The chief of these were the Horus falcon-god of Lower Egypt and Set of the Upper Kingdom, represented with the head of a crocodile or the strange 'Typhonian' animal. These and other animal deities gradually became assimilated to the sun cult of Heliopolis, which had probably been introduced by immigrants from Syria or the Caucasus. Although gods continued to be depicted with animal heads and various creatures were sacred to them, it seems that it was only in the late decadent period, under the Macedonian Ptolemies (early fourth century B.C.) that the Egyptians can be said to have actually worshipped animals.

In its heyday, one of the most distinctive aspects of ancient Egyptian religion was the part played in it by the pharaoh, who came to be regarded not simply as the gods' intermediary and chief priest, but as himself a god, son of the supreme being.

Throughout its long history, Egyptian religion was essentially synchronistic. Each city had its own deities, but these were subordinate to the gods of the capital. The advent of a new dynasty, or even, as in the case of Akhenaten, of a new pharaoh, could lead to a change in the gods particularly favoured by the monarch, and so the rôles of all the other deities also changed, as they were now seen in relation to the royal favourite(s). Thus Horus (161–172), the early falcon-god and supreme deity, came to be regarded as an aspect of the sun-god Atum (119–121). When Atum himself was assimilated to Ra (125–140), Horus too was said to exemplify an aspect of Ra's nature and was spoken of as his son. With the rise of the Osiris

(147–158) cult, he was assimilated to that, as Osiris's son. Thus ancient Egyptian gods have a bewildering variety of attributes and the myths a similarly large number of variants since they too were constantly being modified.

The Egyptians recorded their beliefs on coffins and on the walls of pyramids and other tombs, as well as on stone tablets and papyri. The earliest of these texts dates from *c.*2300 B.C. Cults of the later periods are described by a number of Classical writers, of whom the most useful are Plutarch and Herodotus.

COMMON THEMES

The myths and legends of this whole region offer fascinating similarities and contrasts. It is easy to understand how, watching the earth spring to life as the annual innundation receded, men in Mesopotamia and Egypt should have conceived of the world as emerging from water and mud (1, 20, 119–121). But while geographical and climatic features have affected some mythological concepts, others seem to have been influenced by different factors. For example, the importance of the Mesopotamian god of water and irrigation and of the Anatolian Storm God is clearly related to the regions' climate and physical geography, but some other influence seems to have determined the Egyptians' choice of the pitiless African sun as an appropriate image of the supreme being. Some scholars believe the concept of the sun-god was introduced by conquering invaders from further north. It certainly seems to be related to the essentially aristocratic nature of Egyptian society and the pharaoh's awesome power and splendour.

Other similarities and differences of like kind may be traced in the recurrent stories of the battle between the forces of civilisation and chaos. In Mesopotamia the latter became associated with the uncontrolled power of the sea, in Egypt with darkness. In both it also came to be thought of in terms of a cthonic dragon or serpent. A parallel theme is expressed in the different vegetation myths, the earliest of which, the Sumerian story of Inanna and Dumuzi (39–46) remains tantalisingly incomplete.

Impression of a Sumerian cylinder-seal *c.*2180–1800 B.C. shows a priest before Enki, the Mesopotamian god of water and irrigation. British Museum. (*Photo: Mansell Collection.*)

Time Chart of Egyptian dynasties

	Dynastic Nos.	Period (B.C.)	Pharaohs mentioned in text
OLD KINGDOM	1	*c.* 3100–2890	Narmer (Menes)
	2	*c.* 2890–2686	
	3	*c.* 2686–2613	Djoser
	4	*c.* 2613–2494	
	5	*c.* 2494–2345	
	6	*c.* 2345–2181	
1st Interregnum	7–10	*c.* 2181–2133	
MIDDLE KINGDOM	11	*c.* 2133–1991	
	12	*c.* 1991–1786	
	13	*c.* 1786–*c.* 1663	
2nd Interregnum	14–17	*c.* 1663–1567	
NEW KINGDOM	18	*c.* 1567–1320	Amenophis I, 1546–1526 Amenophis III, 1417–1379 Amenophis IV (Akhenaten), 1379–1362
	19	*c.* 1320–1200	Ramesses II, 1304–1237
	20	*c.* 1200–1085	
	21	*c.* 1085–935	
Libyan or Bubastite	22	*c.* 935–730	
	23	*c.* 817(?)–730	
	24	*c.* 730–709	
Late Period			
Nubian or Ethiopian	25	*c.* 750–656	
Saïte	26	*c.* 664–525	
Persian Rule	27	*c.* 525–404	
	28–29	*c.* 404–378	
	30	*c.* 380–343	
MACEDONIAN KINGS		*c.* 332–304	
THE PTOLEMIES		*c.* 304–30	Ptolemy I Soter, 304–282

Note: Overlapping dates usually indicate co-regencies.
Source: British Museum.

Bas-relief from a Theban tomb shows the scarab and the ram-headed man, symbolising the sun at dawn and at the dead of night. (*Photo: Mansell Collection.*)

A NOTE ON SPELLING AND PRONUNCIATION

In general, where variant spellings exist, the most common have been preferred. In the case of a few Sumerian place-names the well-known Hebrew versions, Erech and Ur, are used instead of the unfamiliar Sumerian, Uruk and Uru.

It is thought that the final syllables of all Sumerian words remained unpronounced. In the cuneiform texts of the Hittites and Hurrians, the letters for p/b, d/t and g/k are indistinguishable, so the sounds for these consonants are uncertain. Ugaritic names were written without vowels, but translators usually supply these. The version here followed is that of H. L. Ginsberg from Pritchard's anthology, *Ancient Near Eastern Texts Relating to the Old Testament* (1969).

PART 2

Narrative Outlines

MESOPOTAMIA

Sumerian Stories of the Creation and Organisation of the World
1–16

(i) THE BEGINNING

1 In the beginning Nammu, the primordial sea, bore An and Ki, deities of the heaven and earth, that formed a single mountain. One fragmentary story says that An carried off the sky, Enlil (the air god) took Ki and Kur (the underworld) carried off the goddess Ereshkigal. 'Father' Enki (god of water and of wisdom) set sail for Kur, apparently to rescue the goddess. In this, it seems, he failed.

2 Although An was probably the first head of the Sumerian pantheon, and, according to one story, created all the other gods by naming their names, in most of the stories so far discovered and deciphered Enlil and Enki are the more active deities and the poems about them contain many references to their creative activities, although no specific creation myths are yet known.

(ii) ENLIL

3 Originally, it was said, the gods lived in the holy city of Nippur, and Nunbarshegum ('the old woman of Nippur') suggested to her daughter Ninlil (the evening star) that she walk by the river Nunbirdu, so that Enlil might notice her and find her attractive. This Ninlil did, but she was nervous of the god's ardour. Unable to restrain his passion, Enlil raped her. The other gods were outraged and banished him to the underworld.

4 Pregnant with his son, the moon-god Nannar, Ninlil followed Enlil into the depths, where she encountered three of the underworld's guardians, the gatekeeper, the riverman and the boatman. As she approached, Enlil impersonated each of these in turn. As the gatekeeper he impregnated her with the god Meslamtaea (often identified with Nergal, ruler of the underworld). As the riverman, Enlil gave her the god Ninazu and as the boatman he fathered a third underworld deity whose name is yet unknown.

5 As no-one could leave the underworld without providing it with a substitute for himself, these three gods took the place of their elder brother Nannar, who then ascended into the sky and brought light to the world as he traversed the heavens in his circular boat, accompanied by the stars and lesser planets. He married Ningal and their children were the sun-god Utu and Inanna, Queen of Heaven.

6 Enlil made the whole earth rich and prosperous. He fashioned the pickaxe, so that men could till the soil and build houses, and he created two demi-gods Emesh (Summer) and his brother Enten (Winter) to furnish the land with plants and animals and make it fertile. Emesh created trees, fields, byres and sheepfolds, but his brother Enten was the superior for he presided over water supplies, and so gave all things their fertility. The brothers quarrelled over their respective importance but Enlil confirmed Enten's authority and Emesh did him homage.

(iii) ENKI

7 Enki is generally considered to have been the third god of the Sumerian pantheon, ranking below An and Enlil but in a number of myths from Eridu in southern Sumer he is responsible for the creation of gods and men and for the organisation of the world.

Enki and the Paradise of Dilmun

8 In the land and city of Dilmun (Bahrein?) there was neither sickness nor old age and all creatures lived peaceably together. Only freshwater was lacking and this the god Enki provided. At the request of his daughter Ninskilla (the guardian goddess of Dilmun) he ordered the sun-god Utu to draw fresh water up from the earth and when this was done Dilmun became like a garden.

9 There Enki's wife Ninhursag bore him a daughter, Ninsar or Ninmu, a goddess of vegetation, and Ninsar bore her father a second daughter, Ninkurru. Ninkurru also bore Enki a daughter, Uttu, goddess of plants and clothing. Ninhursag told Uttu that Enki would approach her also and she advised the young goddess how to receive him. In accordance with Ninhursag's counsel, Uttu asked Enki for a gift of cucumbers, apples and grapes. These he brought her and she became his mistress. Uttu bore Enki eight different plants, but he ate them all before the great earth-mother Ninhursag had had chance to name them and allot their functions. In fury she cursed Enki and abandoned him.

10 Diseases now attacked eight parts of his body and as the great god of water grew progressively weaker, all the other deities sat helpless in the dust. Then, for a consideration, a fox induced Ninhursag to return and heal Enki. This she did by bearing eight deities, each with a name associated with one of his afflicted parts. They were the god Abu, king of plants; Nintul, lord of Mangan—his birth healed the damage to Enki's hip; Ninsutu, who married Nintul and cured Enki's toothache; Ninkasi, the goddess who overwhelms the heart with pleasure, who healed his sore mouth; Nazi, the god who married Ninsar, Dazimus, the goddess who healed the weakness

A statue of the goddess
Ningal from Ur.
Pennsylvania University
Museum, Philadelphia.
(*Photo: Pennsylvania Univ.
Museum.*)

of Enki's side, Ninti, the goddess who healed his damaged rib and Enshag, the god who became Lord of Dilmun.

11 No parallel to this story has yet been found in later Babylonian and Assyrian myths and scholars have yet to elucidate its full significance. Some believe that it may have influenced Hebrew myths.

Enki and the Creation of Man

12 A myth usually referred to as *Enki and Ninmar* (Ninmah, Ninhursag) says that after Enki had fathered the great gods, the Anunna, who were born of his mother Nammu, goddesses were created and divided between heaven and earth as wives of the gods. However the deities were far from happy, for they had to toil unceasingly, digging canals and tilling the soil, to feed and clothe themselves. Bitterly they complained of their lot, but Enki, fast asleep in Engur, his home in the Absu (the abyss of waters beneath the earth), did not hear the gods' laments. At length their mother Nammu went and called him. She suggested he create deputies for the gods so that they themselves need toil no more. Enki summoned into existence the Sigensigdu and made them stand by his side as he mused on the nature of the being his mother-wife had asked for. Then he said the Sigensigdu would bring her clay from above the Absu. This she should model into the form of the being she desired. A number of deities (possibly the Sigensigdu) were to stand by to help at the birth and Nammu was to decide the offspring's fate, while Ninmar, the goddess of birth, would assign his life's work as servant of the gods.

13 To celebrate the creation of man, Enki held a great feast for Nammu and Ninmar. During the revels, he and Ninmar grew drunk and she boasted that she too could create men. Enki undertook to assign a destiny to anyone she made. The drunken goddess formed a man with a paralysed arm, another with defective sight, a third who was crippled and a fourth who suffered from uncontrollable ejaculations. Finally she made a barren woman and a eunuch. Enki decreed a kindly fate for each unfortunate, making the eunuch a king's vizier, the barren woman a harem beauty, the blind man a singer. Now he in turn created two beings, telling Ninmar she should decree their fates. The first he formed was a fruitful woman, the second an old man in the last stages of helpless senility. When Ninmar saw him, instead of assigning him a fate which would enable him to live and support himself, as Enki had done for her unfortunates, the goddess turned away in horror and, cursing the great god, banished him from the earth.

The Organisation of the World

14 Enki journeyed to Nippur, the city of Enlil, and there made a splendid banquet for his great brother. In return, Enlil presented him with the *me's* tree, the tree of life and destiny. Having planted it in the Absu, Enki named the names of all things, and so gave them life. Then he blessed the land of Sumer and the city of Ur and gave them their *me's*. Next he journeyed to the lands of Meluhha, Dilmun, Elam, Marhashi and Martu and blessed them and gave them their *me's* also. He filled the rivers Euphrates and Tigris with living waters, appointed the god Enbilulu to guard canals and rivers

and filled the waters and marshes with fish and vegetation. He appointed Nanshe as goddess of floods and of the land and sea. He made Ishkur god of the weather, organised farming and placed it in charge of Enlil's farmer Enkimdu (39) and made Ashnan goddess of the harvest. Kulla, he appointed god of the brick-kilns and tool-making and Enlil's builder Mushdamma he made ruler of all temples. To Sumuqan he gave the lordship of the wild creatures of the plains and hills and placed Dumuzi in charge of flocks and herds. He appointed the sun-god Utu as the judge of the universe and made Uttu goddess of cloth-making and all women's work. However, he gave no particular charge to the great goddess Inanna, who consequently took umbrage, for An and Enlil had already given office to other goddesses and she felt unjustly neglected, although in fact as Queen of Heaven she already wielded great powers.

15 Another fragmentary myth says that both men and animals were created by the gods An, Enlil, Enki and Ninhursag (the mother-goddess) working together and subsequently one or more of them sent the kingship to earth and appointed tutelary gods for each city.

Enki and Inanna
16 Inanna decided to attempt to bring the *me's* which Enlil had given Enki to her own city of Erech, and so obtain supreme power. She sailed to Eridu, Enki's home, where he welcomed her, giving a banquet in her honour, and during the feast, while befuddled with beer, gave her the *me's*. When he was sober again and noticed they were gone, he sent his vizier, Isimud, with sea monsters to stop Inanna's heavenly boat at one of the seven boat stations between Eridu and Erech and recover the *me's*. At the first station Isimud and the monsters seized the Queen of Heaven's boat and Inanna was forced to continue on foot until her vizier Ninshubur came to her rescue. At the second station the same thing happened, again at the third and each of the following ones, until eventually Inanna arrived home, still carrying the *me's*. So Erech won all the arts of civilisation and became the chief city.

Gypsum trough *c.* 2900–2800 B.C. found at Erech, depicts sheep and lambs around a reed byre. The crook-like bundles are emblems of the fertility goddess, Inanna. British Museum. (*Photo: B. Museum.*)

Akkadian Creation Stories
17–28

(i) A BABYLONIAN MYTH

17 A ritual myth used during ceremonies at the repairing of a temple says that Anu (Sumerian An) created Heaven and Nudimmud (Ea, the Sumerian Enki) created the Apsu (the Abyss) his home. Then Ea nipped off some clay in the Apsu and made the god Kulla to be responsible for restoring temples. Ea also created reed marshes and forests to provide temple building-materials. He made the gods Ninildu, Nisimug and Arazu to put the finishing touches to the buildings. He made the mountains and oceans to furnish ritual offerings and the gods Gushkinbanda, Ninagal, Ninzadim and Ninkurra to do the temples' work. Ea created Umunmutamku and Umunmutamnag to make the offerings, Ashnan, Lahar, Sikis, Ningizzida and Nisar to enrich the temples. He created Kusug to be the gods' high priest, the king to be 'the power' and men to be 'makers'.

Symbols of the gods Enlil and Anu from Assyrian boundary stone *c.* 1120 B.C. British Museum. (*Photo: Michael Holford.*)

(ii) THE ENUMA ELISH

18 Akkadian myths contain a number of other accounts of creation—one (*The Worm and the Tooth-ache*) forms part of the ritual to be used when drawing a tooth! The most complete is that known as the *Enuma Elish*. This takes its name from the opening words of the liturgy, *Enuma elish*—'When on high'—which was chanted, or recited, at two points in the great Akitu (New Year) festival.

19 The *Enuma Elish* is written on seven tablets and in this form probably dates from the beginning of the second millennium B.C., though its origins are almost certainly much older. Readers will notice similarities between it and the fragmentary Sumerian myths already outlined.

20 At first there was nothing but Apsu, the ocean of fresh water, Tiamat, the ocean of salt water, and Mummu (probably the mist which hovered above them), their son and vizier. The primordial oceans gave birth to twin deities, Lahmu and Lahamu (possibly esturine silts), who also bore twins, Anshar and Kishar, the horizons of earth and heaven. The children of Anshar and Kishar were Anu the sky-god (Sumerian An) and Ea or Nudim-mud, god of earth and water (Sumerian Enki).

21 Their noisy descendants irritated the primaeval oceans and, although Tiamat was against it, Apsu and Mummu planned to kill the younger gods, the Anunnaki. However the Anunnaki learned of this scheme and Ea, fount of all wisdom, frustrated it. He bewitched Apsu, stole his glory and slew him. Then Ea built himself a sacred chamber, which he called Apsu. There he lived with his consort Damkina and there his only son, the glorious Marduk, was born.

22 Goaded by the reproaches of her older children, the ocean Tiamat planned to avenge Apsu's death. She created a host of monsters, including scorpion-men, lions, mad dogs and dragonflies (or flying dragons) and made her son, Kingu, their commander, fastening the Tablets of Destiny (cf. Sumerian *me's*) to his breast, thus giving him supreme power.

23 Led by Anshar, the Anunnaki took council and suggested that Ea should destroy Tiamat as he had Apsu, but for some reason, as yet unknown, this plan fell through. Later Anu made an unsuccessful attempt to ward off Tiamat's host and finally Marduk was persuaded to accept the rôle of champion, on the condition that he was given supreme power.

24 Invested with the kingship, Marduk filled himself with fire and created seven hurricanes. Gathering his arms—bows and arrows, mace, lightning and a net of the four winds—he rode against Tiamat in his chariot of storms.

25 Tiamat agreed to engage him in single combat and Marduk slew her. He netted her monstrous host and took prisoner its leader Kingu, from whose breast he took the Tablets of Destiny and bound them to his own.

26 Now Marduk divided Tiamat's huge corpse and fixed one half of it in the heavens, as the roof-like sky; then he went to his father's house, Apsu, and having measured it carefully built the great canopy of the earth above it as its counterpart Esharra. Next he established the Anunnaki in their homes, Anu in the sky, Enlil in the air and upon the earth's surface, Ea in the waters.

27 Marduk created the stars and signs of the zodiac as images of the Anunnaki and established a lunar calendar, assigning three constellations to each month and appointing Nibiru (the planet Jupiter) as their governor. At the same time he set Enlil's heavenly road in the northern sky, that of Anu at the zenith, that of Ea in the south.

28 Now Marduk decided to make men. Following a suggestion of his father, Ea, he had Kingu slain and men formed from his blood to relieve the great gods of their labours. In gratitude the Anunnaki built him his great sanctuary of Babylon, with the Esagila temple. There they proclaimed the fifty great names of the supreme god, Marduk.

Bas-relief of Marduk fighting Tiamat. British Museum. (*Photo: B. Museum.*)

The Flood
29–38

(i) THE SUMERIAN STORY OF ZIUSUDRA

29 So far, only fragments of this myth have been discovered. It tells how the gods decided to destroy mankind, but Enki warned the devout king Ziusudra of their intentions and, whispering to him through a wall, told him how to escape the coming flood. Ziusudra rode it out in a great boat. Eventually the storm died down and the sun-god Utu lightened the sky. Ziusudra opened one of his ship's windows and Utu shone through it into the vessel. There Ziusudra sacrificed an ox and a sheep to him.

30 Eventually Ziusudra came before the great gods An and Enlil and did them homage. They made him immortal and sent him to live in the land of Dilmun.

(ii) THE OLD BABYLONIAN STORY OF ATRAHASIS

31 The gods asked Mami (Ninhursag) to create the man Lullu to carry the burden of the world's work. Enki commanded that a god be slain and his flesh and blood mixed with clay to form man, and so Ninhursag gave birth to mankind in the House of Fate.

32 However, as people grew more numerous upon earth the noise they made was so appalling that the gods could not sleep. Enlil therefore sent a terrible drought and famine to decimate mankind. When this did not quell their noise—indeed with suffering their cries grew even louder—Enlil decided to destroy the entire human race in a great flood. However, Enki disputed Enlil's authority to do so, since it was he, not Enlil, who brought mankind to birth in Ninhursag's womb.

33 Enki descended to King Atrahasis of Shurruppak, who begged the god to speak, but Enki could not tell his fellow gods' secrets to a man, so he whispered to the reed wall of the king's house, saying, 'Build a ship.' Atrahasis built a great ship and loaded it with his family and their goods and with birds and animals, wild and domesticated. So man survived the flood.

34 It will be noticed that this epic includes not only material from the Ziusudra story, but also elements from Enki and the Creation of Man (12–13) and material later included in the *Enuma Elish* (18–28).

(iii) THE ASSYRIAN STORY OF UTNAPISHTIM

35 Utnapishtim was a man of Shurruppak, the oldest city of Akkad. The god Ea whispered to him through the reed walls of his house, telling him that the gods had decided to destroy mankind. He commanded Utnapishtim to build a boat, giving him precise instructions and measurements, from which it seems the vessel was to be a perfect cube.

36 Having carried out the orders, Utnapishtim placed in the boat all his gold and silver, all his animals, his family, relatives and workmen and all kinds of domesticated and wild creatures. He explained his activities to his neighbours by telling them that the god Enlil was angry with him and

Cuneiform tablet recording the Assyrian flood myth, once part of Ashurbanipal's library at Nineveh. British Museum. (*Photo: Mansell Collection.*)

Impression of an Akkadian cylinder-seal, *c.* 2340–2180 B.C., shows Ishtar standing on a fire-breathing dragon with rain pouring from her hands. Behind rides Enlil in a storm-chariot. Pierpoint Morgan Library. (*Photo: P. M. Library.*)

had banished him from Shurruppak, so he was going away to live on the sea. However, Enlil was going to demonstrate his favour for them by showering them with riches. Completely deceived, all the city's inhabitants perished in the terrible storm which followed. Even the lesser gods shrank back against heaven's walls as Nergal tore down the skies' floodgates and the Anunnaki set the land ablaze with their flaring torches.

37 On the seventh day the storm fell and Utnapishtim looked out upon a plain of water stretching to the horizon. He realised that but for him and his family all mankind had perished. Eventually his ship ran aground on Mt. Nisir (Pir Omar Gudrun, or Pir-i-Mukurun, in the Lesser Zab Basin, east of the Tigris). After a further seven days he sent out a dove, but finding nowhere to rest, it returned, so did the swallow that Utnapishtim sent next. Finally however he sent a raven, which found food and did not come back. Then Utnapishtim and all his company left the ship and sacrificed to the gods, who congregated like flies around the savoury-smelling offering.

38 Ishtar (**39–52**), who had it seems instigated the flood, vowed on her lapis-lazuli necklace never to forget the disaster and harangued Enlil for having destroyed mankind. He however was furious that anyone had escaped and Ninurta blamed Ea for having betrayed the gods' secrets. Ea however justified himself and interceded with Enlil, who, pacified, blessed Utnapishtim and his wife and made them immortal, ordering them to make their home far away at the rivers' mouth, beyond the Mountains of Mashu and the waters of death (i.e. in Dilmun).

Inanna and Dumuzi—Ishtar and Tammuz
39–52

(i) THE SUMERIAN STORIES

39 The goddess Inanna, daughter of Nannar the moon-god, had two suitors, the shepherd Dumuzi and the farmer Enkimdu. She inclined to Enkimdu but her powerful brother Utu, the sun-god, preferred Dumuzi. When he learned that Inanna favoured his rival, Dumuzi pressed his suit vigorously, declaring that he could not only match but outdo anything Enkimdu could offer her. Eventually Dumuzi was successful and Enkimdu, who bore him no grudge, tried to win his friendship, offering various gifts, all of which were spurned. However, Dumuzi's arrogance seems later to have been his downfall.

40 Inanna decided to descend to the underworld of Kur, ruled by her sister Ereshkigal, whose authority she seems to have determined to challenge. At the gates of Kur she was stopped by Neti, its guard, and told him she was come to attend her brother-in-law Gugalanna's funeral. Granted entry, she passed the underworld's seven gates and at each, in accordance with Kur's laws, she was divested of a garment or one of her insignia until at length she came naked before Ereshkigal and the Anunnaki, the Seven Judges, whose deathly gaze killed her, for her power had been lost with her regalia. Ereshkigal ordered the corpse to be hung from a stake.

41 When, after three days, Inanna had not returned home, her vizier Ninshubur ordered mourning; then, in accordance with her previous instructions, he went to the great gods Enlil, Nannar and Enki, asking them to intercede and save Inanna's life. Enlil and Nannar refused, saying she had courted her fate, but Enki responded (cf. **50, 68**). From the dirt of his scarlet-painted fingernail he created Kurgarru and Kalaturru and sent them to the underworld with the food and water of life, telling them to sprinkle it upon Inanna sixty times. This they did.

42 Restored to life, Inanna returned to earth accompanied by seven *galla* (demons), who were to carry back a substitute for her, since none might leave Kur without providing one. The galla first claimed Inanna's vizier Ninshubur, who had come to welcome her, but him she rescued, as she also did the gods Shara of Umma and Latarak of Badtibira, who were the next potential victims. Eventually the party came to Inanna's own city of Erech and there found her husband Dumuzi, who, far from grieving at her loss, had cheerfully assumed her throne. In fury Inanna gave him to the demons.

43 Terror-stricken, Dumuzi appealed to the sun-god Utu to turn him into a snake that he might escape. We do not know if Utu responded, but other tablets of the story say that Dumuzi fled into the desert. There he had a terrible dream of the world's desolation and summoned his sister Geshtinanna to interpret it for him. Warning him that the demons were very near she promised not to reveal his hiding place.

Billy-goat peering through a 'tree of life' whose starry flowers are associated with the goddess Inanna. An offering stand *c.* 2500 B.C. from the 'royal graves' at Ur. British Museum. (*Photo: B. Museum.*)

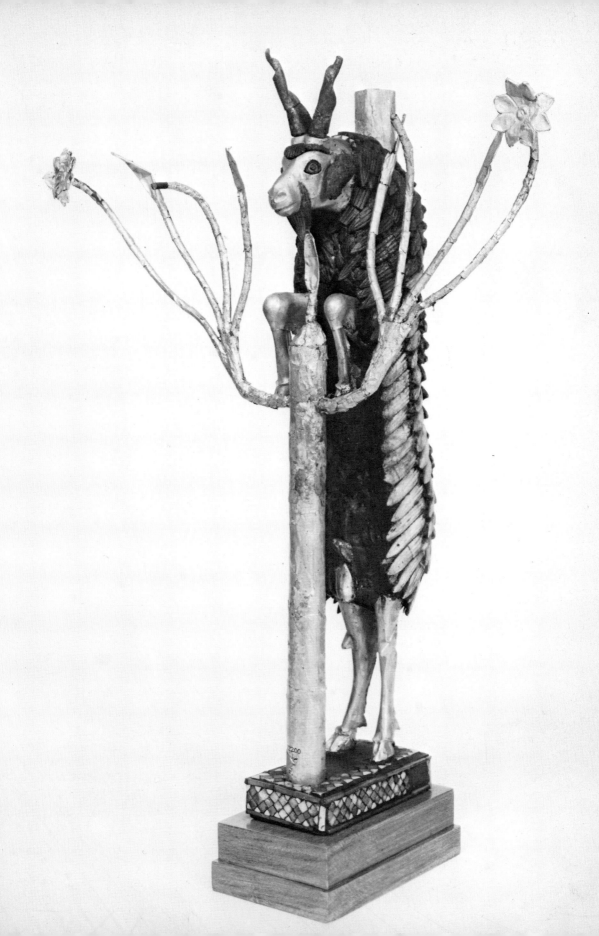

44 When the galla arrived they captured her and tried to bribe her into betraying her brother. Perhaps because he feared for her life, Dumuzi now returned to the city. There the galla fell upon him. Dumuzi begged his brother-in-law Utu, to save him. Utu responded by transforming him into a gazelle and so Dumuzi fled to the home of the wise old goddess Belili, who gave him food and drink.

45 Hardly had he eaten than the demons once more caught up with him. A third time Utu changed him into a gazelle. Dumuzi fled and took refuge in his sister's sheepfold but five of the galla broke into it and killed him.

46 It seems that although Dumuzi's mother and wife Inanna wandered, mourning, seeking him, it was his sister who rescued him. She descended to the underworld in a boat and there apparently became his substitute for six months of the year, so that he might return to earth, but at present this conclusion exists only in fragments and is uncertain.

(ii) THE AKKADIAN STORIES

47 The Akkadian version of the Ishtar-Tammuz (Inanna-Dumuzi) myth exists in two forms, the older, known as *A*, dates from the end of the second millennium B.C., the other, *N*, comes from Ashurbanipal's library at Nineveh. There are a number of differences between these texts and the older Sumerian story.

48 When Ishtar arrived at the gates of Cutha, the underworld, she threatened that if she were refused admittance she would break down the doors and set the dead upon the living, thus depriving her sister Ereshkigal of all her subjects.

49 When, divest of her clothes and power, Ishtar came before Ereshkigal, the goddess of the underworld called her vizier Namtar and ordered him to imprison her sister and loose the sixty 'miseries' to attack every part of her.

50 As a result of Ishtar's imprisonment the earth lost all its fertility, plants wilted and neither animals nor men desired their mates. Papsukkal, the gods' vizier, begged Ishtar's father, the moon-god Sin, to rescue her and save the world, but it was the great god Ea who responded to the plea (cf. **41**, **68**). He created the eunuch Ashanmer or Asushunamir, whom he ordered to descend to Cutha and induce Ereshkigal to give him the water of life. Such was Asushunamir's charm that Ereshkigal complied and ordered Namtar to sprinkle Ishtar with the water in the presence of the Seven Judges, the Anunnaki. The goddess's clothes and jewels were restored to her and she was set free, though Ereshkigal ordered her vizier to bring the goddess back if she failed to pay her ransom (which probably means provide a substitute for herself).

51 The story ends strangely with Ereshkigal ordering that Tammuz, who was it seems already in the underworld, should be royally entertained. When Ishtar has dressed and is sitting with her lap full of 'fish's eyes' (pearls ?), she apparently hears Tammuz playing a lapis-lazuli flute and welcoming courtesans. Throwing down her jewels, Ishtar calls upon Tammuz, invoking him to do her no harm; then she prays that the dead

Eighth-century B.C. stele from Tell Ahmar showing Ishtar as a warrior goddess riding her cult animal, the lion. Louvre. (*Photo: Michael Holford.*)

may rise when he and the wailing men and women welcome her.

52 Scholars await the discovery and decipherment of additional material which may enable them to elucidate the significance of this ending, to which, so far as is known, no parallel exists in the older Sumerian stories.

16

Gilgamesh
53–68

53 According to the Sumerian King Lists, Gilgamesh was the fifth ruler of Erech, during the second dynasty after the flood and lived 120 years. Gilgamesh, who certainly existed and probably ruled in *c.*2600 B.C., captured the imagination of most of western Asia, and poems about him have been discovered in several languages, including Hurrian, as well as Sumerian and Akkadian, but the most complete version of his story, *The Epic of Gilgamesh*, comes from Ashurbanipal's library.

(i) THE EPIC

54 The giant Gilgamesh was two-thirds god, one-third man. His subjects complained of his tyranny, so the goddess Aruru made the wild-man Enkidu to be his foil. She fashioned him from clay in the image of the great gods Anu and Ninurta.

55 Enkidu fed on grass and was friendly with all the wild creatures of the steppe. Intrigued by huntsmen's tales of this wild-man, Gilgamesh sent a temple prostitute to the pool where Enkidu usually drank, ordering her to seduce and tame him. This she did and after six days and seven nights of ecstasy Enkidu came to himself to find he was a changed man. All the wild creatures now fled before him in terror.

56 Telling him that he was now like a god, the woman induced him to accompany her to Erech. There Enkidu and Gilgamesh met and quarrelled, wrestling together till they shattered a door post and the walls shook around them, but the match ended in friendship and the two heroes then set out together in pursuit of Humbaba (Huwawa) a fire-breathing giant who guarded the great cedar forest of Amanus (Lebanon), home of the goddess Irnini (i.e. Ishtar).

57 Aided by the sun-god Shamash, who sent eight strong winds against Humbaba, the two heroes slew the giant and cut off his head. As they returned in triumph to Erech, Ishtar followed, begging Gilgamesh to marry her, but he, citing the unhappy fate of others who had succumbed to her wiles, spurned the goddess's proposal. Infuriated, she asked Anu to avenge her, which he did by creating the monstrous Bull of Heaven, whose scorching breath ravaged the whole countryside.

58 However, Gilgamesh and Enkidu fought the monster and killed it, Enkidu making the fatal thrust. They offered its heart to Shamash and scornfully threw a hind quarter into Ishtar's face. Returning to Erech, they were greeted by women dancing and chanting antiphons in praise of their great king (cf. *Samuel* 18, vi–vii). The rejoicing was however short-lived for the gods condemned Enkidu to death for his slaughter of the heavenly Bull and after an illness lasting twelve days the hero expired.

59 Realising that he too eventually must die, Gilgamesh, overcome with horror, decided to seek immortality, and set off in quest of his ancestor Utnapishtim, the only man to have acquired eternal life.

Eighth-century B.C. bas-relief from Khorsobad showing Gilgamesh carrying a lion. Louvre. (*Photo: Giraudon.*)

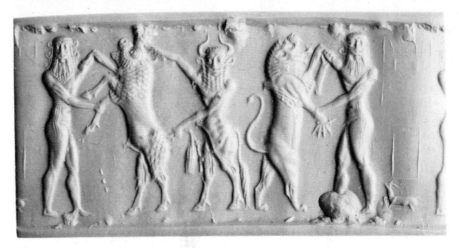

Impression of an Akkadian cylinder-seal c. 2360–2180 B.C. shows the sun-god Shamash rising between two mountains as attendant deities open heaven's gates. British Museum. (*Photo: Michael Holford.*)

Impression of an Akkadian cylinder-seal late third millennium B.C. thought to depict, left to right: Gilgamesh, the Bull of Heaven, Enkidu, a lion wrestling with Gilgamesh. British Museum. (*Photo: B. Museum.*)

60 Coming to the Mountains of Mashu, Gilgamesh was challenged by guards, a scorpion-man and his wife, who attempted to dissuade him from continuing, but, impressed by his resolution, they eventually let him pass. Gilgamesh went on, following the path of the sun through pitch darkness, until he came before Shamash. The great sun-god warned Gilgamesh that his quest was futile, but the hero continued, undeterred, and came to the waters of death, where an ale-wife, the goddess Siduri, again warned him

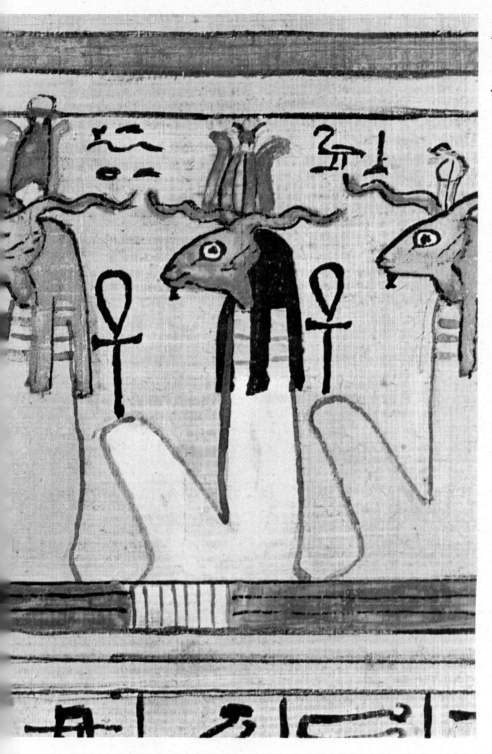

Egyptian papyrus painting shows goat-headed manifestations of the Hermopolitan deities riding in the solar barque. Tefnut, goddess of moisture, in white, is followed by her son, Geb, the earth-god. (Photo: Michael Holford.)

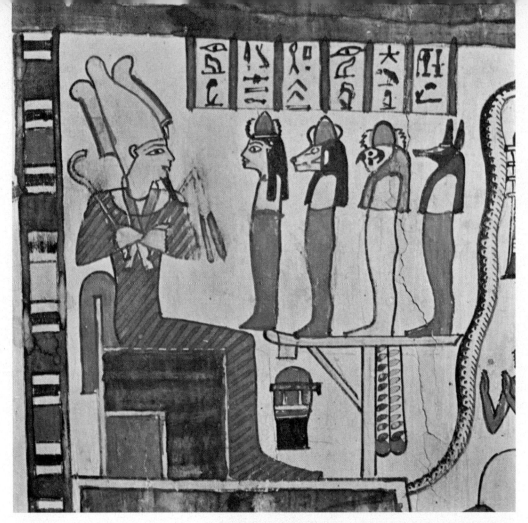

Above—Painting from a
Theban coffin, c.900 B.C.,
shows the four Amenti:
Imset, Hapy, Quebehsenuf,
Duamutef, before Osiris,
judge of the dead. British
Museum. (Photo: Photo-
resources.)

Right—Statuette of the
Egyptian god Osiris,
carrying the crook and flail,
symbols of judgement. The
Louvre. (Photo: Michael
Holford.)

he would fail in his task. She urged him to enjoy the life he had instead of wasting it in such an hopeless endeavour. Spurning her epicurean homily, Gilgamesh went on to the shore, where he met Urshanabi, the man who had been Utnapishtim's boatman at the time of the great Flood (37).

61 Urshanabi told the king that in order to cross the waters of death in safety he must cut 120 poles, each 60 cubits long, and punt himself across the river, letting each pole fall as he used it, so as to avoid the slightest contact with the deathly waters.

62 Furnished with poles from the nearby forest, Gilgamesh crossed the river and so came at last to Utnapishtim's home. He implored his great ancestor to tell him how he had won immortality. Utnapishtim answered by recounting his experience of the Flood (35–38), and then, like others before him, told Gilgamesh that his quest was doomed. The gods had decreed that all men should die. He showed the hero that he was powerless to resist even sleep, let alone the last sleep of death, but as the disconsolate king prepared to take his leave, Utnapishtim said there did exist a rejuvenating plant, growing on the seabed. If Gilgamesh could reach it he might win his desire.

63 Diving to the bottom of the sea, Gilgamesh pulled up the plant, but on his journey home, while stopping to bathe at a pool he foolishly put the treasure down. Attracted by its scent, a serpent appeared and carried it off, shedding its skin as it went. So the unhappy hero was robbed of immortality.

Impression of an Akkadian cylinder-seal *c.*2340–2180 B.C. showing Gilgamesh's journey to find Utnapishtim, who lives at the source of the waters, beyond the gates at the ends of the earth, which are guarded by two deities. British Museum. (*Photo: Michael Holford.*)

Impression of an Akkadian cylinder-seal *c.* 2360–2180 B.C. shows the Zu bird, symbol of drought and chaos, led captive before Ea. British Museum. (*Photo: Michael Holford.*)

(ii) GILGAMESH AND THE HULUPPU-TREE

64 Among the Sumerian stories of Gilgamesh, many of which were incorporated in the Akkadian *Epic,* is one called *Gilgamesh and the Huluppu-Tree.* This only appears at the end of the Akkadian poem and in truncated form, evidently as a late addition:

65 Inanna took a sapling *huluppu*-tree (willow ?) from the banks of the Euphrates and planted it in her garden in Erech, where she tended it carefully, intending to have a chair and couch made for herself from its wood. However, when the time came to fell the tree, Inanna found it commandeered by three monsters. At its foot a snake which no magic could charm had built its nest, in its crown the malicious Zu bird had set its young, and in the middle Lilith the 'maid of desolation' had built her house.

66 Overhearing the goddess telling her brother Utu of this misfortune, Gilgamesh came to her aid, killing the snake and frightening away Lilith and the Zu bird; then his companions felled the tree, and presented it to Inanna. The goddess rewarded Gilgamesh with a *pukku* and a *mikku* (probably a ritual drum and its stick), made from the tree's crown and base.

67 In some way, because of 'the young maiden's cry', these gifts fell through into the underworld. Enkidu proposed to rescue them. Gilgamesh told him of the rules he must observe if he was to return safely, but Enkidu ignored them and so was trapped below.

68 In vain Gilgamesh appealed to the gods Enlil and Nannar for aid. Eventually Ea agreed to help him (cf. **41, 50**) and commanded Nergal to make a hole in the ground so that Enkidu's spirit might ascend. It came up like a puff of wind. When Gilgamesh asked it to describe the underworld and its inhabitants, the spirit replied that its body, that Gilgamesh had loved, was now eaten by vermin, its bones filled with dust. Convulsed with tears, Gilgamesh threw himself to the ground.

The Akkadian Legend of Etana and the Eagle
69–70

69 After the Flood men lacked the guidance of a king, a 'shepherd of the people', and the royal insignia were returned to heaven. Then the Anunnaki decided that the time had come to send the kingship back to earth and so Etana became king, but he had no son. Every day he sacrificed to Shamash and prayed for an heir. Eventually the god told him to cross the mountains to a pit where an eagle was imprisoned. If he released it the bird would lead him to the plant of birth.

70 Etana found the eagle, which Shamash himself had imprisoned for breaking its oath of friendship with its neighbour the serpent. When it was freed, the bird carried Etana high into the heavens, earth's landscape growing fainter and fainter until it vanished from sight; then they came to the throne of Ishtar, from whom Etana received the plant of birth.

The Akkadian Legend of Adapa
71–73

71 Adapa, son of Ea, was priest-king of Eridu, fisherman to the gods. One day, when his boat was overturned by a strong gust of south wind, he angrily cursed the wind and broke its wing, so for seven days it could not blow.

72 Anu sent his messenger Ilabrat to discover what had happened and learning of Adapa's deed, commanded that he be brought before him. Ea advised his son to dress in mourning. On reaching heaven he would be met by its gatekeepers, the gods Tammuz and his father Ningizzida. When they enquired his business he should tell them he was grieving for the two gods Tammuz and Ningizzida, who had disappeared from earth. This would please them and induce them to speak to Anu on his behalf. When he came before Anu himself he would be offered deathly bread and water, which he must refuse, and a robe and oil, which he should accept.

73 Adapa followed all his father's advice and when Anu, having heard his explanation of why he had broken the south wind's wing, ordered the bread and water of life to be offered to him, Adapa declined it, although he accepted the robe and oil which were offered next. Laughing, Anu demanded the reason for his strange preference and hearing it, explained that Adapa had in truth been led to reject the chance of immortality. Sending him back to earth, Anu decreed that his city, Eridu, should thenceforward be free of all feudal obligations and its priesthood especially honoured. Misfortune and sickness would henceforward dog mankind, but Ninkarrak, the goddess of healing would, in some measure, alleviate these ills.

ANATOLIA AND NORTHERN SYRIA

The Hittite Myth of Telepinus
74–82

74 A number of versions of this fertility-ritual myth have been found. In one the protagonist is the Storm God, in another several deities including the Sun God play the leading part. (The chief deities of the Hittite pantheon are referred to in the tablets by the ideogram suggesting their function— e.g. Storm God—and not by any name.) The most complete version centres on the vegetation god Telepinus. It will be noticed that some details of the myth—the seven gates of the underworld, for example—suggest Sumerian influence.

75 Telepinus's activities were, it seems, questioned or interrupted. Beside himself with fury, he put his shoes on the wrong feet and taking all the land's fertility with him, went away into the steppe. No one knew his whereabouts.

76 The land was wreathed in clouds of dust (?) which permeated even houses and temples, extinguishing their fires and quelling even the gods' vitality. All vegetation shrivelled and the land was devastated by famine.

77 The gods sought Telepinus everywhere. The Sun God sent the Eagle to seek him on the mountain tops, in valley bottoms and in the depths of the sea, to no avail. Then Telepinus's father, the great Storm God, asked his wife Hannahannas, mother of the gods, for advice. She suggested he himself seek Telepinus, so the Storm God searched throughout the city, but could not find him. Then Hannahannas proposed to send out a Bee, and although the Storm God was annoyed at the suggestion, scoffing at the idea that this tiny insect should be sent on a quest which had defeated all the gods including himself, Hannahannas nevertheless persisted. She ordered the Bee to seek until it found Telepinus; then it was to sting his hands and feet and make him get up. Next it should clean his feet and eyes with wax and bring him back to her. (This command seems related to the widespread folk belief that honey expels evil spirits. A parallel to this Hittite incident is found in the Finnish *Kalevala*, where the dead hero Lemminkainen is revived with honey brought to him by a bee at his mother's request. See vol. 2: 3.2.**278**)

78 Off flew Hannahannas's Bee and searched until it was on the point of collapse. At last it found Telepinus sleeping in a meadow at Lihzina. It stung him, so that he leaped up; then it cleaned his feet and eyes with wax, as Hannahannas had commanded; but being roused made Telepinus even more furious than before. Now he dammed the springs and rivers, causing disastrous floods. He inundated clay pits, broke windows, destroyed houses and drowned both men and their flocks.

79 Bewildered and distraught, the gods tried to fathom the cause of his fury. At length the Sun God suggested fetching a man and telling him to carry the spring Hattara on Mt. Ammuna, and, with the eagle's wing force

Bas-relief showing the Hittite Moon God and winged Sun God riding on a lion. (*Photo: Hirmer.*)

Telepinus to move. (The significance of these instructions has yet to be elucidated, and there follows a break in the tablets.)

80 After an interval in which Kamrusepas, goddess of healing, is summoned to restore Telepinus to his senses, there follows her ritual incantation, culminating in Telepinus's return in a black thundercloud. He is now purged of his fury. Kamrusepas orders a sacrifice of twelve rams from the Sun God's flock to ensure Telepinus's longevity. All the gods assemble under a *harikeshnash* tree (an evergreen ?) for the sacrifice.

53

81 Next the man who had been sent after Telepinus also performs a ritual invoking the god and asking him to lose his anger, remove its curse from the land and send it down into the underworld on the path of the Sun God. The seven doors of the underworld will open to reveal seven metal cauldrons. Anything which enters them dies for ever. The man implores Telepinus to send his fury into the cauldrons.

82 This was done and Telepinus returned home. The dust (?) cloud left the houses and temples and fertility returned to the land. Telepinus tended the king and queen and ensured them a long and vigorous life. Then an evergreen tree was raised in front of the god and from it was hung a fleece, symbolising fertility and long life.

The Hittite Story of the Dragon Illuyankas
83–88

83 This story which was associated with the Purulli festival (probably a New Year ritual) exists in two versions, one of which was obsolete at the time it was recorded.

84 The older version says that the dragon Illuyankas defeated the Storm God in a battle at Kiskilussa. Then the Storm God summoned all the other deities to come to his aid. He ordered the goddess Inaras to prepare a sumptuous banquet for them with gallons of strong drink.

85 Having done so, Inaras went to Zigaratta, where she met the man Hupasiyas, who promised to do anything she wished if he might be her lover. She granted his request and, hiding Hupasiyas in the palace, put on her finest clothes, went to the dragon's lair and persuaded him to come to the feast she had prepared. Illuyankas came with all his children and they drank the palace dry. While they lay drunk Hupasiyas crept out and trussed Illuyankas securely with a rope. Then came the Storm God and slew the dragon.

86 Hupasiyas also came to a sad end. Inaras built a cliff-top house for herself in Tarukka. One day she prepared to go into the countryside and before leaving told Hupasiyas he must not on any account look out of the window while she was away. After twenty days had passed and Inaras still had not returned, Hupasiyas defied her. Opening the window he looked out and saw his wife and children. When Inaras returned he begged to be allowed to go home. Furious the goddess killed him and went back to Kiskilussa.

87 The later version of the story says that having defeated the Storm God, Illuyankas stole his heart and eyes. The Storm God brooded on revenge. Eventually he married a poor man's daughter who bore him a son and this son he married to the dragon's daughter. The Storm God told his son that when he went to his wife's home he should ask to be given his father's heart and eyes. This the young man did and, receiving them, returned them to the Storm God.

88 Now restored to his full strength the Storm God went to the sea and prepared to do battle. The dragon came accompanied by his son-in-law, who shouted to the Storm God to kill him as well as Illuyankas, for he was now the dragon's man. So the Storm God slew them both.

Bas-relief from Malatya showing the Storm God killing the dragon Illuyankas. (*Photo: Hirmer.*)

The Hurrian Myth of the Birth of the Storm God 89–91

89 It is almost certain that the Greek Hesiod derived his story of Uranos (2.2.1–4) from a version of this myth.

90 Alalus was king of heaven and for nine years the great god Anus served him as his cupbearer; then Anus rebelled and fought the king and vanquished him. Alalus fled and descended into the dark earth. Anus sat upon his throne and the great god Kumarbis served him as his cupbearer. In the ninth year of his reign Anus's power was challenged by Kumarbis and they fought a great battle. Anus fled, pursued by his enemy, who caught up with him and, biting his 'knees' (*sic*) emasculated him and swallowed his manhood. Kumarbis's triumphant laughter was cut short as Anus warned him he was now pregnant with three terrible beings, the Storm God, the irresistible River Aranzahas (the Tigris) and the great god Tasmisus. Having spoken Anus disappeared, hiding himself in the sky, while Kumarbis apparently spat out onto Mt. Kanzuras at least one and probably two of the gods whom he had swallowed. However he was still pregnant with the Storm God. Furious, he went to Nippur (the Mesopotamian city of Enlil, also a god of storms). There he waited, counting the months of his pregnancy.

91 The remainder of the story is difficult to decipher but it seems that Anus spoke to the as yet unborn Storm God telling him how to escape from Kumarbis's body. Eventually the god was born and, allying himself with Anus, fought and apparently defeated Kumarbis.

The Hurrian Story of Ullikummis
92–97

92 A second myth bears some resemblances to the Greek story of Typhon (2.2.**14–15**). It tells how Kumarbis created a stone monster as rival to his son the Storm God, who had deposed him.

93 Brooding on how to avenge himself on the Storm God, Kumarbis conceived a plan. He called his messenger Imbaluris and sent him to the Sea Goddess, who acknowledging Kumarbis's supremacy, invited him to visit her and entertained him royally. Soon afterwards a son was born to Kumarbis. It is unclear whether the mother was a river goddess, the Sea Goddess's daughter, or whether she was a mountain deity. However, the child, born from the rocks, was formed of diorite. Kumarbis named him Ullikummis and summoning deities called the Irsirra, ordered them to carry the infant down into the earth's depths and set him like a column on the right shoulder of Ubelluris, the giant who supported the world (cf. Atlas 2.3). Before doing this, the Irsirra showed the boy to Ellil (Sumerian Enlil) who forecast he would be a fighter of terrible power, and commented on Kumarbis's unexampled vileness in creating such a monster to rival his older son.

94 Once placed on Ubelluris's shoulder Ullikummis grew at amazing speed. Soon he attracted the attention of the Sun God, who hurried to Kummiya, the Storm God's city, and told him of the terrible monster he had seen.

95 Accompanied by his sister, Ishtar, the Storm God climbed Mt. Hazzi (Mt. Casius near ancient Ugarit) and gazed at Ullikummis. The sight made him weep in fury and despair.

96 Led by the war-god Astabis, the divinities attacked Ullikummis but were helpless against him and all fell into the sea, so Ullikummis continued to grow unchecked and the earth trembled. He pushed the sky higher and higher, blocking it off from the earth as he reached the boundaries of the gods' heavenly home, the *kuntarra,* and towered above the gates of Kummiya.

97 Unable to see or gain any news of her husband and his supporters, the Storm God's wife Hebat sent her messenger Takitis to discover what was happening, but he was unable to find out, for Ullikummis completely blocked the road. Then Tasmisus, the Storm God's brother, came to the watch-tower where Hebat stood and told her her husband had been forced to abdicate. Stumbling with shock, Hebat almost fell off the tower, but her women just managed to catch her.

Bas-relief from Yazilikaya showing the Hurrian Storm God (Teshub) standing on the deified mountains Nammu and Hazzi. Before him is his wife Hebat or Hepatu. The third deity is probably their son Sharrumas, who is also symbolised by the bulls at his parents' feet. (*Photo: Mansell Collection.*)

UGARIT

El
98

98 El, whom the Greeks equated with Cronos (2.2.1–7) was creator of all things. The Hebrews seem to have identified him with their Lord God Most High, El Elyon (*Genesis* 24). He was known as The King, or The Bull, and lived in the Fields of El at the source of the rivers, among the headwaters of the two seas. Occasionally the other gods travelled there to consult him, but he had relinquished effective power to the younger deities Yamm-Nahar, ruler of the sea and judge of the rivers, Mot, king of the desert and underworld, Baal, lord of heaven and Anath, goddess of fertility and war. By his wife, the sea goddess Asherah, El had seventy other children, known as the Children of Asherah.

Baal
99–110

99 Baal, the most vigorous of the Ugaritic pantheon, was the son of the corn-god Dagon, whose temple stood next to his in Ugarit (see also I *Samuel* 5). He was usually shown as a youthful warrior, armed with battle-axe and lightning-spear, wearing a helmet adorned with bull's horns. His name means Lord and he was known also as 'Al'eyn, the Mighty, 'Al'eyn Qrdm, the Mightiest Hero, and Zebul, the Prince. In his rôle as god of thunder, he was called Baal Hadhad.

100 The story of his battle with chaos, symbolised by the sea- and river-god Yamm-Nahar, is a ritual myth. Similar material in the Hebrew New Year Psalms makes it clear that the rite was associated with the coming of the autumn rains.

THE BAAL EPIC
101 El designated Yamm-Nahar as his Beloved Son (cf. *St. Mark* 1, xi); then Yamm sent messengers to El asking that Baal, son of Dagon, who commanded the greatest following of all the gods, should be made to acknowledge his supremacy. All the assembled deities, who were in council with El on Mt. Lala, bowed to Yamm's messengers as they arrogantly delivered this request, which El granted. Furious, Baal abused the assembly for its craven manners and turned on the messengers, whom he would have killed had not the goddess Ashtoreth restrained him.

102 Kothar wa-Khasis, the gods' craftsman, then gave Baal two enchanted maces, Yagrush, the Chaser, and Ayamur, the Driver, with which Baal attacked Yamm, felling him with a blow to the forehead. Just as he was about to despatch his foe, Ashtoreth reminded him that it would be dishonourable to slaughter one who was now his prisoner; so Yamm-Nahar's life was spared.

Bas-relief of Baal Hadhad brandishing a mace and carrying a spear. Stele from the temple of Baal Hadhad at Ugarit, *c.* 2000 B.C. Louvre. (*Photo: Giraudon.*)

103 Having established his supremacy over Yamm, Baal decided he would like a new palace, suitable for his enhanced position. He and his sister Anath persuaded Asherah to be their intermediary and ask El to grant permission for the work. This given, messengers were sent to Kothar wa-Khasis, for whom Baal and Anath prepared a noble feast. Baal and the craftsman god disagreed about the design of the building. Kothar felt it should have a window, but Baal did not want one, apparently because he felt that Yamm-Nahar would peer through it at his wives Padriya and Talliya (Flashing Light and Dew). However, reassured of Yamm's powerlessness, Baal eventually consented to Kothar's plan. His former cedarwood home was demolished and a new palace of gold, silver and lapis-lazuli raised upon the same foundations (a common Mesopotamian practice when building temples, the gods' 'houses'). It had a single window, through which Baal sent rain, thunder and lightning upon the earth.

104 Baal held a great house-warming banquet, at which the gods acclaimed him as king. He announced he would spurn his father's new favourite, Mot.

105 In the battle with Yamm-Nahar, Baal had proved his supremacy over the previously uncontrolled might of the sea and rivers, now he faced the power of sterile heat and dust, personified by Mot. Baal sent his envoys, Gapn and Ugar (Vine and Field) to Mot, announcing his refusal to pay him tribute, but Baal was very frightened when Mot replied that although he might have slain the primaeval two-headed serpent Lotan, Baal would find himself powerless against him. Mot proposed to eat him! Apparently Baal was cowed and sent a humble reply.

106 Messengers came to El, saying that Baal was dead. El threw himself on the ground and rent his clothes, covering his head with dust and lacerating his cheeks and body in mourning. Anath meanwhile sought everywhere for her brother's body. Having found it she and the sun-goddess Shapash carried it to Mt. Zaphon. There it was buried.

107 Asherah suggested that her son Ashtar (the evening star?) should succeed to Baal's throne, but Ashtar was so short that when he sat upon it his head was far below its top while his feet dangled in mid-air, so he immediately abdicated.

108 There followed seven years of famine and drought; then Anath fell upon Mot and clove him with a sickle, winnowed him, parched him with fire, ground him like corn and scattered his body like seed upon the earth. (cf. *Leviticus* 2, xiv). Now El dreamed that Baal yet lived. All the gods believed him immediately, but none could find Baal until Shapash, the torch of the gods, went in search of him in the underworld.

109 Baal returned to his throne and the land ran with oil and honey, wine and milk (cf. *Deuteronomy* 11, ix, *Joel* 3, xviii) but after seven years Mot reappeared and challenged him. They wrestled, biting and kicking each other until at length Mot was thrown and Baal fell upon him, but Shapash drew them apart and they were reconciled.

110 Mot's reappearance in the seventh year may be related to a septennial fertility rite, for we know from *Exodus* 23, x and *Leviticus* 25, iii–vii that in ancient Israel the land was left fallow every seventh year. Gray suggests that this artificial dearth was arranged so as to give the powers of sterility and death free play that, exhausted, they might then be quiescent during the next six years.

Anath
111–118

(i) ANATH THE FERTILITY GODDESS
111 At once a virgin and the Mother of Nations (Yabamat Liimmim) Anath was Baal's sister. One story tells of how, when he went hunting she followed him and Baal was overwhelmed with desire for her. They united in the forms of a bull and cow and later, much to his joy, Anath bore her brother a wild ox.

(ii) THE WAR GODDESS
112 The tablets of the Baal epic vividly illustrate the warlike aspect of this fertility goddess's character. She killed Yamm-Nahar's supporters, the flood-god Rabbim, the slippery, wriggling sea-serpent (Lotan?) the seven-headed monster Shalyat, as well as the god 'Atak and goddess Hashat. She muzzled the sea dragon Tannin and destroyed the whole house of El-Dhubub.

113 Carefully made up with henna and perfumed with coriander and amber-gris, Anath went out to do battle between two towns and slaughtered both their peoples, those of the east and those of the west. Wading knee-deep in blood she slung the victims' severed heads over her shoulder, their hands about her waist. Returning home, still relishing battle, she imagined it continuing in the palace, chairs, tables and footstools taking the places of the soldiers. Only later did she clean her blood-stained hands and bathe herself. (Cf. vol. 2: 3.2.51–52)

(iii) ANATH, DANIEL AND AQHAT
114 King Daniel (who may be he whom the Hebrews honoured for his wisdom and godliness, *Ezekiel* 14, xiv), was a man of Rapha. Being without an heir, he sacrificed to the gods for seven days, spending each intervening night on a bed of sackcloth. At length Baal heard his prayer and going to El asked him to grant Daniel's petition, for the king had no son to tend his ancestral spirits, to care for him when he was drunk, to repair his house, to defend him from his enemies or to perform his funeral rites. Granting the prayer, El sent Daniel a son, Aqhat.

115 One day as Daniel sat outside his gate under a tree on the threshing floor, dispensing justice to widows and their children, he saw in the distance the craftsman god Kothar wa-Khasis, lord of Hikpat-El, approaching with bow and arrows. Daniel called his wife Danatiya to prepare a feast for the god, and when Kothar wa-Khasis had gone home gave Aqhat the bow and arrows he had brought.

116 The goddess Anath offered Aqhat great riches in return for them, but he refused. When Anath offered him immortality he scorned her, replying that she had no power to bestow such a gift, all mortals must die. Mockingly he added that a bow and arrows were no weapons for a woman.

117 Furious, the goddess demanded revenge from her father El, offering him violence when he demurred, so the old god gave her permission to do what she would. Anath went to Abelim, the city of the moon, and sought out a drunken soldier, Yatpan by name. She told him how she wished Aqhat to be killed, then, carrying Yatpan in her girdle, flew like a vulture over Aqhat's head and loosed the man upon him. Yet when Aqhat was dead she regretted it.

118 The earth withered at his passing. His sister, the seer Paqhat, told her father Daniel of his murder, prophesying that the drought which had come upon them would last seven years. Daniel buried his son and cursed the land where he had died, the city of Abelim whence his murderer had come. For seven years he mourned his son; then he sent the weeping women away from his house and, putting on clean clothes, sacrificed to the gods. Seeing her father making the sacrifice, Paqhat asked him for a blessing; then, disguising herself as a handsome youth, she went to the city of Abelim and slew Yatpan her brother's murderer as he lay drunk in his tent.

ANCIENT EGYPT

Atum and His Children
119–122

119 Originally there was only a waste of waters, Nun (Nu), from which the great god Atum emerged. Some say he was Nun's child, others that he created himself by uttering his name, hence his titles, *the complete one* and *Neb-er-djer,* lord of the world.

120 Realising that Nun's waters offered him no resting-place, Atum created a hillock. (According to some he himself was the hillock.) In this aspect as the androgynous god Iusau, Atum now engendered and vomited forth twin divinities, Shu (god of air), and his sister-wife Tefnut (goddess of moisture). Shu (see also **141–144**) was the principle of life, Tefnut (see also **143**) of order, this aspect of her nature being personified in the goddess Mayet.

121 While they were young, Shu and Tefnut were either cared for by Nun or by Atum's Eye. Once they were lost in the dark waters of chaos and Atum sent his Eye to seek them, meanwhile creating a second Eye for himself. This was far brighter than the first and when that returned with the children it was angered to find itself outshone. To placate it, Atum set it on his forehead to rule the world he was about to create. Men associated this eye with the sun's burning power and with the cobra goddess Buto (Edjo), the rearing serpent symbolised by the snake-like *uraeus* the pharaohs wore as an emblem of their power.

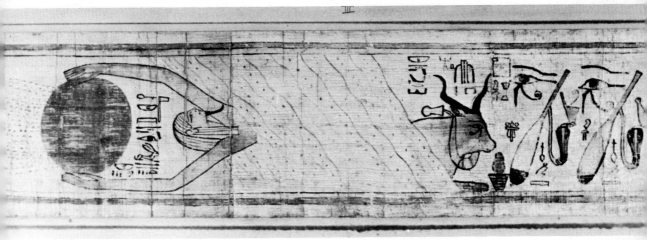

122 When Atum's Eye returned with Shu and Tefnut, the great god wept for joy and from his tears came men.

Geb and Nut
123–124

123 Shu and Tefnut bore the twin gods Geb (the earth) (see also **128, 142, 145**) and Nut (the sky), his sister-wife. At first they clung together but Shu (god of air) separated them (cf. **1** and vol. 4: 7.2.**46–48**). Some say this was on Atum's orders, others that Shu was spurred by jealousy of his children's love.

124 Although thus separated from her husband by day, at night Nut was allowed to descend and rejoin him, and so darkness fell. Occasionally she slipped earthwards during the day, when the heavens grew dark with

The winged *ba* (soul) of the pritestess Pa-Shebut-n-Mut pays homage as the sun disc is carried forth from the Western Desert by the air-god Shu. To the right are the cow goddess Hathor, guardian of souls, and four of the 'rudders of heaven' each watched over by a protective Eye of Horus or *udjat*. XXI Dynasty papyrus. British Museum. (*Photo: Michael Holford.*)

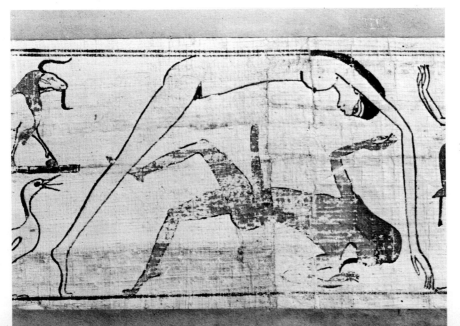

Nut and Geb are separated. To the left a ram symbolises Osiris; a goose, Geb as the Great Cackler. Papyrus of Tameniu, XXI Dynasty. British Museum. (*Photo: Michael Holford.*)

storm clouds. Nut was depicted as a cow or, sometimes, as a huge sow, suckling her piglets, the stars, whom she swallowed each morning and bore anew at dusk. Alternatively, the stars were said to be the souls of the dead lying in her bosom (see also **133, 147**).

Ra
125–140

(i) THE BIRTH OF RA

125 Ra, whose name means 'sun', was sometimes said to have been fathered by Atum, the god of Heliopolis with whom he was early identified, but it was more generally believed that, like Atum, he was self-created. As Ra's cult gained wider acceptance, Atum became identified with the setting sun as an old man tottering towards death, while Ra was the sun at the zenith of its power.

126 Every morning a lotus grew up from the waters of Nun and as its petals unfurled, Ra emerged from them as the Bennu bird to perch on the Benben stone, a gilded obelisk which caught the sun's first rays. Every evening at dusk he returned and was enfolded within the lotus blossom.

127 Although as Atum-Ra the god was said to have fathered Shu and Tefnut, according to another tale Ra was the offspring of these divinities' children, the earth-bull Geb and the sky-cow Nut. One popular story said that every morning he was born as Nut's calf. By midday he was the mature bull Kamephis and fertilised his mother. In the evening he died to be reborn, as his own son, next morning as Nut's blood stained the dawn sky.

128 A Hermopolitan story told how Ra emerged from a cosmic egg laid by the Great Cackler, Geb (**123**) in the form of a goose. The bird's cries broke the silence of chaos as it deposited its egg on the Isle of Flames, a hillock rising from the Sea of the Two Knives, the sacred Hermopolitan lake symbolising the primordial waters. A later version of the tale, said the egg was laid by an ibis, emblem of Thoth.

(ii) RA THE PHARAOH

129 In the First Time, at the beginning of the world, Ra ruled the earth as pharaoh. Daily he left the House of Benben (his temple in Heliopolis) and, attended by Shu, journeyed through the twelve *nomes* (Egypt's provinces) which symbolised the twelve daylight hours. Occasionally he came unpleasantly close to his people and burned them, which led the serpent Apep or Apophis (probably an earlier solar god) to lay a plot to kill him at dawn, but after a day-long battle Apep was worsted. Sometimes it is said that Ra destroyed him by assuming the form of a lion or cat and biting his head off. (See also **135–138**.)

130 Another rebellion was engineered by Set, the great god of Upper Egypt. At Ra's command his son Horus, of the Delta city of Behdety, assumed the form of a winged sun-disc and fell upon the enemy at Edfu, driving all

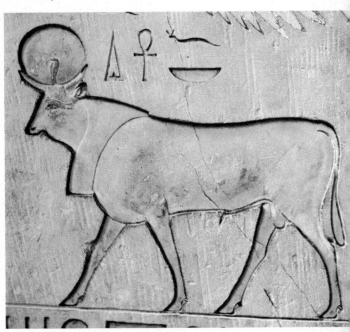

Left—XXVth Dynasty statuette of the Egyptian god Anhur wearing the war crown. His features may be modelled on those of an Ethiopian king. British Museum. (Photo: Michael Holford.)

Below—Bas-relief of the Egyptian bull-god Apis wearing the solar disc and uraeus. The Louvre. (Photo: Photoresources.)

Below—XXIst Dynasty papyrus painting from The Book of What is the Underworld shows the deceased Hent-Taui, musician-priestess of Amon-Ra, kneeling behind a sacred ape and adoring the Eye of Ra in the solar disc as it rises from the Eastern Mountain. British Museum. (Photo: Michael Holford.)

Bronze statuette of Khnum, creator god of Elephantine. British Museum. (Photo: Michael Holford.)

Bronze head of Ra, c. 850
B.C., probably from the
prow of a solar barque. It
originally bore a solar disc
and *uraeus* of which only
the *uraeus'* tail remains.
British Museum. (*Photo:
Michael Holford.*)

Bas-relief of the lion-goddess Sekhmet. (*Photo* *Mansell Collection.*)

before him and winning himself the title of Horus of Edfu. However, Set's forces renewed their attack, this time in the guise of crocodiles and hippopotomi. Again Horus Behdety attacked them, and, standing in the prow of Ra's boat, harried them throughout the Two Lands until at last he captured Set and dragging him before Ra, there beheaded him.

131 In another version of the story Horus Behdety was merged with Horus son of Osiris (**164–172**), and attacked Set in the form of a staff with a falcon's head and triangular spear-point. In this shape he defeated Set and put down a further rebellion too, and Ra awarded him with the insignia of the winged sun-disc, which was placed on the temples of all the gods to defend them from their enemies.

132 As Ra grew old and senile his strength failed till even men realised his frailty and challenged his authority. After consulting with the other gods, Ra sent his Eye in the form of his daughter Hathor, to subdue the rebels. This she easily did in the shape of the lion-goddess Sekhmet, but once her bloodlust was aroused it seemed unquenchable and all mankind was endangered. So Ra ordered great quantities of beer to be dyed red and poured over the earth. Lapping it up in mistake for blood, Sekhmet grew incapably drunk and so men were saved.

133 Dispirited by the rebellion, Ra decided to leave the earth. He mounted the cow Nut, who lifted him up to the heavens, while all the other gods clung to her underside and so became the stars. As Nut trembled with the effort of raising this precious burden, four gods Horus, Set, Thoth and Sopdu were ordered to support her legs, Shu her belly. (Some say Nut, the sky, was supported by the mountains that encircled the world.)

(iii) THE SUN-GOD

134 Every day after his abdication, Ra rose from behind the Mountain Manu (cf. vol. 3: 5.2.**74**) and sailed along the heavenly Nile in Manjet, his Barque of Millions of Years. He wore the Double Crown of the Two Lands, bearing the *uraeus* serpent, which spat fire at all his foes. The boat was crewed by many divinities personifying various aspects of the sun-god's power. They included Hu, the Divine Word, Sia, the Divine Intelligence, and Hike, Magic. Falcon-headed Horus was the helmsman. Thoth stood in the prow defending Ra from enemy attacks.

135 The most dangerous of these came from Apep (**129**) who every morning attempted to halt the heavenly barque. Sometimes he was temporarily successful; then storms raged. Occasionally he even swallowed Ra's boat and all its passengers; then there came an eclipse.

136 At night, Ra voyaged through the twelve provinces of the underworld of Duat in a second boat, Mesektet. Now a mummy, the god was called Auf or Auf-Ra, the Body. His attendants Hu, Sia and Hike still accompanied him, while Upuaut, the Opener of Ways (of the underworld) stood at the vessel's prow. Beside him was the warrior-god Mont of Hermonthis with lance at the ready, for on this night journey Ra was again menaced by Apep and also faced many other dangers.

137 Since the air of the underworld was always deathly still, the Mesektet was drawn along the underworld Nile by relays of demons and hydra-headed serpents, under the command of the goddess of each hour, who spoke the secret word which opened the watergate into the next province. Although subservient, the monsters were hostile to Auf-Ra, who now personified the spirits of the dead whom they sought to swallow.

Nun, god of the primordial waters, raises the boat of day as Khepri pushes forth the dawn sun. Supported by Osiris, Nut receives the solar disc. Papyrus of Anhia, XX Dynasty. British Museum. (*Photo: Photoresources.*)

138 Passing from one province to another, the god brought a faint, transient illumination to the dead souls, who joyfully hailed his coming and fell back in anguish as he departed. He opened their nostrils so that they might breathe. He admonished the bad and relieved the pains and sorrows of the good. At length, having survived all perils, and left Apep chained and transfixed with knives, guarded by the scorpion goddess Selket, Auf came to the twelfth and final region of Duat. Some said this was a huge snake through whose body Auf passed, emerging from its mouth.

139 As his attendants hauled up the boat of day, Auf was reunited with Khepri, his youthful self and became the dawn sun. Khepri's very name means 'he who comes to life' and men identified him with Atum in his aspect as *Neb-er-djer* (119). His emblem was the scarab beetle pushing the ball of the sun before it.

(iv) THE PHARAOH'S FATHER

140 As his wife, Ra chose the daughter of one of his priests at Heliopolis and, taking human form, came to her as her husband. She bore him three sons, the first three pharaohs of the Fifth Dynasty and from that time every pharaoh was the son of Ra and just as Ra was reborn every day so the pharaoh was reborn in his son and his commands were the commands of the god.

The Deposition of Shu
141–145

141 Some stories say that Shu (120–123) became the second ruler of the earth in succession to his father Atum-Ra, although others hold that Thoth succeeded Atum-Ra. Shu was the Heart of Ra, the personification of his divine intellect and so an expression of Atum's creative power. Some said that Shu, Nun and Atum were all born at once and in later texts the god of air was identified with Ra-Harakhte (see 3: Harakhte).

142 When Shu succeeded Atum as ruler of Egypt, he divided the land into *nomes*, organised irrigation and built innumerable temples, all facing east toward his own palace Het Nebes, set between the four pillars of heaven (133). As he grew older however the country was invaded from the desert by the sons of Apep (129, 135–138) who ravaged the whole land before the gods eventually expelled them. Soon afterwards, Shu's sight began to fail and his government grew weaker. One day, while he was away in heaven, his son Geb (123–124), who had fallen in love with Queen Tefnut (120–123) his mother, seized both her and the throne.

143 For nine days the world was battered by storms and all was dark, but gradually calm returned and Geb was acknowledged as pharaoh. Seventy-five days later he began a tour of his realm. While in the east he heard how his father had strengthened himself by placing the *uraeus* serpent on his head. Resolving to follow this example, Geb opened the chest containing the great snake, but the serpent's breath was so venomous that all the pharaoh's retinue fell dead, while he himself was terribly burned and stricken with fever. Eventually the gods suggested he study the *aart* of Ra. This was placed upon his head in a stone box and the pharaoh's sickness left him. Sometime later, the *aart* was taken to be washed in the sacred lake adjoining Het Nebes. When placed in the water it turned into the crocodile Sebek, and quickly swam away.

144 Now, following the traditions of Atum and Shu, Geb restored the temples and cities, repaired the canals which had fallen into decay during

Bronze figure of Sebek,
Ptolemaic period. British
Museum. (*Photo: Michael
Holford*.)

the latter years of his father's reign. Egypt once more grew rich. Indeed she
prospered so greatly that for ever after the throne was called the Throne
of Geb in memory of the great benefits he had brought the land.

145 When Geb reached the age of 1,773 he decided to abdicate and made
Horus (**161–172**) pharaoh of the Northern Kingdom, Set (**130–131, 161–171**)
ruler of the Southern. He himself took the place of Thoth as Atum-Ra's
herald and judge. He also became an attendant upon Ra's solar barque.

Isis and Osiris
146–160

146 The authenticity of the myth as told by the Greek Plutarch in his *Moralia* has been confirmed by Egyptian inscriptions.

147 The sun-god Ra forbade the marriage of Nut and Geb (**123–124**, whom Plutarch identifies with Rhea and Cronos 2.2.3–**9**). When they defied his interdict, Ra cursed Nut, declaring she should bear no children in any month of the year. Taking pity on her, Thoth (Hermes 2.2.**90**–**98**) gambled with the moon at draughts and won from it five days' light. On these inter-calculate days, belonging to none of the year's months, Nut bore the five gods Osiris, Horus (Apollo 2.2.**68**–**80**), Set (Typhon 2.2.**14**–**15**), Isis and Nephthys (Aphrodite 2.2.**57**–**63**).

148 At the birth of Osiris a voice was heard crying, 'The lord of all things comes towards the light' or, according to other accounts, 'A great and benevolent pharaoh, Osiris, is born.'

149 One story says that Osiris was fathered by Ra, Isis by Thoth, Set and Nephthys by Geb. Isis and Osiris loved each other even in the womb and, according to some, Horus was the fruit of their prenatal union.

150 At this time the Egyptians were still barbarous, but Osiris taught them the arts of irrigation and agriculture and established ethical and religious codes; then he set out to civilise the rest of the world, drawing all people to him by his compelling words and his retinue's mellifluous singing.

151 Meanwhile, Isis, helped by Osiris's scribe Thoth, ruled as his regent. She was much embarrassed by Set, her brother, who sought to win both her and the throne.

152 Set conspired with Aso, Queen of Ethiopia, and seventy others to bring about Osiris's death. He had a beautiful casket made to the pharaoh's exact measurements and produced it at a feast, promising to give it to the first man who found it fitted him when he lay in it. When Osiris tried the casket the plotters slammed the lid, hammered it down and sealed it with lead. Carrying the box to the river they flung it in. The day of this terrible deed remained for ever accursed.

153 Stricken with grief, Isis wandered over the earth asking all whom she met if they had seen or heard of the casket. Eventually she traced it to Byblos, where it had come ashore. A huge tamarisk tree had grown up around it and later been felled to form a pillar in the royal palace of King Malacander and Queen Astarte.

154 As the tearful goddess sat to rest by a spring, her grief was interrupted by the arrival of Queen Astarte's waiting women, to whom Isis taught a new fashion of plaiting their hair. This immediately attracted the queen's attention and, intrigued by what she was told of the stranger, Astarte sent for Isis and made her nurse of her newborn son.

155 During the night, the goddess placed the infant in the fire, to burn away its mortality, so that it might become like a god. Meanwhile, transforming herself into a swallow, she flew wailing around the pillar which held Osiris's body. Disturbed by the noise, Astarte entered and snatched her child from the flames. Isis, revealing her true nature, rebuked the queen for her impetuosity (cf. 2.3: Demophon (i)). The royal parents begged the goddess to accept as a gift anything in their palace. Isis asked for the pillar. Cutting it open, she revealed Osiris's coffin. This she carried back to Egypt and hid in the marshes near Buto, for she wished to conceal from Set the fact that she had found the corpse and also that she was now pregnant with Osiris's posthumous son, for by her magic arts she had conceived a child of her dead husband.

156 Set however came upon the coffin while hunting. He tore Osiris's body into fourteen pieces and scattered them throughout the land. Discovering this sacrilege, Isis searched everywhere until she had found thirteen of the fragments. These she carefully preserved, holding funeral ceremonies on the site where each had been found, hoping to deceive Set into thinking the pieces had been buried there.

157 The last piece of the corpse, its phallus, was lost for ever, for Set had thrown it to the fish of the Nile, the pike, the sea bream and the lepidotus, and they had eaten it, an act for which they were eternally accursed. By her arts, Isis however fashioned a new member and mended the broken body, anointed it with oils and restored her husband to life. In these rites she was helped by her sister Nephthys and, some said, by Thoth, Horus and Anubis (Osiris's son by Nephthys. See also glossary).

158 Although Osiris could now have regained his throne he chose to remain in the world of the dead and so became Khenti-Amentiu, the First of the Westerners, King of the Dead.

159 Set now reigned as the undisputed Lord of the Two Lands and Isis, left to raise the infant Horus in secret, was reduced to beggary. One day while she was out seeking food, Set, in the form of a poisonous snake attacked Horus, whom she had concealed among the reeds. Powerless to heal the virulent poison, Isis in despair called upon Ra, who ordered his barge to hove to and sent Thoth to enquire what ailed her.

160 In Ra's name Thoth promised to cure the infant, declaring that the solar boat would remain at anchor, leaving the world in darkness, until Horus had recovered. This meant that Ra was committing the whole of his power to combat Set's evil. Thoth charmed the poison in Ra's name. Horus was healed and thenceforth Ra called him his son.

Bronze statuette of Isis
suckling Horus. British
Museum. (*Photo: Michael
Holford.*)

Horus and Set
161–172

161 In early days Horus was a sky-god of the Delta, worshipped in the form of a falcon. The sun and moon were his eyes. Horus was the Divine Pharaoh, and the human ruler, the god in human form. Later Horus was said to be the son of Ra, or the child of Amon's son Geb. On his abdication Geb gave him the throne of Lower Egypt, as we have seen, and he and his brother Set were known as the Nuoni (the 'two lords') and portrayed as a man having two heads, one a falcon's, the other an animal's.

162 Dissatisfied with his inheritance, Set lay claim to Horus's crown as well. After a fierce battle in which he himself was castrated, Set, taking the form of a black pig, gouged out his brother's weaker eye, the moon, causing a lunar eclipse. However the other gods restored the eye and at a subsequent tribunal Set was deposed and Horus given both crowns, even although Set claimed that, since he defended Ra on his voyage through the underworld (**136–139**) and nightly slew the monster Apep, Ra could not afford to alienate him. However, once Apep was dead, Ra commanded that Set should be driven from his barge, which proceeded without him.

163 Some say Set now went to live in the desert (a symbol of the underworld) and became the god of foreigners, others that he ascended to the sky and, taking the form of the Great Bear, became lord of the storms and winds.

164 Horus, the falcon-god, later became assimilated to Harsiesis (Horus son of Isis and Osiris) and the myth of the rivalry between Horus and Set developed new forms. Set was now held to have displayed a devilish character from the very first, and to have kicked his way out of his mother's womb, emerging through her side. His hair and eyes were an evil red.

165 When he grew to manhood, Harsiesis, determined to avenge his father Osiris and regain the throne, declared war on Set. Many times he decimated Set's forces and once even beheaded Set himself, but to no avail, for the older god, far more powerful than his youthful nephew, always staged a miraculous recovery.

166 At length, Set decided to bring his case before the heavenly tribunal. First he disputed Osiris's original claim to the throne, but lost his plea. Next he summoned Horus, declaring him a bastard pretender.

XXV Dynasty statuette of Neith of Sais wearing the red crown of Lower Egypt. British Museum. (*Photo: Michael Holford.*)

167 The gods were willing to accept Horus as Osiris's son, but their chairman, Ra-Harakhte, felt that Set would be the better ruler, being so much more experienced. After eighty years' argument between the claims of might and right, Thoth and Shu asked the court to prefer Horus's claim. Triumphant, Isis, assuming the battle was won, demanded the *uraeus* should be given to her son. Outraged at this pre-emption of his verdict, Ra refused. To resolve the deadlock the deities summoned Ptah and Bandebdetet of Mendes and asked them to adjudicate between the claimants. They refused to, but advised the court to ask the advice of the oldest goddess, Neith of Sais. She favoured Horus, but again a final verdict was prevented by Ra's injured dignity and deadlock once more ensued.

168 Disguising herself as a ravishing beauty, Isis now captivated Set, telling him a pitiful story of how her son was being swindled out of his inheritance by a brutal stranger. Set declared her son the rightful heir. Isis now revealed herself and Set, being condemned out of his own mouth, lost his case. However, the gods agreed that there should be a trial of strength between him and Horus in which each must assume the form of an hippopotomus. Anxious, since this form was natural to Set, the hippopotomus being one of his emblems, Isis again took a hand and eventually speared Set. However, when he begged for mercy, reminding her that he was her brother, she withdrew the harpoon.

169 Furious at being thus baulked once more, and now by his mother's treachery, Horus leaped from the river and beheaded her. The gods declared he must be punished. Set tracked him down, tore out his eyes and buried them. From them grew two lotus blooms. Meanwhile Hathor, or, some say, Thoth, found the blinded god and bathing his wounds with gazelle's milk restored his sight and brought him back to the divine assembly.

170 The war between him and Set was now virulently renewed until, at Thoth's advice, the gods asked Osiris to give a binding decision on their claims. Osiris pronounced in his son's favour and when Ra challenged the verdict, and questioned Osiris's power, the god of the dead reminded him that, great and powerful as Ra was, it was not to be gainsaid that under Set the rule of divine justice, Mayet, had been long denied upon earth. Moreover, he, Osiris, as the judge of the underworld appointed by Ra himself, was the ultimate judge of all, for gods as well as men passed into the West and came before his throne.

171 So Osiris won acceptance for his decision. Set was brought before the tribunal in chains and ordered, as god of storms and winds, to propel Osiris's boat.

172 Horus became Lord of the Two Lands, Har-pa-Neb-Taui, and restored the rule of Mayet, repaired damaged cities and their temples and brought new prosperity to the land, becoming the model for all pharaohs who succeeded him. He was the intermediary between men and the gods of heaven and conducted the souls of the dead into the presence of Osiris, his father, in the halls of the underworld.

PART 3

Index and Glossary

The following abbreviations are used:
A: Anatolia and N. Syria; C: Classical;
E: Egypt; M: Mesopotamia; T: Turkish;
U: Ugarit.
Bold numbers refer to the numbered
paragraphs of Part 2 unless otherwise
indicated.

Aah (E) ancient moon-god later
assimilated to Thoth (q.v.).
aart of Ra **143**
Abelim, the city of **117, 118**
Abibaal (Phoenician) a god of Byblos.
Abimilki see Athtar.
Absu 12, 14.
Abu 10.

Abuba (Akkadian, M) a winged being,
ally of Marduk in his fight with
Tiamat. See **24–26.**
Adad (Akkadian) god of storms, also
called Addu.
Adapa 71–73.
Addu a variant of Adad (q.v.) and also
one of Marduk's fifty titles. See **28.**
Adonis (Phoenician) the third most
important god of Byblos. His name is
that used by the Greek Philo, the
Phoenician one being uncertain, but
adoni in Semitic languages means 'my
master', so the Greek may be correct.
See also p. 26 and **2.2.62.**
Agaku one of Marduk's titles. It implies

love, anger and perfection. See **28.**
Agga (Sumerian, M) a historic king of
Kish who challenged the power of
Gilgamesh but, according to the poem
Gilgamesh and Agga, was defeated by
him.
Agilma another of Marduk's titles,
implying waves and creativity. See **28.**
Ahmes-Nefertari see Amenophis I.
Akitu festival 18.
Akki see Sargon.
Alalus 90.
'Al'eyn 99.
'Al'eyn Qrdm 99.
Allatum (Hittite-Hurrian, A) deity of
unknown attributes.

Lightning symbol of the Assyrian storm-god Adad, from a boundary stone *c.* 1120 B.C. British Museum. (*Photo: Michael Holford.*)

Ninth-century Phoenician
ivory caryatids of Astarte,
found at Nimrud in
Assyria. British Museum.
(*Photo: Mansell Collection.*)

Papyrus painting of the *ba* hovering over its mummified body. British Museum. (*Photo: Michael Holford.*)

Bronze figure of Bast with
attendant cats, *c.* XXII
Dynasty. British Museum.
(*Photo: Mansell Collection.*)

Aya (Akkadian, M) goddess of dawn, wife of Shamash (q.v.).

Ayamur 102.

---

ba (E) the individual soul, represented as a human-headed falcon. It was born when the person died. Bulls were especially associated with the *ba*. See also *ka*.

Baal (i) (U) 98–109, 111, 112, 114.
(ii) (Phoenician) the chief god of Sidon, but less active than Astarte (q.v.).

Baal Addir (Phoenician and Punic) a deity whose name means 'Powerful Lord', referred to in inscriptions of King Shipitbaal of Byblos and in Punic and Neo-Punic African ones. He may possibly be identifiable with the Jupiter Valens worshipped by the Roman African legions.

Baal Hadhad 99.

Baal Shamin (Phoenician) the 'Master of the Heavens' referred to in inscription of King Yehaumilk of Byblos (cf. **98–99**).

Baalat (Phoenician) the goddess of the city of Byblos and its most important deity. Her name means 'Lady'.

Babel, Tower of p. 21

Babylon, city of p. 22 and **28**.

Bahrein p. 21 and **8**.

Bandebdetet (E) fertility god whose cult animal was the ram. He was the god of the city of Mendes and later held to be as aspect of Amon (q.v.). See also **167**.

Barque of Millions of Years 134.

Bast (E) a prehistoric fertility goddess associated with happiness and the warmth of the sun, she was also known as Bastet and depicted with a cat's head. Originally the goddess of Bubastis she became a national deity in the Twenty-Second Dynasty (c. 935–730 B.C.) when Bubastis was the Egyptian capital. She was associated with the moon and said to be Ra's (q.v.) daughter-wife and bore him Maahes. Cats were sacred to her and a huge cat cemetery existed in Bubastis. Her cult was associated with cheerful river festivities and ritual orgies.

Bau (Sumerian, M) goddess of the poultry farm, wife of Ningirsu (q.v.).

Bel (Akkadian, M) word meaning 'Lord', cognate with Baal (q.v.). Often applied to Marduk (q.v.).

Bel Matai (Akkadian) Marduk's fiftieth 'Name'. It means 'Lord of the World'. See **28**.

Belataiakkis (Hittite, A) a deity whose cult centre was the as yet unidentified city of Samuah.

Belili 44.

Belit-Seri see Geshtinanna.

Beltiya (Akkadian) goddess, consort of Bel, i.e. Marduk (q.v.)

Bennu bird (E) created at dawn from the sun's fire burning the sacred Heliopolitan persea tree, or said to have sprung from Osiris's heart. Herodotus says it was born in Ra's temple meadows but was only seen once every 500 years when it came to bring to the temple an egg of myrrh containing the body of its newly dead father, hence its identification with the phoenix. It was depicted as a huge golden hawk with a heron's head. See also **126**.

Benben, House of 129.

Benben stone 126.

Bes (E) introduced from Sudan during the Twelfth Dynasty, Bes was a grotesque dwarf figure particularly associated with domestic happiness.

Bigirhush (Akkadian, M) a god of the Apsu, ocean, also called Shuzianna.

Birhuturre (Sumerian, M) a hero of Erech who volunteered to act as Gilgamesh's messenger to Agga (qq.v.) during the siege of Erech.

birth, plant of 70.

Buchis (E) the third most famous of the Egyptian bull gods was held to be the incarnation of Mont of Hermonthis, but was also identified with Ra and Osiris (qq.v.). He is also known as Bacis, and Bkha.

Bull of Heaven 57–58. See also Gugalanna.

Bull of the Ennead (E) a title of Atum (q.v.).

Busiris (E) Greek name for the Delta city Djedu, early centre of the Osiris (q.v.) cult and named after him, Per Usire, House of Osiris.

Buto (E) a cobra goddess more properly called Udjat or Edjo. Her chief cult centre was at Buto. She represents the left eye of Atum-Ra which he placed on his brow as the *uraeus*. She was called Lady of Heaven, Queen of Gods. In the Osiris cult she became the daughter of Anubis and foster-mother to Horus (q.v.). One of the most famous oracles was in her temple. See also **121**.

Buto, city of 155.

Byblos, city of p. 26 and **153**.

Chusor (U) ancient god also referred to by Philo as a Phoenician deity, the inventor of iron and smith's work.

Cutha 48, **50–51**.

Dagon (U) ancient corn-god and father of Baal, according to Philo in Phoenician times he was regarded as the inventor of both wheat and the plough. See 99, **101**.

Damgalnunna see Ninhursag.

Damkina 21.

Damu (Sumerian, M) a name meaning 'child', sometimes applied to Dumuzi (q.v.) in ritual laments.

Danatiya 115.

Daniel, King 114–115.

Dazimus 10.

Dilmun p. 21 and 8–11, 14, 30, 38.

Dimtabba (Sumerian) goddess to whom a temple was built by Dugi, a king of the Third Dynasty of Ur (c. 2112– c. 2015 B.C.).

Dingir (Sumerian) generic term for gods.

Djed (E) originally the trunk of an evergreen in which Osiris was said to be embodied. Later an ornate pillar which some texts describe as the god's spine. See **155**.

Duamutef see Amenti.

Duat 136–138.

Dumuzi (Sumerian, M) the shepherd god, also a title of kings. It means 'True and faithful son'. See 14, **39–46, 47**.

Duranki (Sumerian) an early name for Nippur, meaning 'the bond uniting heaven and earth'. Here, it was said, Enlil (q.v.) broke the earth's crust with his pickaxe, allowing man to emerge.

Ea 17, 20–21, 23, 26–28, 35, 38, 50, 60, 71–73.

Edjo see Buto.

El (i) (U) 98, 101, 103–108, 114, 117.
(ii) (Phoenician) the principal god of Byblos, but inactive.

El, the fields of **98**.

El-Dhubub (U) a god who chased Baal (q.v.) from his throne on the heights of Zaphon. Anath (q.v.) killed him. See 112.

Elam 14.

Elibaal (Phoenician) a god of Byblos.

Ellil (i) (Hurrian, A) Hurrian version of the name Enlil (q.v.). See **93**.
(ii) (U) dutiful son of Keret (q.v.).

Emesh 6.

Enbilulu 14.

Endin (Sumerian, M) the waste land or desert, a symbol of the Underworld.

Endukugga (Sumerian) Underworld god, also called Enmul, father of Enlil, husband of Nindukugga (qq.v.).

Engur (Sumerian) Enki's (q.v.) shrine in the city of Eridu. See also **12**.

Winged goddess possibly Beltiya or Ishtar from the palace of Ashurbanipal II (883–859 B.C.). British Museum. (*Photo: Mansell Collection.*)

Enki 1–2, 7–17, 20, 31–34, 41.

Enkidu 54–58, 67–68.

Enkimdu 14, 39.

Enlil (Sumerian and Akkadian, M) in Babylonian Tammuz (q.v.) liturgies, a title of Tammuz, but generally refers to the god of air and storms. See 1–7, 14, 15, 16, 26, 27, 30, 32, 34, 38, 41, 68, 90, 93.

Enmul see Endukugga.

Ennead of Heliopolis the gods Isis, Osiris, Nephthys, Set (qq.v.).

Ennugi (Akkadian, M) god of canals and irrigation and agriculture, also called Sabarragimgimme.

Enshag 10.

Enten 6.

Enuma Elish, the 18–28, 34.

Epadum a title of Marduk, associating him with irrigation. See 28.

Erech, city of (Sumerian, M) modern Warka. The well-known Biblical name Erech is usually used in preference to the Sumerian, which was Uruk. See 16, 42, 53, 56, 58, 65.

Ereshkigal 1, 40, 49–51.

Eridu, city of 16, 71, 73.

Ernutet (E) cobra goddess of harvests who was assimilated to Renenet (q.v.).

Esagila 28.

Eset a variant of Isis (q.v.).

Esharra 26.

Eshmun (Phoenician) the third god of the Sidonian pantheon, he seems to have been the Sidonian equivalent of Adonis (q.v.). The Greeks identified him with Asclepios.

Etana 69–70.

Etemenanki (Akkadian, M) the great ziggurat (step-pyramid) of Babylon, not a tomb but the centre of the temple complex.

Euphrates, River 14, 65.

Eye, of Atum 121–122.

Eye, of Horus see Thoth.

Eye, of Ra 132.

First of the Westerners 158.

First Time, the 129.

Flames, Isle of 128.

galla 42–45.

Gapn 105.

Gazbayas (Hittite-Hurrian, A) a god whose chief cult-centre was at Hupisna (C: Cybistra).

Geb 123–124, 127–128, 142–145, 147, 149, 161.

Geb, the Throne of 144.

Geshtinanna (Sumerian, M) sister of Dumuzi (q.v.) and Recorder of Heaven and Hell, a singer and wise interpreter of dreams. Her name means Vine of Heaven. She is also called Nin-Edin, Lady of the Wilderness (Underworld) or, in Akkadian, Belit Seri. See 43–44.

Ghazir a title of Mot (q.v.).

Gibil a title of Marduk, originally name of the god of metalworkers. See 28.

Gil another of Marduk's titles, meaning 'exalted'. See 28.

Gilgamesh 53–68.

Gilgamesh and the Huluppu-Tree 64, 68.

Gilgamesh, the Epic of 53–63.

Gilma a title of Marduk, meaning 'flame'. See 28.

Great Bear (Ursa Major) 163.

Great Cackler, the 128. See also Geb.

Great Green (E) the Mediterranean Sea.

Gugal a title of Marduk meaning 'great wealth'. See 28.

Gugalanna (Sumerian, M) a name of Ereshkigal's (q.v.) husband. It means, Great Bull of Heaven. See also 40, 57–58.

Gushkinbanda 17.

Hadhad See Baal Hadhad.

Haia (Sumerian) god of Lagash, husband of Nanshe (q.v.).

Halkis see Kait.

Hanish (Akkadian, M) herald of storms.

Hannahannas 77–78.

Hapantalli (Hattic, A) Hattic original of Hittite Hapantalliyas.

Hapantalliyas (Hittite, A) the 'patron god'.

Hapi (E) androgynous god of the Nile and its floodwaters, supremely a fertility deity. His devotees considered him greater even than Ra (q.v.). The Nile was believed to flow all round the world, through the underworld and across the skies. As lord of the underworld river Hapi was identified with Nun (q.v.). He lived on the island of Bigeh at the Nile's First Cataract, in a grotto guarded by Khnum (q.v.). Sometimes he was thought of as two gods, one personifying the Nile's upper reaches, the other its lower. In the Osiris (q.v.) cult he became identified with Osiris, or, sometimes was said to personify the Nile's waters, while Osiris expressed the indundation. The river was then held to derive from Osiris's perspiring hands, while Isis's (q.v.) tears caused the floods.

Hapy see Amenti.

Har-pa-Neb-Taui (Lord of the Two Lands) 172.

Harakhte (E) Horus of the Horizon, sometimes called Horus of the Two Horizons, an aspect of Horus (q.v.) that developed as his rôle as a sun-god became more prominent. Later, he was

A Phoenician figure of the Egyptian god Bes. Barracco Museum, Rome. (*Photo: Mansell Collection*.)

The cow-goddess Hathor, wearing the solar disc and
uraeus, suckles the (obliterated) Queen Hatshepsut
(c. 1503–c. 1482 B.C.). (*Photo: Ronald Sheridan.*)

Horus Behdety wearing the white crown of
Upper Egypt. Statue from his temple at Edfu.
(*Photo: Michael Holford.*)

identified particularly with Ra in Ra's aspects as the rising and setting suns Khepri and Atum (qq.v.). Eventually Ra and Horus Harakhte were identified and as Ra-Harakhte became the chief god of the Egyptian pantheon.

harikeshnash tree **80**.

Harmakhis (E) Horus on the Horizon, best known as the Great Sphinx of Giza, he was identified with the rising sun but was also a fount of wisdom.

Haroeris see Harwer.

Harpokrates (E) the infant Horus, son of Isis and Osiris (qq.v.).

Harsaphes (Herishef) (E) the god of Hercleopolis Magna, nationally worshipped during the First Inter-

regnum (*c.*2181–*c.*1233 B.C.), when he was considered an aspect of Horus (q.v.). A fertility god, he was depicted as a ram or ram-headed man.

Harsiesis (E) Horus son of Isis. See Harpokrates and Horus and **164–172**.

Harwer (E) The falcon-cult of Horus early assimilated that of the indigenous god, Wer, whose eyes were said to be the sun and moon. Harwer or Haroeris, was thus referred to as Mekhenti-irty or Hor-merti, 'He who wears two eyes in his forehead' and as Mekhenti-en-irty, 'He who bears no eyes', the god of moonless nights and patron of the blind. The son and/or husband of Hathor (q.v.) he lost his eyes in a

battle with Set, a story later assimilated to the Osiris cult, see **166–172**.

Hashat 112.

Hasikasnawanzas (Hittite, A) god of the as yet unidentified city of Lawzantiya.

Hat-Mehit (E) dolphin goddess, wife of Banebdetet (q.v.).

Hathor (E) early sky-goddess and personification of the Great Mother, she is often shown as a cow, and was sometimes said to have created the world. In early myths she is the daughter of Ra and the sky-goddess Nut (qq.v.). She was also Ra's wife and bore him Ihy, the god of music. She and Nut were often confused in the popular mind. She was both the mother and

breathed its last, the *ka* left it and travelled to the West. There welcomed and refreshed by Hathor (q.v.) it met its heavenly counterpart. The *ka* then returned to the tomb, where it lived by the mummy, although existing simultaneously in heaven. The funeral food was for its consumption. See also *ba*.

Kait (Hattic, A) god known to the Hittites as Halkis and invoked in curses.

Kaka (Akkadian, M) messenger of Anshar (q.v.).

Kalaturru 41.

Kalevala **77** and vol. 2: 3.2.**247–279**.

Kamephis 128.

Kamrusepas 80.

Kanzuras, Mt 90.

Karibatu see Lamassu.

Kashku (Hattic, A) the moon-god.

Katahhas (Hittite, A) a god whose cult centre was in Tawiniya (Cl: Tavium).

Kataziwuri (Hattic, A) Hattic original of the Hittite Kamrusepas (q.v.).

Kauket see Ogdoad.

Keb a variant form of Geb (q.v.).

Keret (U) legendary king of Hubar, a Job-like figure who lost all his family—wife, children and relatives—but later was blessed by El (q.v.).

Khenti-Amentiu (E) the First of the Westerners, i.e. King of the Dead, an ancient god whose attributes were assimilated first by Anubis, later by Osiris (qq.v.). See also **158**.

Khepera a variant of Khepri (q.v.).

Khepri 139.

Khnum (E) He controlled the Nile's dispersion to the north and south from two caverns on the island of Elephantine, where, it was said, the river rose from the underworld. His name means 'creator' and he was said to have created not only himself but also the world and raised the heavens on four pillars. As a potter, he made gods and men from clay and he was sometimes held to be Lord of the Afterworld. Where he was not accepted as the creator *sui generis* he was held to be an aspect of Ra (q.v.). See also Hapi.

Khons (E) Theban moon-god later said to be son of Amon and Mut (qq.v.). Originally he seems to have symbolised the royal placenta, which was identified with the moon, just as the pharaoh himself was identified with the sun, as the offspring of Ra (q.v.). Khons was identified with Thoth (q.v.) as Lord of Time, with Shu (q.v.) as Lord of the Air and was worshipped as a powerful oracle god and magician.

Khonsu a variant of Khons (q.v.).

Ki 1.

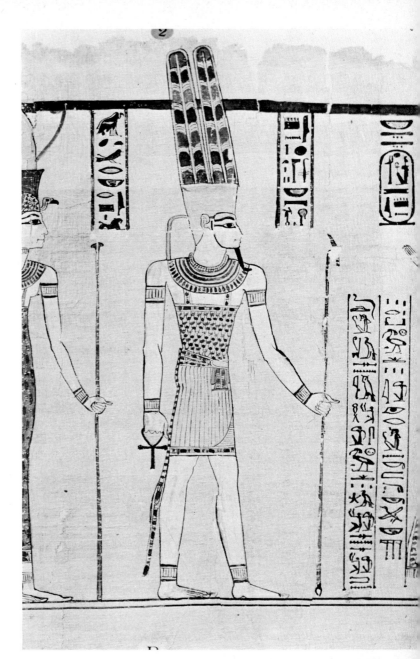

Papyrus painting of the Egyptian god Khons wearing the war crown. (*Photo: Michael Holford*.)

Bronze statuette of the god Min wearing the war crown and solar disc. British Museum. (*Photo: Michael Holford*.)

Limestone statue of the Assyrian god Nebo from Nimrud, *c.*800 B.C. British Museum. (*Photo: Mansell Collection.*)

chief god Amon and absorbed the characteristics of the sky-goddess Amaunet (q.v.). In a great annual festival Amon's image was carried from Karnak to Mut's temple in Luxor. Her function as a fertility goddess was emphasised by her androgynous nature.

Nammu 1, 12–13.

Namru a title of Marduk signifying brilliance, purity and enchanting power. See **28**.

Namtar (Sumerian and Akkadian, M) an underworld demon, in Akkadian myths vizier to Ereshkigal (q.v.) and see **49–50**.

Namtillaku, a title of Marduk meaning 'god of life, comforter, sustainer'. See **28**.

Nannar 4–5, 39, 41, 68.

Nanshe (Sumerian, M) goddess of Lagash, she was particularly concerned with social justice and also interpreted the gods' dreams. See also **14**.

Naram-Sin (Sumerian, M) a king of Agade (Akkad) who sacked the holy city of Nippur and desecrated its temples. A myth explains that the subsequent devastating invasion by Gutian hill peoples was prompted by Enlil's (q.v.) wrath at this outrage. Eight of the other chief gods and goddesses pleaded with Enlil to save Sumer and in return they cursed Agade for ever.

Nari Lugaldimmerankia (Akkadian, M) a title of Marduk (q.v.) meaning 'deliverer and supreme king'.

Narunte (Assyrian, M) an Elamite (West Iran) goddess of victory, whom the late Assyrians called a 'sister of the evil-giver'.

Naunet see Ogdoad.

Nawtiyalas (Hittite, A) a deity whose cult centre was the as yet unidentified city of Zarwisa.

Nazi 10.

Neb-er-djer 119, 139.

Nebhet Hotep (E) a wife of Atum (q.v.).

Nebiru see Nibiru.

Nebo (Akkadian, M) son of Marduk (q.v.) and mediator between gods and men. His chief shrine was at Borsippa.

Nedu Akkadian form of Sumerian Neti (q.v.).

Nefertum (E) an ancient god early taken into the Memphite pantheon as son of Ptah and Sekhmet (qq.v.). His name means 'lotus' and he was said to have risen from the cosmic lotus blossom as

King Urnashi of Lagash (c. 2630 B.C.) attended by his heir Akurgal and retainers, helps to build a temple to the god Ningirsu and later celebrates its completion. Louvre. (*Photo: Mansell Collection.*)

a weeping child. From his tears came men. In Heliopolitan solar myths he was therefore associated with Atum-Ra (see Ra) and considered to be a manifestation of him.

Neheh see Heh.

Neith (E) goddess of Sais and of hunting, she was known as the Great Goddess, Mother of the Gods, and said to have born Ra (q.v.) even before she emerged from Nun's primaeval waters, which she sometimes personified. Subsequently she was said to be Ra's daughter. Her husband was Khnum (q.v.). A guardian of the dead, she stood at the head of a mummy's coffin with Nephthys (q.v.) and was goddess of the canopic jar guarded by Duamutef (see Amenti). See also **167** and p. 75.

Nekhebet (E) vulture-goddess of Upper Egypt with a cult centre at Nekheb, opposite Nekhen (Hierakonpolis), Horus's city. She was assimilated into the solar cult as Ra's daughter and right Eye (q.v.), into the Osiris cult as wife of Khenti-Amentiu (q.v.) but she was also wife of Hapi (q.v.) and so an expression of the Great Mother. She was depicted as the pharaoh's guardian, shielding him with wings outstretched.

Nemur (E) a black or piebald bull, also called Mnevis, venerated at Heliopolis as Ra's incarnation.

Nephthys (E) sister of Isis, wife of Set, whom she deserted after his murder of Osiris (qq.v.). Though she had no children by her sterile husband she

bore Osiris a son, Anubis (q.v.). In funeral rites, she stood in the form of a kite at the coffin's head, Isis at its foot, folding the dead within their wings. Nephthys was also the goddess of the canopic jar guarded by Hapy (see Amenti). See also **147, 149, 157.**

Nergal 4, 36, 38.

Neti 4.

Nibiru 27.

Nidaba (Sumerian, M) patroness of writing, music and bookkeeping, and goddess of Lagash.

Nin-Edin see Geshtinanna.

Ninagal 17.

Ninattas (Hurrian, A) attendant on Shaushkas (q.v.).

Ninazu 4.

Nindukugga (Sumerian, M) underworld

he was worshipped in Egypt and, sculptures suggest, associated with the frightening power of the desert.

Statuette of the Egyptian god Ptah from the tomb of Tutankhamun (c. 1361–c. 1352 B.C.). (Photo: Ronald Sheridan.)

Sabarragimgimme see Ennugi.

Sahassaras (Hittite, A) goddess of the city of Tuwanuwa (Cl: Tyanna; T: Bor) and consort of the Storm God (q.v.). See also Hebat, Huwassanas, Tasimis.

Sandon see Santas.

Santas (Luwian, W or SW coasts, A) deity of uncertain attributes whom the Hittites identified with the Assyrian Marduk (q.v.). During the Greek period he had a cult centre at Tarsus, where he was known as Sandon.

Sargon of Agade (Akkadian, M) great Akkadian king of Sumer (c. 2370 B.C.). Legend says his mother concealed his birth and placed him in a rush basket on the river. He was found by Akki who reared him as a gardener. In this rôle, Sargon won the love of Ishtar (q.v.) who made him king.

Sartiyas (Hittite, A) goddess known as Queen of Katapa, a city near the modern Kügük Köhne.

Satis (E) Satis, Sati or Satet was a fertility goddess of Siheil, an island near the Nile's First Cataract. In early beliefs she purified the pharaoh with lustrations as he entered the underworld. She became associated with Khnum (q.v.) as his wife, and in the Northern Kingdom was thought of as queen of the gods.

Sea Goddess, the (Hurrian, A) goddess of unknown name. See **93**.

Sea of the Two Knives 128.

Sebek (E) ancient water and fertility god whose cult centre was at Crocodilopolis in the Faiyum. The son of Neith of Sais (q.v.) he was early held to serve the sun-god and caught the four Amenti (q.v.) as they rose from chaos. During the Twelfth Dynasty (c. 1991–c. 1786 B.C.) he became a royal god, identified with Geb (q.v.) and worshipped throughout Egypt as Sebek-Ra. His most important sanctuary in Upper Egypt was Kom Ombo (Ombos) and as his cult animal was the crocodile he became associated with Set (q.v.). At another cult centre, in Hake Moirs, a sacred crocodile, his incarnation, was kept, its ears and front feet decorated with jewels and gold. In the *Coffin Texts* of the Middle Kingdom (c. 2133–1633 B.C.) Sebek is identified with Maka (q.v.) as a manifestation of evil, but otherwise he was seen as benevolent, though awesome. See also **143**.

Seventh-century B.C. clay tablet with outline map of the world, surrounded by the waters of the Persian Gulf. Beyond lie various mysterious regions denoted by the triangles. The text describes the conquests of King Sargon of Agade. British Museum. (Photo: B. Museum.)

The Egyptian goddess Selket protecting the canopic chest of Tutankhamun.
(*Photo: Roger Wood.*)

Sehem (E) a personification of the divine energy which caused and sustained the world. See also Hu, Heh and Sia.

Seker (E) early sparrow-hawk-god of the necropolis of Memphis, he governed the underworld kingdom known as the Western Desert, standing at its gate, the Gate of the Ways, eating the hearts of the dead. See also Ptah-Seker-Osiris.

Sekhemtaui (E) Power of the Two Lands, Upuaut as an aspect of Osiris (qq.v.).

Sekhmet (E) lion-goddess, Ra's daughter and his Eye (q.v.), called the Mighty One. In Memphis the wife of Ptah (q.v.) and one of the Great Triad of Memphis. Occasionally she was linked with Mut (q.v.) and also identified with Hathor (q.v.). See **132**.

Selket (E) scorpion-goddess of fertility and the after-life. Also called Serquet, she guarded one of the underworld's four gates, the sources of the Nile. Her husband was Nekhebkau. Sometimes said to chain dead souls, at other times she was seen as kindly. She helped Isis to rear Horus (qq.v.) and stood with her on guard at the foot of coffins. She was the goddess of the canopic jar guarded by Qebehsenuf (see Amenti). See also **138**.

Serquet see Selket.

Seshat (E) originally goddess of writing and mensuration, a deity of the royal household she recorded the pharaoh's name on a leaf of the Tree of Life, so assuring him immortality. The number of his mortal years was recorded on her notched palm wand. Having fore-knowledge of fate she was associated with Anubis (q.v.) but her husband was Thoth (q.v.).

Set (E) early predynastic god probably introduced from Lybia, his emblems were the crocodile, hippopotomus and the Typhonian animal (q.v.). Originally his cult centre was Nubt, later known as Ombos, and he was Lord of Upper Egypt at least until the late Middle Kingdom. His title was Majesty of Set and only Ra (q.v.) was addressed in similar terms. See also p. 26 and **130–131, 133, 145, 147, 149, 151–152, 157, 161–171**.

Seth variant of Set (q.v.).

Seven Judges, the 40, 50.

Shadrapa (Phoenician and Punic) a god of healing, referred to in sixth and fifth century B.C. inscriptions from Amrit and also in Punic and Syrio-Greek references.

Shai (E) god who determined the individual's fortune, life-span and mode of death and led the soul into the after-world for judgment before Osiris. He was at first depicted as a man, later as a goat, finally as a serpent and was said to be Meshkent's (q.v.) husband.

Shalyat 112.

Shamash (Akkadian, M) sun-god, god of justice, 'the great judge of heaven and earth'. cf. Utu and see **57, 58, 60, 69, 70.**

Shapash 106, 108–109.

Shara (Sumerian, M) god of Umma. See **42.**

Sharmas see Sharrumas.

Sharrumas (Hurrian-Hittite, A) son of Teshub and Hebat (qq.v.) he was referred to as 'the calf of Teshub' and depicted as a bull in the Yazilikaya rock sculptures. See p. 57

Sharuk see Ninurta (i).

Sha'tagat (U) goddess El (q.v.), made from clay and sent to heal Keret (q.v.) of a mortal illness.

Shaushkas (Hurrian-Hittite) important goddess whom the Hurrians identified with Akkadian Ishtar. The Hittite king Hattusilis III adopted her as his patroness. Ninattas and Kilittas were her attendants. See also Lelwanis.

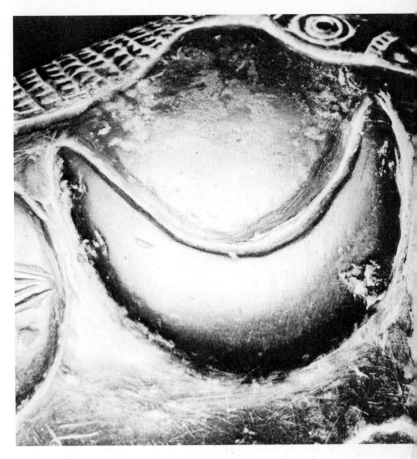

Symbol of the Akkadian moon-god Sin, from a boundary stone, *c.* 1120 B.C. British Museum. (*Photo: Michael Holford.*)

Shazu a title of Marduk (q.v.) signifying his power to read men's minds. Possibly cognate with Shazi, the name of the Iranian Elamite river-god and judge of ordeals—accused criminals were thrown into the river to be saved or destroyed by Shazu.

Shed (E) ichneumon-god, worshipped as the destroyer of snakes and crocodiles' eggs. He was held to be an aspect of Atum (q.v.).

Shipit Baal (Phoenician) a god of Byblos referred to in an inscription of King Yehaumilk.

Shu 120–123, 127, 129, 133, 141–144, 167.

Shukalletuda (Sumerian, M) a gardener. Tortured by summer dust and heat he was inspired by the stars to plant trees in five parts of his garden. Plants flourished in their shade and so attractive grew the garden that Inanna (q.v.) came to rest in it. Unfortunately Shukalletuda was tempted to become the goddess's lover and as a result the whole country was afflicted with plague.

The Egyptian goddess Tefnut as the lynx, kills the wicked snake Apophis.
XIX Dynasty papyrus of Hunefur. British Museum. (*Photo: Photoresources.*)

Shullat (Akkadian, M) herald of storms.

Shulpae (Akkadian) god of feasts.

Shunem (U) Father Shunem, this title, of uncertain meaning, was given to El (q.v.).

Shurruppak, city of **35**.

Shuzianna see Bigirhush.

Sia (E) a bearded man symbolising the divine intelligence, and therefore in Memphis called the Heart of Ptah. He was associated with Thoth and shared with Hu the task of carrying the Eye of Horus (qq.v.). He also personified the human conscience. See also **134, 136**.

Siduri (Akkadian, M) goddess of wine and beer. See **60**.

Sigensigdu 12.

Sikis 17.

Sin (Sumerian and Akkadian, M) a Sumerian title of Nannar (q.v.) and the name of the Akkadian moon-god. See **50**.

Sirsir a title of Marduk (q.v.) and see **28**.

Sirtur another name of Ninsun (q.v.).

Sobk variant of Sebek (q.v.).

Sokaris see Seker.

Sopdu 133.

Storm God (Hurrian and Hittite, A) the chief god of the Hittite pantheon, his name is unknown, being written by the symbol for Storm God. In Anatolia he is depicted as driving a chariot drawn by bulls, his sacred animal. The Storm God standing on a bull and known to the Romans as Jupiter Dolichenus is probably a later form. In Syria, where the Hurrians called him Teshub (q.v.) he is usually depicted unaccompanied and brandishing a lightning-axe. cf. Taru and see also **74**, **77, 84–85, 87–97**.

Suchos a variant of Sebek (q.v.).

Suhgurim a title of Marduk (q.v.).

Sumukan (Hittite, A) fertility god and patron of animals.

Sumuqan 14.

Sun God, the Hittite (A) In many lists of gods attached to treaties the Sun God has first place. He was thought of as the god of justice and as the 'shepherd of mankind', ideas possibly of Mesopotamian origin (cf. Shamash and Dumuzi). He may have been introduced into the Hittite pantheon by lakeside or coastal people from the east or assimilated to one of their gods, for one text speaks of him as rising from the sea, another as bearing fish on his head. There were other distinct aspects of the god, known as Sun-God-in-the-Water and Sun-God-of-the-Underworld, through which the sun was said to pass at night. (cf. Ra). See **74, 77, 79–80, 81, 94.**

Sursunabi (Akkadian, M) the Old Babylonian form of Urshanabi (q.v.).

Sutekh (E) god of the Hyksos pharaohs who identified him with Set (q.v.).

Suwanzipas (Hittite, A) a deity whose cult centre was the as yet unidentified city of Suwanzana.

———————————

Tablets of Destiny 22, 25.
Takitis 97.
Talliya 103.
Tammuz 39–47, 51–52, 72.
Tannin 112.
Tarhuntas (Luwian, W or SW coast, A)

the Storm God, alternatively called Tarhuis. His name means the Conqueror and is the origin of the Etruscan Tarchon.

Taru (Hattic, A) the Storm God and head of the Hattic pantheon. cf. Storm God, the Hittite, and Teshub.

Tarukka 86.

Tasimis (Hittite, A) goddess, consort of the Storm God in the area immediately north of the Taurus foothills. See also Hebat, Huwassanas, Sahassaras.

Tasmisus 90, 97.

Taueret (E) predynastic mother goddess depicted as an hippopotomus. She was the wife of Bes (q.v.) and the especial protectress of pregnant women. She was also known as Thoeris and Apet.

Tefnut (E) wife of Shu (q.v.) and sometimes said to be the left Eye of Horus,

i.e. the moon. As the Eye of Ra (q.v.) she fled into the Nubian desert in the form of a lioness or lynx and Shu went with Thoth (q.v.) to bring her back. They transformed themselves into baboons and eventually caught her, after which, it was sometimes said, she married Thoth and when they returned to Ra she was placed on Ra's forehead as the *uraeus* (q.v.). See also **120–123, 127.**

Telepinus 75–82.

Tem a variant of Atum (q.v.).

Teraphim (Sumerian, M) household gods, roughly comparable with the Roman Lares and Penates, but also the personal gods of the household, who interceded with the great gods on behalf of their people.

Teshub (Hurrian, A) the Storm God and

The ibis-headed Egyptian god Thoth. Painted relief from the tomb of Amon at Karnak. (*Photo: Roger Wood.*)

chief of the pantheon. (cf. the Storm God of the Hittites, and the Hattic Taru). His wife Hebat (q.v.) was almost his equal in importance and they were worshipped jointly in Aleppo, Smuha (modern Malatya?), Kummanni (Cl: Hyde), Hurma and Apzisna.

Theoris see Taueret.

Thitmanet (U) dutiful daughter of Keret (q.v.).

Thoth (E) predynastic god thought to have been originally a funerary deity. The Ogdoad of Hermopolis (q.v.) were known as his 'souls'. He was said to have created himself by speaking his own name and appeared enfolded in a lotus blossom which rose from the waters of chaos. With the spread of the cult of Ra (q.v.) this story was applied to Ra and Thoth was assimilated to the new god as his Heart, i.e. as a personification of the divine intelligence. He became identified with the moon, weaker Eye of Horus (q.v.), whose attributes Ra had also assimilated. It was said that Ra created the moon for Thoth as a reward for rescuing his Eye, which Tefnut (q.v.) had carried into the desert. Alternatively, Ra allowed Thoth to create the moon and made him the governor of the night sky. As the moon deity Thoth was also god of time and said to have invented astronomy, engineering and mathematics. He acted as the gods' scribe and was Lord of Magic. In the Osiris (q.v.) cult he became Osiris's vizier and taught him those arts of civilisation that the divine king brought to man (**150**). In Osiris cult myths he was the god of truth and justice. See **128, 133, 141, 145, 147, 149, 151, 157, 159–160, 167, 169–170**.

Tiamat 20–26.

Tigris, River 14.

Tiy see Amenophis III.

Triad of Elephantine (E) Khnum, Satis and Anuket (qq.v.).

Triad of Memphis (E) Ptah, Sekhmet and Nefertum. Later Imhotep replaced Nefertum (qq.v.).

Triad of Thebes (E) Amon, Mut and Khons (qq.v.).

Tuku a title of Marduk (q.v.) refers to the binding words of a spell.

Tum variant of Atum (q.v.).

Tutu a title of Marduk (q.v.) meaning 'father and restorer of the gods'.

Two Knives, the Sea of the **128**.

Typhonian animal (E) a strange beast with long curved snout, square, pricked ears and a tufted tail. An emblem of Set (q.v.).

Ubara-Tutu (Akkadian, M) father of Utnapishtim (q.v.).

Ubelluris 93–94.

Ubshuukkina (Sumerian, M) the assembly court of the gods, and so, by association, the assembly of the holy city of Nippur.

Udjat (E) the sun-god's eye. See Ra, Amon, Haroerus.

Uduran (Assyrian, M) a god of the seventh century B.C. originally worshipped by the Iranian Elamites under the name Hutran.

Ugar 105.

Ullikummis 92–97.

Umunmutamku 17.

Umunmutamnag 17.

Upuaut (E) wolf-god, at first the local deity of Asyut in Middle Egypt, later identified with Khenti-Amentiu and so associated with Anubis. He was thought to lead the pharaoh's army into battle. With the rise of the Osiris (q.v.) cult he was said to be Osiris's son and was shown at the prow of his boat as it sailed through the underworld. He was now worshipped chiefly as the god who guided souls through the underworld. Sometimes he appeared under the name Sekhemtaui, Power of the Two Lands, as an aspect of Osiris. See also **136**.

Ur, city of p. 21 and 13.

uraeus (E) serpent image symbolising supreme power, worn by the pharaohs as descendants and reincarnations of the sun god. See **121, 134, 143, 167**.

Urash (Sumerian, M) goddess wife of An (q.v.).

Urbadda see Kusug.

Urbadgumgum a name of Ninsar (q.v.).

Urshanabi 60–61.

Urt-Hikeu (E) sometimes said to be Ra's (q.v.) wife. Her name means 'powerful with magic'.

Uruk see Erech.

Utanapishtim (Akkadian, M) Old Babylonian form of Utnapishtim (q.v.).

Utnapishtim 35–38, 59–60, 62.

Uttu 9, 14.

Utu (Sumerian, M) sun-god, and, in two funeral songs dating from *c.* 1700 B.C. is also referred to as judge of the dead. cf. Shamash and see also, **5, 8, 14, 29, 39, 43–45, 66**.

Washaliyas (Hittite, A) deity whose cult centre was the as yet unidentified city of Harziuna.

Wepwawet (E) ancient wolf-god later identified with Upuaut (q.v.).

Wer see Harwer.

Worm and the Toothache, The **18**.

Wurukatti (Hattic) important deity

whose name means King of the Land. He was identified with the Sumerian war-god Zababa and worshipped especially in the area immediately north of the Taurus foothills, around Tuwanuwa (Cl: Tyana).

Wurusemu (Hattic-Hittite, A) sun-goddess, wife of Taru (q.v.) and chief deity of the holy city of Arinna (q.v.).

Yabamat Liimmim 111.

Yagrush 102.

Yamm-Nahar 98, 100–103, 112.

Yassib (U) rebellious heir of Keret (q.v.).

Yatpan 117–118.

Zababa (Sumerian, M) war-god. See also Wurukatti.

Zahgurim a title of Marduk (q.v.) meaning 'scourge of the wicked, saviour of his friends'. See **28**.

Zahrim 'scourge of the wicked', a title of Marduk (q.v.).

Zamamas (Hittite, A) god whose cult centres were at Hipisna (Cl: Cybistra) and the as yet unidentified cities of Illaya and Arziya. He was known as God of the Throne.

Zaphon, Mt 106.

Zebul 99.

Zigaratta 85.

Ziku a title of Marduk (q.v.) signifying he was the essence of goodness.

Zintuhi (Hattic-Hittite, A) granddaughter of the great sun-goddess Wurusemu (q.v.).

Zinuhiyas (Hittite, A) deity whose cult centred at Arinna (q.v.).

Ziparwas (Hittite) deity referred to in omen texts.

Zisi a title of Marduk (q.v.). See **28**.

Ziukkinna 'sustainer, leader, and king of the gods', a title of Marduk (q.v.). See **28**.

Ziusudra, King 29–30, 34.

Zu (Akkadian, M) a bird-man, god of storms and darkness and enemy of the great gods. He stole the Tablets of Destiny (q.v.) from Enlil (q.v.) while the latter was washing (cf. **63**) and flew away with them. Eventually Lugalbanda (q.v.) undertook to recover the Tablets. He killed Zu. In later Assyrian hymns Marduk (q.v.) is credited with his death. For Sumerian reference see **65–66**.

Zulimas (Hittite, A) deity whose cult centre was the as yet unidentified city of Sugazziya.

Zulum a title of Marduk (q.v.) meaning 'the cutter of the clay'.

PART 4

Bibliography

The standard edition of the texts is

PRITCHARD, JAMES B. (ed.) *Ancient Near Eastern Texts Relating to the Old Testament*. Princeton, N.J.: Princeton University Press, 3rd ed., extended, 1969.

Other works:

ABBATE, FRANCESCO (ed.) *Egyptian Art*. Translated by H. A. Fields. Octopus Books, 1972.

*ALDRED, CYRIL *The Egyptians*. Thames & Hudson. 1961.

BARNETT, R. D. *Assyrian Palace Reliefs in the British Museum*. British Museum. 1970.

BECK, M. A. *Atlas of Mesopotamia*. Nelson. 1962.

BENITO, CARLOS ALFREDO *'Enki and Ninmah' and 'Enki and the World Order'*. University of Pennsylvania Ph.D. thesis 1969. Ann Arbor, Michigan: University Microfilms Inc. 1970.

BIBBY, GEOFFREY *Looking for Dilmun*. Collins. 1970.

*BRATTON, FRED GLADSTONE *Myths and Legends of the Ancient Near East*. New York: Thomas Y. Cromwell Co. 1970.

BRITISH MUSEUM (T. C. Mitchell & D. Collon) *Sumerian Art*. British Museum. 1969.

CAMPBELL, JOSEPH *The Masks of God*, Vol. II. Secker & Warburg. 1962.

CASSUTO, U *The Goddess Anath. Canaanite Epics of the Patriarchal Age. Texts . . . Commentary and Introduction*. Translated from the Hebrew by Israel Abrahams. Jerusalem: The Magnes Press: Hebrew University. 1971.

DESROCHES-NOBLECOURT, CHRISTINE *Tutankhamen*. Penguin Books. 1965.

DRIVER, G. R. *Canaanite Myths and Legends*. Edinburgh: T. & T. Clark. 1956.

EDWARDS, I. E. S. *The Pyramids of Egypt*. Penguin Books. rev. ed. 1961.

FINEGAN, JACK *Light from the Ancient Past*. Princeton, N.J.: Princeton University Press. 1959.

GARSTANG, JOHN & GURNEY, O. R. *The Geography of the Hittite Empire*. British Institute of Archaeology at Ankara. 1959.

*GRAY, JOHN *The Canaanites*. Thames & Hudson. 1964.

GURNEY, O. R. *The Hittites*. Penguin Books. 2nd. ed. 1954.

*HAWKES, JACQUETTA *The First Great Civilizations*. Hutchinson. 1973.

HEIDEL, ALEXANDER *The Babylonian Genesis, a complete translation of all the published cuneiform tablets of . . . Babylonian creation stories*. Chicago, Ill: Phoenix Books, University of Chicago Press. 2nd. ed. 1963.

HERODOTUS *The Histories*. Translated by Aubrey de Selincourt. The Penguin Press. 1954.

HINDSON, EDWARD E. *The Philistines and the Old Testament*. Grand Rapids, Michigan: Baker Book House. 1972.

*HOOKE, S. H. *Middle Eastern Mythology*. Penguin Books. 1963.

*IONS, VERONICA *Egyptian Mythology*. Paul Hamlyn. 1965.

*JAMES, E. O. *Seasonal Feasts and Festivals*. Thames & Hudson. 1961.

—— *The Ancient Gods*. Weidenfeld & Nicolson. 1960.

*KRAMER, SAMUEL NOAH *The Sumerians, their History, Culture and Character*. Chicago, Ill.: The University of Chicago Press. 1963.

—— *Sumerian Mythology*. Memoirs of the American Philosophical Society Vol. XXI. Philadelphia: American Philosophical Society. 1944.

LAMBERT, W. G. AND MILLARD, A. R. *Atrahasis. The Babylonian Story of the Flood*. Oxford: The Clarendon Press. 1969.

LANGDON, S.*Tammuz and Ishtar*. Oxford: The Clarendon Press. 1914.

*MALLOWAN, M. E. L. *Early Mesopotamia and Iran*. Thames & Hudson. 1965.

*MOSCATI, SABATINO *The World of the Phoenicians*. Translated from the Italian by Alastair Hamilton. Weidenfeld & Nicolson. 1968.

*PARROT, ANDRÉ *Nineveh and Babylon*. Translated by Stuart Gilbert and James Emmons. Thames & Hudson. 1961.

PLUTARCH *Moralia* Vol. V. Translated by F. C. Babbit. Heinemann: Loeb Classical Library. 1962.

PRITCHARD, JAMES B. (ed.) *The Ancient Near East: An Anthology of Texts and Pictures*. Oxford University Press. 1958.

*REISMAN, DANIEL DAVID *Two Neo-Sumerian Royal Hymns*. University of Pennsylvania Ph.D. thesis 1969. Ann Arbor, Michigan: University Microfilms Inc. 1970.

*ROUX, GEORGES *Ancient Iraq*. George Allen & Unwin. 1964.

*SANDARS, N. K. (trans.) *The Epic of Gilgamesh. An English Version with an Introduction*. Rev. ed. incorporating new material. Penguin Books. 1972.

—— *Poems of Heaven and Hell from Ancient Mesopotamia*. Penguin Books. 1971.

*SOLLBERGER, EDMOND *The Babylonian Legend of the Flood*. British Museum. 3rd. ed. 1971.

*WILLIAMS, GWYN *Eastern Turkey: A Guide and History*. Faber & Faber. 1972.

WOOLLEY, SIR LEONARD *Excavations at Ur*. Ernest Benn. 1954.

*Works including detailed bibliographies.

CHAPTER 2

Classical Greece and Rome

PART 1

Introduction

THE GREEKS

Because of their extraordinary vitality and pervasiveness, some familiarity with Greek myth and legend is almost indispensable to a full appreciation of our European culture.

Great painters like Botticelli, Veronese and Rubens made the ancient stories the subject of their pictures, and writers from Shakespeare to James Joyce have enriched their work by constant reference. The French dramatists from Racine to Giraudoux are notable for relying on them for the basic plot of their dramas. Today, when good and inexpensive translations enable us to go direct to Homer's *Iliad,* or to see Euripides's *Medea* on the stage, it is especially useful to have some general knowledge of the mythical background to the particular epic or play.

Not only to those who love art and literature is the knowledge of Greek mythology rewarding. Psychologists have found here suggestive symbols for the profound mental processes they are endeavouring to elucidate. Through Freud the term 'Oedipus complex' is now a commonplace. Philosophers also have found it profitable to return to the myths. Bertrand Russell has emphasised the influence of Greek religion on Greek philosophy, and, through such philosophers as Pythagoras and Plato, on Christianity.

Perhaps the most exciting of all recent investigations are those of the archaeologists working on sites once considered only legendary. The German Schliemann, trusting to the fidelity of his Homer, actually unearthed the foundations of Priam's Troy and Agamemnon's Mycenae, finding fabulous treasure and proving to the astonished world that these antique tales were indeed rooted in fact. Through Schliemann's trust in Homer we have added an early chapter to history, that of the Mycenaean culture of pre-classical Greece, which flourished from about 1550 to 1200 B.C.

Another centre of ancient story, the island of Crete, was the field of Sir Arthur Evans's enquiries, and his excavation of the magnificent Palace of Cnossos not only pushed back the frontiers of history yet further, to about 3000 B.C., but also showed how many Cretan legends had some factual basis.

More recent excavations at legendary Mycenaean sites on the mainland have led to the discovery of the 'Palace of Nestor' at Pylos, and the 'House of Cadmus' at Thebes.

Tablets found at Mycenaean towns and in Cnossos inscribed in an entirely unknown script, 'Linear B', challenged scholars with a fascinating

The lion gate of the citadel at Mycenae, thirteenth century B.C., looking towards the plain of Argos. (*Photo: Charisiades, Athens.*)

puzzle. After years of study Michael Ventris and others were able to decipher the script and establish that the language used is archaic Greek. We now know therefore that the Greeks of the Mycenaean age could write, and that Homer's single reference to writing is once more a faithful record of fact. (See Book VI of the *Iliad* and the reference to Bellerophon's 'folded tablet'.)

Linear B script on a Minoan tablet found in the 'Palace of Nestor' at Pylos. (*Photo: Mansell Collection.*)

The Historical Background to the Myths and Legends

Archaeological evidence now makes it possible to trace the probable course of Greek history from *c.* 3000 B.C. when the Neolithic Age was succeeded in the eastern Mediterranean by the Early Bronze Age, and people, akin to those of early Crete and the Cyclades, entered Greece and fused with the Neolithic folk already there. These invaders were of Mediterranean stock, and they worshipped the Great Goddess, a fertility goddess who appeared in many guises. She was unmarried, and in many instances her lover appeared to her in the form of a bird.

The Hellenes or Greeks, an Indo-European people from the north, for

107

whom transport and conquest were easy by reason of their horses and wheeled vehicles, invaded the country in three main groups, beginning in about 2000 B.C. with Minyans and Ionians.

Penetrating far south to the islands, and to Sicily, southern Italy, and Asia Minor, the Hellenes became expert navigators. They were much influenced by a brilliant and sophisticated Minoan culture already flourishing at Cnossos in Crete, and this began to have considerable effect on the mainland of Greece from about 1580 B.C. onwards.

In about 1400 B.C., however, Cnossos fell, destroyed either by earthquake or by invaders, for the Achaeans, the second wave of Hellenes, had now begun to enter Greece, and from about 1400 to 1100 B.C. Mycenae on the mainland was probably the centre of civilisation in the Aegean world. It is the Mycenaean culture of the Late Bronze Age which, seen through legend, is depicted in Homer's *Iliad* and *Odyssey*. Mycenae is Agamemnon's own citadel, and archaeological remains of other cities named in the *Iliad*'s 'Catalogue of Ships' are also being found. The Achaeans as Homer shows them were a conquering feudal aristocracy and a concerted attempt probably made by them in the beginning of the twelfth century B.C. to seize the Black Sea trade may be reflected in the epic of the siege of Troy.

But the Achaeans themselves were soon to be defeated, for at the end of the twelfth century B.C. the last influx of invading Hellenes, the Dorians, ancestors of the classical Greeks, entered the country. They practically destroyed the Mycenaean civilisation, and the Late Bronze Age now gave way to the Iron Age.

The close fusion between the early non-Aryan Mediterranean people, with their matriarchal culture, and the successive waves of patriarchal Hellenes was reflected in the Greek worship of Olympians. The ancient earth-goddess of fertility lived on in such guises as Aphrodite or Hera, and Zeus, sky-god of the Hellenes, appropriately took Hera to wife. Indeed, many deities, such as Demeter and Athene, combined, in the single divinity, both Mediterranean and Hellenic traits.

A third element in Greek Olympian religion derived from a Hittite-Hurrian culture flourishing in Asia Minor in about 1300 B.C. Hesiod writing in about 750 B.C. incorporated some violent Hurrian myths in his *Theogony* or *Birth of the Gods* (see **2–9** and **1.2.89–98**).

The 'Epic Cycle'

By the eighth century B.C. there was in existence a rich store of myth and legend known as the *Epic Cycle*, which was drawn on by Homer and also by later poets and dramatists.

Homer, whose epics were probably completed at the end of the eighth or in the seventh century B.C., presents the composite myth and legend of Greece in highly civilised form, as the beliefs of a successful war-like aristocracy. The twelve deities dwelling on Olympus acknowledged the supremacy of Zeus, and Dionysus the god of wine and ecstasy, who entered from Thrace in the eighth century B.C., was still an outsider, a god of the lower orders.

The Coming of Dionysus

By the fifth century B.C. Dionysus had been accepted as an Olympian, taking the place of Hestia. The growing popularity of his worship, which induced an ecstatic union with the god in a frenzy partly stimulated by wine, partly mystical, shows the need of the recently civilised Greeks for an impulsive religious expression which was not always satisfied by the prudent cults of the serene Olympians.

Orpheus

From the worship of Dionysus developed that of Orpheus, which aimed at mystic union with the god through enthusiasm wholly mystic, and through purification. The Orphics, believing in the transmigration of souls and an after-life had much influence on the Greek philosopher Pythagoras, and this influence was transmitted through Plato into Christianity itself.

THE ROMANS

While the discoveries of archaeologists have done much to confirm the historical bases of Homer and other Greek writers, they have on the other hand progressively undermined the traditional accounts of Roman history, demonstrating that much once accepted as fact is rather a mythical version of the past. This is not to suggest that the historical bases of Roman myths are now considered to be less solid than the Greek, simply that like the Greek they are an amalgam of 'fact' and 'fiction'. For example, while the Romans' sack of Veii (461–466) undoubtedly took place, it is on the whole most improbable that it did so at the end of a ten-year siege closely modelled on the Greeks' legendary siege of Troy (307–333).

The early Romans worshipped nature gods and agricultural deities such as Consus (the Storer), Pomona (goddess of fruit) and Robigus (Blight). Of their early mythology practically nothing survives. Indeed the Romans seem always to have been a people more concerned with practical ritual observances than with religious speculation. They did later adopt stories about the gods, both from the Greeks and elsewhere, but considerably modified the presentation of divine intervention in human affairs, which seemed to them generally beneath the dignity of august beings. They also adopted and invented stories to account for the origins of their own ritual practices, whose true genesis they had long forgotten, or to explain the names of geographical features such as the Lacus Curtius (442). In these as in other aspects of their mythology, what chiefly interested the Romans was the significance of their own past.

Thanks mainly to the work of Dumézil, we are beginning to have a clearer understanding of the Romans' historical myths and to see them as embodying patterns found elsewhere among Indo-European peoples. Thus, Dumézil plausibly suggests that the first three legendary kings of Rome,

Romulus, Numa Pompilius and Tullus Hostilius may be understood as at least to some extent exemplifying the same 'functions' as the Vedic gods Varuna, Mitra and Indra (vol. 3: 5.1.).

The story of the Sabines' attack on Rome (**440–443**), leading to the unification of the Roman and Sabine peoples, has been convincingly elucidated as expressing an acknowledgement of the interdependence of the various social groups, particularly the merchant-farmers' claim to recognition by the ruling priestly and warrior classes. In the story this is expressed particularly by Titus Tullius's elevation to the joint kingship with Romulus. This is not to suggest that an amalgamation of Roman and Sabine populations did not take place, it almost certainly did at a very early stage, and possibly some incident such as the rape of the Sabine women (**440**) played a part in it, but the story as presented has a pattern very similar to that found in the Norse battle of the Vanirs for recognition by the Aesir, and the fight of the Vedic Ashvins for acknowledgement by Indra (vol. 2: 3.2.**155–157**, vol. 3: 5.2.**100**), and is susceptible to a similar interpretation.

While the forms of some Roman myths may thus echo those of other Indo-European peoples (and are apparently peculiar to them) the material which the Romans used to give flesh to their themes is a hybrid tissue of diverse origins, and the Romans' individual character and preoccupations led them to present this material in pseudo-historical terms (a process familiar enough among other people, including the Hebrews and Chinese and far from unknown among the Greeks). At the same time Roman 'history' was constantly being rewritten for political purposes, to glorify one important family or to denigrate another, to support conservative or liberal factions, the patricians against the plebeians, or vice versa. (Again, this is a practice by no means peculiar to the Romans.) Some knowledge of Rome's history therefore helps us more fully to appreciate the complexity of its myths and to realise that they are something far more interesting than bronze versions of golden Greek originals.

The Historical Background

Bronze-age immigrants from central Europe, who probably spoke an Indo-European language, began to enter Italy in *c.* 1600 B.C. settling in the Po valley and southern Tuscany, and as far south as the area of modern Rome, which has almost certainly been continuously occupied ever since. Further inland were groups of other Indo-European settlers, the Sabines, whose origin is unknown.

In *c.* 1200 B.C. a further wave of immigrants reached Latium (now southern Lazio), the area south of the Tiber. They were of mixed stock and talented bronze engravers, who seem to have known something of the Minoan culture, but were also of central European background and familiar with iron. Their colonies centred on the Alban Mount in whose vicinity there gradually arose the towns of Alba Longa (Castel Gandolfo), Aricia, Ardea, and Lavinium. Settlements were also established on the hills of Rome itself.

Material from the Palatine Hill and the Forum area suggests a community particularly associated with Alba Longa, while remains from the Esquiline Hill are more characteristic of southern Latium. By tradition the Quirinal was a Sabine settlement area but there is no evidence to support this claim or any other traces of distinctive Sabine communities, which must very early have amalgamated with the Latin settlers, and by the early seventh century all the Roman hill villages were coalescing.

From c. 700 B.C. city states began to develop in southern Tuscany and northern Lazio. They were inhabited by Etruscans, a mysterious people whose language remains little understood, though we are beginning better to appreciate the considerable influence they exerted on Rome. They were not it seems of Indo-European stock and their culture was in many respects distinctly Asiatic, though this could be due to their extensive trade contacts with the Asian coast. Most classical authorities believe them to be Lydians, but this is uncertain. By the mid-seventh century they were trading with all the Middle Eastern countries and particularly with the Phoenicians, who had commercial settlements in Etruscan ports. They were also in close contact with the Hellenic colonies of southern Italy, particularly with the great settlement at Cumae.

Like the Greek the Etruscan cities were independent states. One of the oldest and most splendid was Tarquinii, some forty miles north of Rome. In its neighbourhood stood the almost equally powerful Vulci. Nearer Rome, only fifteen miles to the north-west, was the great metal-working centre of Caere. It had several dependent ports and a large Phoenician population, but was one of the most Hellenised of all Etruscan cities, though Veii bid fair to rival it in this respect. Only twelve miles from Rome, Veii controlled the Tiber's crossing at Fidenae and thus exerted a powerful sway over the whole area to the south, including a vital salt route. Later, towards the end of the sixth century, further inland rose Clusium, governing the route through central Italy.

As the Etruscans' power expanded, Rome inevitably came beneath its sway, though the Romans retained their distinctive Latin tongue. Archaeological evidence confirms the tradition that, like other Etruscan cities, Rome was early governed by kings, but subsequently became a republic, probably towards the end of the fifth century B.C. It was now it seems dominated by six powerful families, the Aemilii, Claudii, Cornelii, Manlii and Valerii, all of whom decisively affected its myths and legends.

In 474 B.C. the Etruscans, who had been attacking Cumae, were routed at sea by the Sicilian Greek King Hiero I and subsequently exercised less dominant power over their neighbours.

During the fourth century B.C. Rome was therefore encouraged to expand. At this period it was engaged in conflicts both external and internal, externally against a host of rival cities Etruscan, Latin and Sabine, internally between the patricians and plebians, and the claims of rival families for a decisive say in the city's government. The subsequent expansion of Rome and continuing internal conflicts led, on the one hand, to a vast expansion of Roman cultural experience and, on the other, to much rewriting of history in order to boost the claims of rival groups and factions.

The Sources of Roman Myths and Legends

It is increasingly clear that the material of Roman mythology owes much to Etruscan stories as well as to Greek, but little Etruscan material has survived. Our chief sources of the myths and legends come from the Augustan period. They are the writings of the historian Livy (c. 60–c. 15 B.C.) and the poet Virgil (70–19 B.C.) supplemented by the Greeks Dionysius of Halicarnassus (fl. 30–7 B.C.) and Diodorus the Sicilian (d. c. 21 B.C.). All these writers, and particularly the two Romans, drew upon earlier material now lost to us, or preserved only in fragmentary form, as is the important *Origin of the Roman Nation* by the elder Cato (d. 149 B.C.). On a generally more light-hearted level are the poems of the Hellenised Ovid, whose *Metamorphoses* in particular is a storehouse of charming tales, such as the immortal stories of Pyramus and Thisbe, Pygmalion and Galatea. These are clearly of non-Roman origin but it is to Ovid we owe their preservation.

PART 2

Narrative Outlines

GREECE

The Olympian Creation Myths
1–19

(i) URANOS AND GE

1 The infinite and empty space which existed before creation was known as Chaos. The Earth, or Ge, sprang from Chaos, and herself gave birth to Uranos, the Heavens, and Pontus, the Sea. Ge then became, by Uranos, the mother of the hundred-handed giants, the Hecatoncheires or Centimani (Cottus, Briareus, also called Aegaeon, and Gyes or Gyges); of the one-eyed Cyclopes (Brontes, Steropes and Arges); and of the twelve Titans. Greek writers give inconsistent lists of these Titans, but those most frequently mentioned are Cronos, Oceanos, Hyperion, and Iapetus, and the Titanesses Rhea, Themis, Tethys, and Mnemosyne.

2 Barbarous stories follow of Uranos's dealings with his descendants. These have been influenced by Hurrian stories (cf. 1.2.**89–97**) which Hesiod (eighth century B.C.), a poet whose family had recently come from Asia Minor, incorporated in his *Theogony*.

(ii) THE REVOLT OF CRONOS

3 Uranos had thrown his rebellious sons the Cyclopes into Tartarus, in the Underworld, and Ge persuaded the Titans, with the exception of Oceanos, to rise against their father. She gave Cronos, the youngest, a flint sickle, and with this he unmanned Uranos. Drops from the wound falling upon Mother Earth, she bore the three Erinnyes or Eumenides, the furies Alecto, Tisiphone, and Megaera, and from drops that fell into the sea Aphrodite was born.

4 Uranos deposed, the Titans freed the Cyclopes, but Cronos, now supreme, consigned them again to Tartarus along with the hundred-handed giants.

5 Cronos then married his sister Rhea, and mindful of the curse of Uranos and Ge, that he also would be deposed by his own son, he swallowed each of his children at birth.

(ii) THE BIRTH OF ZEUS

6 When Zeus the youngest was born, Rhea gave Cronos a stone to swallow and saved Zeus, who, according to Minoan tradition, was brought up in the Dictaean cave in Crete. In 1900 the reputed 'birth-cave' was explored by

113

archaeologists—probably the first men to enter for two thousand years, and there they found votive offerings to the god which may have been left there in the second millennium B.C. It was here that the Curetes, Rhea's priests, clashed their weapons to drown the cries of the infant Zeus, while a goat, Amalthea, acted as his nurse, and was rewarded by being placed among the stars as Capricorn, while one of her horns became the Cornucopia or horn of plenty.

7 Zeus when of age was counselled by Metis, the daughter of Oceanos, and with Rhea's help gave to Cronos a potion which obliged him to disgorge first the stone and then his other children, Hestia, Demeter, Hera, Hades, and Poseidon. These now joined with Zeus in a contest against their father and the other Titans, who were led by Atlas.

(iv) WAR BETWEEN ZEUS AND THE TITANS

8 The war, known as the Titanomachia, was waged in Thessaly, and lasted ten years, until Ge promised Zeus victory if he would free the Cyclopes and the hundred-handed giants from Tartarus.

9 The Cyclopes gave to Zeus a thunderbolt, to Hades a helmet of darkness, and to Poseidon a trident. Thus aided, the three brothers overcame Cronos, and the hundred-handed giants stoned the other Titans, who were defeated and consigned either to an island in the west or to Tartarus, guarded by the hundred-handed. Atlas was punished by being made to carry the sky on his shoulders, but the Titanesses were spared. The supersession of the old dynasty of Titans by the new order of gods is the theme of Keats's fine poem, *Hyperion*.

(v) THE OLYMPIANS

10 Zeus and his brothers now divided the government by lot. To Hades fell the Underworld, to Poseidon the sea, and to Zeus the sky, while the earth was common to all. Zeus, the greatest of the gods, lived on the lofty summit of Mt. Olympus between Macedonia and Thessaly, along with Poseidon and their sisters, Hestia, goddess of the hearth-fire, Demeter, goddess of agriculture, and Hera, who became the wife of Zeus. Seven other divinities, Aphrodite, Pallas Athene, Apollo, Artemis, Hephaestos, Ares, and Hermes were also numbered among the twelve great Olympians, and at a later date a new-comer, Dionysus, took the place of Hestia.

(vi) THE GIANTS' REVOLT

11 The troubles of Zeus were not over. A post-Homeric story tells of the giants' revolt. Twenty-four giants with serpents' tails, sons of Ge, tried to avenge the imprisonment of their brothers the Titans by attacking Olympus. Led by Alcyoneus, they included Porphyrion, Ephialtes, Mimas, Pallas, Enceladus, and Polybutes. Only after terrible struggles in Olympus and on earth, were the giants defeated by the gods, who were helped by a magic herb of invulnerability found by Heracles, who always dealt the giants the final blow.

12 The story offered some explanation of huge bones found at Trapezus and volcanic fires at neighbouring Bathos and Cumae, the reputed sites of the battles. The burial of Enceladus under Mt. Etna in Sicily, and of Polybutes under Nisyrus, likewise accounted for their volcanic nature. The inclusion of Heracles before his apotheosis indicates the late origin of the myth.

The Titanomachia depicted on a frieze from Delphi, c.525 B.C. (*Photo: Mansell Collection.*)

(vii) EPHIALTES AND OTUS

13 Another version of the giants' revolt ascribes it to the gigantic Aloeidae, Ephialtes, and Otus, sons of Iphimedeia by Poseidon, but named after Aloeus, whom their mother later married. At the age of nine Ephialtes and Otus first captured and imprisoned Ares, god of war, and then, vowing to outrage Hera and Artemis, they piled Mt. Pelion on Ossa in their attack

on Heaven. Artemis induced them to go to the island of Naxos in the hope of meeting her, but disguised as a doe she leapt between them and they killed each other in error. Hermes then released Ares, and the spirits of the Aloeidae were tied with vipers back to back to a pillar in Tartarus.

(viii) TYPHON

14 After the destruction of the giants, Ge in revenge brought forth the gigantic monster Typhon, fathered on her by her own son Tartarus. His huge limbs ended in serpents' heads and his eyes breathed fire. When he approached Olympus the gods in terror fled to Egypt disguised as animals, Zeus as a ram, Apollo a crow, Dionysus a goat, Hera a white cow, Artemis a cat, Aphrodite a fish, Ares a boar and Hermes an ibis. Athene alone was undaunted and persuaded Zeus to attack Typhon. After a fearful struggle, in which Zeus was temporarily incapacitated and only rescued by Hermes and Pan, he destroyed Typhon with his thunderbolts and buried him under Mt. Etna, which still breathes fire.

15 The flight of the gods to Egypt serves to explain the Egyptian worship of them in animal form.

(ix) PROMETHEUS

16 The creation of mankind is often ascribed to Prometheus, whose name signifies 'forethought', as that of his brother, Epimetheus, means 'after-thought'. These two, unlike their brother Atlas, had supported Zeus during the war with the Titans. But Prometheus, the clever benefactor of mankind, by stealing fire from Olympus and giving it to humans, brought upon himself divine vengeance.

17 The infuriated Zeus ordered Hephaestos to make a lovely woman, Pandora, the Eve of Greek myth, who was endowed by the gods with baleful powers and taken by Hermes to Epimetheus. When he had married her, she opened a box from which escaped all ills which plague mankind.

18 Zeus punished Prometheus by chaining him to a crag in the Caucasus, where all day long an eagle tore at his liver, which grew whole again during the night. Only after many generations did Heracles, with the consent of Zeus, shoot the eagle and free the heroic rebel.

19 The agony of Prometheus is the theme of Aeschylus's tragedy *Prometheus Bound*; the liberator is depicted in his lost drama, *Prometheus Unbound*. Shelley's dramatic poem of the same name takes Prometheus as a symbol of those who challenge tyranny for the sake of mankind.

The Greek Flood Myth
20–22

20 Deucalion, the son of Prometheus, is the Greek Ziusudra (1.2.**29–30, 34**) and his story may well derive from the Sumerian tale, although this cannot be established with any certainty. When Zeus decided to wipe out mankind by releasing a great flood on earth, Deucalion, warned by his father, made an ark which saved both himself and his wife Pyrrha, daughter of Epimetheus. After nine days the flood subsided and the ark came to rest on Mt. Parnassus.

21 Deucalion and Pyrrha then earnestly prayed at the shrine of Themis that the earth might be re-peopled. Themis appeared and commanded them to throw the bones of their mother behind them. They interpreted this as meaning the rocks of Mother Earth and those flung by Deucalion became men, those thrown by Pyrrha women.

22 Their son, Hellen, was the mythical ancestor of all the Hellenes.

The Olympian Deities
23–128

(i) ZEUS

23 Zeus, identified with Jupiter by the Romans, was the greatest of the Olympian divinities, omnipotent king of gods, father of men. Tales of his origin and supremacy are told in **6–20**.

24 Zeus was the bright god of the sky, whom the invading Achaeans introduced into Greece in about 1200 B.C., together with his consort Dione. Her worship, however, did not penetrate south of Zeus's shrine at Dodona in Epirus, where the rustling of oak leaves was interpreted as the voice of the god, and Zeus found other wives. His Olympian consort was Hera, who was in origin the Great Goddess of the pre-Hellenic matriarchal society. This marriage symbolises the fusion of the Achaeans with their predecessors.

25 He first married Metis, daughter of Oceanos and Tethys, but when she was pregnant with Athene he swallowed her and brought forth Athene from his head. His second wife was Themis, daughter of Uranos and Ge, a divinity representing order, and their children were the Horae and the Moerae, or Fates, though some say that the Fates were daughters of Erebus and Night, and that even Zeus was subject to them. To Zeus and Hera were born the deities Ares, Hebe, and Hephaestos, unless the latter was the parthenogenous son of Hera. Zeus was also the father of Persephone by his sister Demeter, of the Charities, or Graces, by Eurynome, and of the Muses by Mnemosyne.

26 By mortal women four Olympian deities were children of Zeus: Hermes the son of Maia, Apollo and Artemis the children of Leto, and Dionysus the son of Semele. Zeus loved many mortal women, and Hera was intensely jealous and revengeful towards them and their children.

27 Although Zeus's earliest oracle was at Dodona, he was said to dwell with his fellow divinities on the summit of Olympus in Thessaly, and was also worshipped at Olympia in Elis. The Greeks dated their era from the first festival of the Olympiad in 776 B.C.

28 Zeus alone used the thunderbolt and was called the thunderer. The oak, the eagle, and mountain summits were sacred to him, and his sacrifices were usually bulls, cows, and goats. His attributes were the sceptre thunderbolt, eagle, and a figure of Victory held in his hand. The Dodonean Zeus sometimes wore a wreath of oak leaves, the Olympian Zeus one of olive.

(ii) HERA

29 Hera, identified by the Romans with Juno, was the Great Goddess of the pre-Hellenic matriarchal society, whom Zeus, supreme god of the Achaeans, appropriately took to wife.

30 She was said to be a daughter of Cronos and Rhea and reluctantly married her brother Zeus, who in the form of a cuckoo sought her out at Cnossos in Crete, or perhaps in Argos, and their wedding night was spent on Samos. Ge gave Hera the tree with the golden apples later guarded by the Hesperides.

31 Though Hera was treated with reverence by the gods, she was greatly inferior in power to Zeus and must obey him, her subordination reflecting the attitude of the Achaeans towards women. Only in her power to bestow the gift of prophecy was Hera equal to her husband.

32 She was often rebellious and jealous of Zeus's intrigues and persecuted his children by mortal women. At one time, with Poseidon and Apollo, she led a conspiracy of all the Olympians save Hestia to put Zeus in chains. He was freed by Thetis and Briareus, and punished Hera by hanging her with wrists chained to the sky and an anvil on each ankle.

33 Hera bore Zeus Ares and Hebe and annually renewed her virginity by bathing in a spring near Argos. As, properly speaking, the only married goddess among the Olympians, she was worshipped as goddess of marriage and the birth of children, the Ilithyiae being her daughters.

34 Hera was of majestic stature, and her attributes were a diadem, veil, sceptre, and peacock. Samos and Argos were seats of her worship.

35 Because of the judgment of Paris she was relentlessly hostile to the Trojans.

(iii) HESTIA

36 Hestia, called Vesta by the Romans, and the eldest sister of Zeus, was a divinity brought to Greece by the invading Achaeans. Though Poseidon and Apollo both sought her love, she swore by Zeus always to remain a virgin.

37 She was goddess of the fire on the hearth, supremely important in those days because so difficult to rekindle, and was naturally thought of as goddess of home life. Each town or city had its sacred hearth, which, like that of the home, was an asylum for suppliants. The first part of all sacrifices offered to the gods was due to Hestia, the most peaceable and kindly of all the Olympians, but at a later date Dionysus took her place among the twelve Olympian gods.

(iv) ATHENE

38 Athene, whom the Romans identified with Minerva, was the embodiment of wisdom and power.

39 The Achaeans brought with them a young warrior goddess, who bore the titles, Core, Parthenos, Pallas, meaning girl, virgin, maiden, and she was in about 1700 B.C. identified with an older pre-Hellenic 'Palace Goddess', worshipped in Crete. The 'Palace Goddess' was one aspect of the Great Goddess, revered not for motherhood but for feminine intuition, and from pre-Hellenic times comes the name Athene.

40 The complex Pallas Athene was thus not only the patroness of women's arts such as weaving, protectress of agriculture, inventor of plough, rake, and ox-yoke, but also a warrior, a wise tactician, appearing in armour and wearing on her aegis or shield the head of Medusa, during the Trojan War the great protagonist of the Greeks. Legends of the birth of Pallas Athene reveal how the patriarchal Hellenes took over, and made their own a matriarchal divinity.

41 She was said to be a daughter of Zeus and Metis, but before her birth an oracle had foretold that she would be a girl, and that if Metis had another child it would be a son who would depose his father. Zeus therefore swallowed Metis, and later, suffered an agonising headache as he walked by Lake Triton. Hermes realising the cause, persuaded Hephaestos, or, according to some, Prometheus, to cleave open Zeus's skull, from which Athene sprang completely armed.

42 The centre of her cult was Attica and Athens, and legend said that when Athene and Poseidon contended for the possession of the city, the gods judged it should belong to Athene, who in planting the olive-tree had conferred the better gift.

43 Preferring to settle quarrels peaceably, Athene established here the court of the Areopagus, where if votes were equal, she herself gave a casting vote to free the accused, as in the trial of Orestes.

44 In 566 B.C. Pesistratus founded the great Panathenaic festival, celebrated every fourth year, and its magnificent procession was represented on the frieze of the Parthenon now in the British Museum, while the birth of Athene was represented in the gable at the east end of the Parthenon, and the contest with Poseidon at the west. Pesistratus also introduced a new coinage, with the head of Athene on one side, and the owl, her bird, upon the other.

Graeco-Etruscan bronze figure of Athene (Minerva) in her aspect as a warrior goddess. British Museum. (*Photo: Mansell Collection.*)

45 Other pre-Hellenic acropolises were sacred to Athene, and her worship flourished in Sparta, Corinth, Argos, and Thebes.

(v) HEPHAESTOS

46 Hephaestos, identified with Vulcan by the Romans, was the smith-god, a superb artist in metals.

47 He probably originated as a pre-Hellenic fire-god near the Mt. Olympus of Lycia in Asia Minor, where gaseous vapour, seeping through the soil, ignited. The Lycians emigrated to Lemnos, where they became known as Pelasgians, and again found fire issuing from the earth, and this fire became the symbol of their god Hephaestos.

48 The cult of Hephaestos spread to Athens, where his artistic genius was so venerated that in the frieze of the Parthenon where two pairs of gods are given positions of honour, Zeus appears with Hera, and Hephaestos with Athene.

49 In Homer's time Hephaestos was one of the twelve Olympians, his exalted position reflecting the importance of the smith in a Bronze Age society when weapons and tools had magical properties. He is, like other smith-gods, represented as lame, possibly because the tribe deliberately lamed their smith to prevent his running away, possibly because work at the forge developed muscular arms but feeble legs.

50 According to Homer, Hephaestos was the son of Zeus and Hera, though later tradition says that he was son of the goddess alone, just as his fire sprang mysteriously from the earth.

51 Born lame and weak, Hephaestos was so much disliked by Hera that she threw him from Olympus, when he fell into the sea and was cared for by the sea-goddesses Thetis and Eurynome in a grotto under the sea.

52 After nine years Hera took him back to Olympus, where he had a smithy, but on one occasion he enraged Zeus by taking Hera's part, so that he was again flung from Olympus, this time by Zeus. He was a day falling, and alighted in the evening on the island of Lemnos, as described in *Paradise Lost*, Book I, lines 740–746. Later writers diverge from Homer in making this second fall the cause of Hephaestos' lameness.

53 He again returned to Olympus and acted as mediator between Zeus and Hera, though the gods laughed at him as he hobbled about.

54 His workshop in Olympus was in his own palace, and all the palaces of the gods were made by him. He also made the magnificent armour of Achilles, as is described in the eighteenth book of the *Iliad,* the necklace of Harmonia, and the bulls of Aeëtes. Later accounts place his workshop on the volcanic island of Sicily, where the Cyclopes served him.

55 In the *Iliad*, Hephaestos' wife was Charis, but in the *Odyssey* she was Aphrodite, who was unfaithful to him with Ares. How Hephaestos caught the two together in an invisible net he had made, and exposed them to the ridicule of the gods, is told in a poem known as the 'Lay of Demodocus', incorporated in the eighth book of the *Odyssey*.

Greek relief *c.* 460 B.C., possibly once part of an altar, shows two nymphs helping Aphrodite from the sea. Ludovici Boncompagni alle Terme Museum, Rome. (*Photo: Mansell Collection.*)

56 Hephaestos' favourite spots on earth were Lemnos, and volcanic islands like Lipara, Hiera, Imbros, and Sicily. In Greek art he is represented as a vigorous man with a beard, carrying a hammer or similar instrument, and wearing an oval cap or chiton.

(vi) APHRODITE

57 Aphrodite, goddess of desire, identified by the Romans with Venus, was derived from the Great Goddess of pre-Hellenic times, her counterpart being the orgiastic Astarte of Syria.

58 She was worshipped as a fertility goddess at Paphos in Cyprus, whence Phoenicians took her worship to Cythera, an island off southern Peloponnesus. Probably as late as the eighth century B.C. her fertility cult was established on Acrocorinthus above Corinth. There was a similar sanctuary on Mt. Eryx in western Sicily. In these places the goddess was served by young girls, but in other Greek states her worship was more that of protectress of the city.

59 According to Hesiod, Aphrodite sprang from the seed of Uranos and rose naked from the sea, as in Botticelli's picture 'The Birth of Venus'. Rising near the island of Cythera, she passed to Paphos in Cyprus.

60 Homer makes Aphrodite the daughter of Zeus and Dione, and represents her as wife to Hephaestos. She was, however, unfaithful to him and in love with Ares. The amusing situation when they were caught together is described in para. **55.** Harmonia was one of their children.

61 Aphrodite also bore sons to Poseidon, and Priapus to Dionysus, and later stories tell that she bore Hermaphroditus to Hermes, and Eros to either Hermes, Ares, or Zeus.

62 Her love for the mortal Adonis (see also 1.3) is the theme of Shakespeare's *Venus and Adonis,* and one of the Homeric hymns tells of her passion for Anchises, cousin of Priam, to whom she bore Aeneas, the hero of Virgil's epic. Unfortunately Anchises, boasting of Aphrodite's love, was struck by Zeus with a thunderbolt.

63 Aphrodite possessed a magic girdle which made the wearer irresistibly lovely and desirable. Doves and sparrows were sacred to her. Her most beautiful statue was that by Praxitiles in the fourth century B.C., a copy of which is preserved in the Vatican. The Venus de Milo may be seen in the Louvre.

(vii) ARES

64 Ares, god of war, who was identified by the Romans with Mars, was a divinity of Thracian origin, whose worship spread through Macedonia to Thebes, Athens, and cities of the Peloponnesus, especially Sparta. Ares was, however, not popular with the Greeks, who disliked purposeless war and despised the Thracians for enjoying it, and their attitude is reflected in the myths of Ares.

65 He was the son of Zeus and Hera, and as he delighted in battle for its own sake he was hated by the other gods, except Eris, Hades, and Aphrodite, who was in love with Ares and he with her. The two were once trapped together in a net which Hephaestos had engineered, as is described in para. **55.**

66 Ares was not always successful in battle. The Aloeidae conquered him and left him imprisoned in a brazen vessel for thirteen months, until he was released by Hermes. Athene twice vanquished him, and Heracles also defeated him and forced him to return to Olympus.

67 According to a late tradition, Ares once defended himself before the gods in a trial where he was accused of murdering Halirrhothius, son of Poseidon. Since he pleaded that he had saved his daughter, Alcippe, from being violated, Ares was acquitted, and the place of the trial became known as the Areopagus.

(viii) APOLLO

68 Apollo's worship probably derived from two sources, from the Dorians, who in about 1100 B.C. entered Greece and reached as far south as Crete, and from Ionians, living in the islands and mainland of Anatolia, or Asia Minor, who became acquainted with a Hittite divinity worshipped in Lycia, and hence called Lycius.

Black-figured painting on an amphora shows Leto holding the twins Apollo and Artemis. British Museum. (*Photo: Michael Holford.*)

69 Apollo's Dorian shrine was at Delphi, near the Castalian spring on Mt. Parnassus, where he was called the Pythian, or Loxias, the Ambiguous. His Ionian shrine was at Delos, where he was called Lycius, and Phoebus, or Shining, and where he was more closely associated with his twin-sister, Artemis.

70 Myths said that Apollo and Artemis were the children of Zeus and Leto, but before their birth, jealous Hera caused Leto to wander from place to place till she gave birth to Artemis under a palm-tree at Ortygia, and to

124

Apollo beside a palm in the isle of Delos.

71 This story is told in the Delian Homeric Hymn of 700 B.C., while the Delphic Hymn tells how Apollo, soon after his birth, sought out the she-dragon Python, on Mt. Parnassus, and there killed her, taking over the Oracle of Earth at Delphi, where his priestess the Pythoness became the mouthpiece of his oracles, which were imparted in hexameter verse. Apollo was commanded by Zeus to visit the Vale of Tempe for purification, and to preside over the Pythian games held in Python's honour.

72 Hera, still implacable, sent the giant Tityus to violate Leto, as she came with Artemis to Delphi, though some say that it was Artemis who was attacked, but the giant was killed by the arrows of Apollo and Artemis.

73 Apollo was not always subservient to Zeus. He once, with Hera, Poseidon, and other Olympians, bound Zeus with chains and was punished by being sent with Poseidon as bondman to King Laomedan, where by playing the lyre and tending the flocks he helped Poseidon to build the walls of Troy. On another occasion, furious that Zeus had slain his son Asclepios, Apollo retaliated by killing the Cyclopes. Zeus now sent him to serve King Admetus of Pherae in Thessaly, and again he kept flocks. He also helped Admetus to win his bride Alcestis and even ensured that the king should be restored to life if one of his family would die in his stead.

74 Apollo loved many mortal women, including Cyrene, mother of Aristaeus, Coronis, mother of Asclepios, the healer, and Aria, mother of Miletus. The nymph Dryope was also seduced by Apollo, but when he pursued the nymph Daphne she cried for help and was turned into a laurel, henceforth Apollo's tree; and the nymph Marpessa preferred his rival, Idas. Apollo loved Cassandra, daughter of Priam, and conferred on her the gift of prophecy, but, when she disappointed him, decreed that she should never be believed. Hyacinthus, a Spartan prince, in origin an earth deity, was beloved by Apollo, and when he was killed by the god's jealous rival, Zephyrus, the hyacinth flower sprang from his blood.

75 Apollo had varied characteristics. He was destroyer, as his arrows indicated, and sudden deaths were ascribed to him. It was he who sent plagues among the Greeks besieging Troy. But he was also protector, warding off evil, as his fatherhood of Asclepios indicated. He protected flocks and cattle, as his service to Laomedan and Admetus showed, and later writers particularly stressed this aspect.

76 As god of prophecy, Apollo could communicate the gift to gods and mortals, and of all the centres of his worship Delphi was the most famous. The shrine had probably been established by pre-Hellenic people, worshipping Mother Earth, and had been seized by invading Hellenes who killed Python the oracular serpent, took over the oracles in the name of their own Apollo, and held funeral games in honour of Python to placate the original inhabitants. The shrine was supposed to contain the Omphalos, or navel stone of earth, and a chasm which occasionally gave out intoxicating vapours. Over this Apollo's priestess, Pythia, sat on a tripod, and uttered his oracle after chewing intoxicating laurel leaf. She was regarded as the mystical bride of the god.

Painting from the inside of a fifth-century B.C. cup, shows Apollo pouring a libation, watched by his cult bird, the raven. Delphi Museum. (*Photo: Photoresources.*)

77 As god of song and music Apollo appears in the *Iliad* delighting immortals. He was said to have received the lyre from Hermes, and its seven strings were connected with the seven Greek vowels. In music none surpassed Apollo, not even Pan, nor Marsyas, the satyr who had found Athene's discarded flute which played by itself. Defeated in a contest, Marsyas was flayed alive by the victorious god. Apollo, as leader of the Muses, was called Musagetes. He valued order and moderation in all things, his favourite maxims being 'Nothing in Excess', and 'Know thyself'.

78 Apollo also delighted in the foundation of towns, and his oracle was always consulted before a town was founded.

79 In later writers he was identified with the sun-god, the result of Egyptian influence, for in Homer, Helios, god of the sun, is completely distinct from Apollo.

80 The worship of Apollo, typical of all that is most radiant in the Greek mind, has no counterpart in the religion of Rome. Not till the end of the third century B.C. did the Romans adopt his religion from the Greeks.

126

(ix) ARTEMIS

81 Artemis, whose Roman counterpart was Diana, had two chief aspects. One was as 'Mistress of Animals', a goddess of the chase, worshipped in primitive matriarchal society, and probably owing something to the Britomartis and Dictynna, worshipped as huntresses in Crete. The other, originating in Asia Minor, was as the age-old mother-goddess, and is most clearly seen in Artemis Ephesia, who was worshipped as an orgiastic goddess.

82 Legends of the birth of Artemis are told in the story of Apollo, and as his sister she shared many of his characteristics. She carried bow and arrows, made for her by Hephaestos, and had power to send plague and sudden death, as when she and Apollo killed the children of Niobe. She was also protectress of children and young animals and goddess of the chase.

83 Like Apollo, Artemis was unmarried, and later writers stressed that she was a maiden goddess and severely punished any lapses. She changed Actaeon to a stag to be torn to pieces by his own hounds, only because he had seen her bathing, and some traditions say that she killed Orion because of his unchastity. The nymph Callisto, who had been seduced by Zeus, was in the form of a bear hunted down by the hounds of Artemis.

84 When Apollo was identified with the Sun, Artemis was identified with Selene, the Moon.

85 The Arcadian Artemis, early worshipped in Arcadia as a huntress among the nymphs, was unconnected with Apollo.

86 Another aspect of the goddess was as the fierce Artemis of Tauris, to whom all strangers were sacrificed. Iphigeneia was once her priestess, and she and Orestes took her image to Brauron in Attica, whence the goddess was called Brauronia. This Brauronian Artemis was worshipped in Athens, and also in Sparta, where boys were scourged at her altar until they sprinkled it with their blood.

87 Artemis as an orgiastic goddess had her chief centre in Ephesus, with its immensely wealthy temple, and it was this Artemis that St. Paul encountered. (See *Acts of the Apostles*, 19.)

88 Though usually regarded as a rural divinity, Artemis was supreme in three great cities, in Ephesus, in Marseilles, to which Ionian Greeks from Asia Minor took her cult between 600 and 540 B.C., and in Syracuse, where she was known as Artemis Arethusa.

89 The goddess was often portrayed as a huntress, as in the so-called Diana of Versailles, now in the Louvre. As huntress her chlamys reached only to the knees, and she carried a bow, quiver, and arrows, or a spear, and was accompanied with stags or dogs. As Selene, she wore a long robe and veil, and a crescent moon on her forehead.

(x) HERMES

90 Hermes, whom the Romans called Mercurius, was originally one of the gods of the pre-Hellenic people, the divinity dwelling in the cairn, or 'herma', set up by the shepherds as a landmark in wild country, and so developing as a protector against predatory animals and a guide to travellers. This Hermes was identified with a similar divinity worshipped in Minoan Crete, a 'Master of Animals', a son or lover of the Great Goddess, and therefore a god of fertility.

91 Legends said that Hermes was the son of Zeus and Maia, an embodiment of the Great Goddess, and a daughter of Atlas, whence Hermes's name Atlantiades.

92 The 'Hymn to Hermes' of 600 B.C. tells that he was born in a cavern on Mt. Cyllene in Arcadia (from which he was sometimes called Cyllenius), and that he grew with amazing rapidity. When only a few hours old he went to Pieria and stole some of the oxen of Apollo, which he drove to Pylos, and then, returning to Cyllene, he invented the lyre by stringing a tortoise-shell with cow-gut. Apollo, on discovering the thief, denounced him to Zeus, who ordered Hermes to restore the oxen. But when Apollo heard the lyre he was delighted, took it in exchange for the oxen, and became the friend of Hermes, leading him back to Zeus.

93 Zeus gave to Hermes supreme power over animals and appointed him his herald, Hermes also acted as herald to Hades, conducting shades to the underworld. (See Virgil's *Aeneid,* Bk. IV, ll. 242 sqq.) As herald he was regarded as god of eloquence, whence St. Paul, 'the chief speaker', was mistaken for him in Lystra of Asia Minor. (See *Acts of the Apostles,* 14.) Heralds promote peace and therefore trade. Thus Hermes came to be looked on as a god of peaceable commerce.

94 He was also god of prudence and cunning, and even of theft, and was said to have helped the Fates in composing the alphabet. Many inventions ascribed to Hermes, such as weights and measures, the musical scale, astronomy, olive-culture, and the arts of boxing and gymnastics, were pre-Hellenic, and the stories of his childhood may indicate how the Hellenes took over these arts in the name of their god Apollo. As a god of fertility and luck, Hermes presided over games of dice.

95 He played a part in such incidents as the rescue of Dionysus, the punishment of Ixion, the selling of Heracles to Omphale, the judgment of Paris, and the leading of Priam to Achilles, but his most famous exploit was perhaps the slaying of Argus, the hundred-eyed giant sent by Hera to watch Io.

96 Hermes had several sons, including Echion, herald to the Argonauts, Autolycus the thief, his son by Chione, and Daphnis.

97 His worship flourished in Arcadia, where he was to be found with Pan and the Muses. It spread to Athens, and he became one of the best loved of the Olympians.

The 'Diana of Versailles', thought to be a copy of a fourth-century B.C. original, perhaps by Leochares. Louvre. (*Photo: Mansell Collection.*)

98 Hermes's attributes were the Petasus, a travelling-hat, in later time adorned with wings, the Alipes, or winged-sandals, and the Caduceus, or herald's staff, whose white ribbons were later mistaken for serpents because he was herald to Hades. Sacred to Hermes were the tortoise, the palm-tree, the number four, and some kinds of fish, and his sacrifices were incense, honey, cakes, pigs, lambs, and kids.

(xi) POSEIDON

99 Poseidon, identified by the Romans with Neptune, derived from a god worshipped by the earliest Aryan invaders of Greece, the Minyans and Ionians, who entered the country in about 2000 B.C. It was with the aid of horses and wheeled vehicles that they quickly overcame any resistance, and their god Poseidon was often thought of as the horse whose hooves thunder on the earth. He is constantly spoken of in Homer as 'earth-shaker', while many legends show him in equine guise. It is possible that he was originally thought of as a sky-god, a thunderer, and the mate of an earth-goddess who later developed as Demeter.

100 But when in about 1450 B.C., another wave of invading Aryans, the Achaeans, entered Greece, they also brought their sky-god, a thunderer called Zeus, possibly in origin identical with Poseidon, and the latter, recognised as an older brother of Zeus, came to be revered as a sea-divinity, for the Minyans were, by now, expert in navigation.

101 According to legend, Poseidon was the eldest son of Cronos and Rhea, and when, after the deposition of Cronos, he and his brothers Zeus and Hades cast lots for sovereignty, the sea became Poseidon's share. He dwelt in an under-water palace near Aegae in Euboea, which is described in the beginning of the thirteenth book of the *Iliad,* and here he kept his horses with brazen hooves and golden manes. When they drew his chariot over the sea it became tranquil.

102 He was said to have created the horse when disputing with Athene for the possession of Athens, and he taught men how to bridle horses. He was the protector of horse races, and horse and chariot races were held in his honour on the Corinthian isthmus.

103 In the form of a horse he raped his sister Demeter, when she was disguised as a mare. Their offspring were the horse Arion and the nymph Despoena, and some say Persephone also, though according to another version Demeter was searching for Persephone, her daughter by Zeus, at the time of the rape.

104 Poseidon, though equal to Zeus in dignity, was less powerful and resented the pride of his younger brother. He once joined with Hera, Apollo, and other Olympians, to put Zeus in chains, and he and Apollo were punished by being sent as bondsmen to Laomedan. Here Poseidon built the walls of Troy, hence called Neptuniia Pergama. When Laomedan refused the wages due, Poseidon sent a sea-monster, which would have devoured the king's daughter Hesione if she had not been rescued by Heracles. In the Trojan War, Poseidon naturally sided with the Greeks, though he became hostile to Odysseus after he had blinded Polyphemus, son of the god.

105 Poseidon desired earthly kingdoms, his attempts to take control possibly being political myths. He disputed with Athene for the possession of Athens, but she was awarded the city because her planting of the olive was judged the better gift. When these divinities, however, disputed the possession of Troezen, Zeus judged they should share it equally. In his claim for Corinth, Poseidon received only the isthmus, where the quadrennial Isthmian games were held in his honour, while the Areopagus was awarded to Helios.

106 Poseidon first intended to marry Thetis, but when it was prophesied that her son would be greater than his father he paid court to Amphitrite, daughter of Nereus. Only after Delphinos had most eloquently pleaded his suit did Amphitrite accept Poseidon, who in gratitude placed Delphinos's image among the stars, as the Dolphin. Amphitrites's reluctance, paralleled by Hera's shrinking from Zeus, and Persephone's from Hades, possibly represents the resistance of an early matriarchal society to a patriarchal system.

107 Poseidon's son by Amphitrite was Triton, but he had many more children by other divinities and mortals.

108 One of them, Scylla, was particularly hateful to Amphitrite, who is said to have turned her into a monster with six barking heads and twelve feet. Poseidon also loved the nymph Tyro, mother of his children Pelias and Neleus, and Aethra, the mother of Theseus. His offspring by Medusa were Chrysaor and Pegasus.

109 Sacrifices to Poseidon were usually black-and-white bulls. His symbol of power was the trident, possibly in origin a thunderbolt, by means of which he could shake the earth or subdue the waves, and which became in Hellenistic and Roman times a symbol of sea-power, as it is today. Poseidon's other attributes were the horse and the dolphin, and he was usually represented as accompanied by Amphitrite, Triton, Nereids, and dolphins.

(xii) DEMETER

110 Demeter, counterpart of the Roman Ceres, was probably in origin a divinity of the Minyans, who entered Greece in about 2000 B.C., and who revered her as an earth-goddess, a mate to their sky-god, who later developed as Poseidon. Both these divinities could take the form of a horse. The worship of this earth-goddess then merged with that of the Great Goddess of the pre-Hellenic matriarchal society, and Demeter was worshipped as the corn-goddess.

111 She was daughter to Cronos and Rhea, and sister to Zeus, by whom she became the mother of Persephone, or Core, the maiden, herself another aspect of the goddess. According to the Homeric Hymn of the seventh century B.C., Hades asked Zeus's permission to marry Persephone, and as he received no downright refusal was emboldened to carry off the maiden as she was gathering flowers. Demeter wandered the earth searching for her daughter until Helios told her what Hades had done. She then shunned Olympus and wandered still on earth, which she forbad to bring forth fruit. Zeus finally told Demeter that her daughter might return, provided she had eaten nothing in the Underworld, and he sent Hermes to escort her back. Hades agreed to let Persephone go, but gave her a pomegranate to eat, and it was at last agreed that she should spend a third of the year with him in Hades, as Queen of the Underworld, and the rest of the year with Demeter, who once more allowed the earth to bear its fruit.

112 Inconsistent accounts are given of the place of the rape. Demeter's priests said it was Eleusis, about twelve miles from Athens, the Latin poets Enna in Sicily, where, according to Ovid, Persephone was gathering poppies. Some say it was Ascalaphus who saw Persephone take food in the Underworld and that because he revealed this, he was turned by Demeter into an owl.

113 It is said that during her wanderings, Demeter punished those, like Abas, son of Celeus, who were unkind to her, but showered blessings on those like Celeus himself and his son Triptolemus who received her hospitably in Eleusis and whom she taught the art of agriculture.

114 The Eleusinian Festival in honour of Demeter and Persephone was probably fully established in Athens by Pesistratus at the end of the sixth century B.C., probably about the time when the cult of Dionysus was instituted. There was an annual procession from Eleusis to Athens, and those who spoke Greek could be initiated into the final rite of the mysteries. The Thesmophoria, celebrating the foundation of laws, was also held in the goddesses' honour, in Athens and in other parts of Greece.

115 The myth originated in the most primitive rites of seed time and harvest at a time when only women practised the arts of agriculture. Persephone, representing the vegetation which dies down during the winter, had her counterpart in the primitive corn-puppet which was buried in winter to be dug up again sprouting in the spring, and later writers saw the story as an expression of the death of the body and the immortality of the soul.

116 In art Demeter was represented with a garland of corn or a ribbon, and holding a sceptre, corn ears, or a poppy, and sometimes a torch and basket. Pigs were sacred to her. There is in the British Museum a fine statue of Demeter of about 330 B.C., which was found at Cnidos in Asia Minor.

(xiii) DIONYSUS

117 Dionysus, god of wine, also called Bacchus by both Greeks and Romans, was not in Homer's time one of the aristocratic Olympian deities, but a god worshipped by humble folk whom wandering bands of ecstatic worshippers brought into Greece from Thrace in the eight century B.C. The cult, which spread through Macedonia and Thessaly, to Boeotia, Delphi, Athens, and beyond, was characterised by a mystic frenzy when the worshippers, intoxicated with wine, believed themselves to be at one with Dionysus or Bacchus, sometimes called Bromius 'the Boisterous'. The men who followed him were known as Bacchoi, the women Bacchae, or Bacchantes or Maenads, or in Athens and Delphi, Thyiads.

118 The immense popularity of the Dionysus cult, especially with women, indicates that among the recently civilised Greeks there was a longing for

Red-figured Attic vase painting, 490–480 B.C., shows Triptolemus honouring Demeter and Persephone. British Museum. (*Photo: Mansell Collection.*)

a more instinctive and impulsive life, valuing enthusiasm rather than prudence, and during the sixth century certain wise statesmen introduced the new cult among the other state religions. Dyonisiac festivals were established in Corinth, Sicyon, Delphi, and Athens. In Delphi the sepulchre of Bacchus was placed near the very tripod of Pythia, and his temple, a theatre, was at the highest point of the sacred precinct. In Athens Pesistratus founded the Dionysia and the Panathenaic Games at about the same time, and a theatre was set up where the worshippers of Bacchus enacted the first primitive drama. In the fifth century, when the Parthenon was finished, the new god had been accepted among the twelve Olympians taking the place of Hestia. This change incidentally secured a majority of gods over goddesses on Mt. Olympus, and is perhaps evidence of a society becoming increasingly patriarchal.

119 Legends said that Dionysus was the son of Semele by Zeus, who visited his beloved disguised as a mortal. When Semele was six months with child, jealous Hera, disguised as an old woman, persuaded her to ask her mysterious lover to appear in his true form. Unwillingly Zeus consented, 'hapless Semele' was consumed by fire, and her unborn child sewn up in Zeus's thigh to be delivered three months later as Dionysus.

120 The child was first entrusted to Athamas and Ino of Boeotia, and reared in the women's quarters disguised as a girl, until Hera, undeceived, punished Athamas with madness so that he killed his own son. Hermes then took Dionysus to Mt. Nysa, where the nymphs cared for him, feeding him with honey, and where he first invented wine. Zeus later placed images of the nymphs among the stars as Hyades.

Dionysus in his transformed boat surrounded by
the erstwhile pirates, now dolphins. Interior of a
black-figured cup by the artist Exekias, *c.* 535 B.C.
Staatliche Antikensammlungen, Munich. (*Photo:
Mansell Collection.*)

121 When Dionysus had grown to manhood Hera drove him mad and he wandered through the world with his old tutor Silenus and a wild rout of Satyrs and Maenads. He went through Egypt, Syria, and Asia to India, overcoming military opposition, teaching the culture of the vine, founding cities and laws. He returned to Europe through Phrygia and then invaded Thrace.

122 Here Lycurgus, King of the Edones, opposed his worship, but, maddened by Rhea, he killed and mutilated his own son, and the Edones caused him to be torn to death by horses.

123 Dionysus now proceeded to Boeotia, and in Thebes was resisted by King Pentheus. But Pentheus was also driven mad and torn to pieces by the Maenads or Bacchae, among whom were his own mother Agave and her two sisters, for in their frenzy they believed him to be a wild beast. This is the legend used by Euripides in his play, *The Bacchae*.

124 Dionysus also visited the islands of the Adriatic. At Icaria he hired a ship bound for Naxos, but the sailors were Tyrrhenian pirates and steered towards Asia, intending to sell Dionysus into slavery. The god, however, turned himself into a lion and the oars into serpents. Ivy grew round the ship and flutes were heard. The terrified pirates, leaping overboard, were transformed to dolphins. Arrived at Naxos, Dionysus found Ariadne deserted by Theseus and at once married her. A Renaissance conception of this incident can be seen in Titian's picture 'Bacchus and Ariadne' in the National Gallery, or in Tintoretto's picture in the Doge's Palace in Venice.

125 At Argos people refused at first to accept Dionysus, but when the women had been maddened by him, they admitted he was a god.

126 His worship established throughout the world, Dionysus was received into Olympus as one of the twelve great divinities, taking the place of Hestia. He brought Semele there from the Underworld, and she was henceforth known as Thyone.

127 Dionysus was worshipped as god of the vital and intoxicating powers of nature, and also, because of his close connection with tillage and early civilisation, as a law-giver. He was also god of tragic art. In art he was represented as young, handsome, and athletic, but later as slightly effeminate. He was accompanied with a wild crowd of Satyrs, and Maenads, the latter frenzied with wine and mystic exaltation, and carrying cymbals, swords, serpents, or the Thyrsus, a wand wreathed with ivy and crowned with a fir-cone. The worship of Dionysus appealed strongly to women, and many would spend the whole night on the mountain in ecstatic dancing and tearing wild animals to pieces. Sacred to the god were the ivy, laurel, and asphodel, and the dolphin, serpent, tiger, lynx, panther, and ass. His sacrifice was usually a goat or ass.

128 The myths of Dionysus are evidence that there was at first much opposition to the ritual use of wine, and the frenzy it engendered. The earlier drink of the Greeks had been a kind of beer flavoured with ivy and mead, and mead was the drink of Homer's Olympians. Wine was not invented by the Greeks, but probably first imported by them from Crete, whither viniculture had probably spread from Mt. Nysa in Libya. The use of wine spread from Thrace to Athens and other civilised cities. The story of Dionysus's wanderings in India represents the spread of viniculture there.

The Heroes
129–218

(i) PERSEUS

129 The ancient folk-tale of Perseus, grandson of Acrisius, has been told by Kingsley in *The Heroes*.

130 Acrisius and Proetus, the twin sons of Abas, King of Argos, eventually agreed, after much discussion, to divide their inheritance. Proetus became ruler of Tiryns, whose massive walls he built by the aid of the Cyclopes, while Acrisius ruled uneasily in Argos, for an oracle had declared that he would be killed by a son born to his daughter Danaë.

131 To prevent this disaster, Acrisius had Danaë immured in a brazen dungeon or tower, with doors of brass, but all in vain, for Zeus visited her in a shower of gold, and she became the mother of Perseus.

132 Not daring to kill Danaë, Acrisius set mother and son adrift on the sea in a chest, which floated to the isle of Seriphos, one of the Cyclades. Here it was found by the sailor Dictys, and he took Danaë and her son to the king Polydectes, who received them hospitably.

133 When Perseus was grown to manhood, however, Polydectes sought to marry Danaë and seized a pretext to send Perseus off to fetch the head of the Gorgon Medusa.

134 Medusa and her sister Gorgons, Stheno and Euryale, who were the daughters of Phorcys and Ceto, and dwelt in Libya, had once been beautiful. But Medusa lay with Poseidon in one of the temples of Athene, and the enraged goddess turned her into a winged monster with brazen claws and serpent hair, so hideous that she turned to stone all who looked upon her.

135 Athene, eager to help Perseus against her enemy, gave him a polished shield whereby he might see Medusa only in reflection. Hermes provided him with a sickle, and told him how to procure winged sandals, a magic wallet in which to carry the decapitated head, and Hades's helmet of invisibility.

136 On Hermes's advice Perseus visited the Gorgons' sisters, the Graeae, three old women grey from birth who had only one eye and one tooth between them, and these they passed from one to another. Perseus found them on Mt. Atlas, and, by snatching the eye and tooth, forced the Graeae to tell him where he could find the sandals, wallet, and helmet. They directed him to the Stygian nymphs, who gave him what he needed.

Black-figured amphora painting showing Perseus and the Gorgon. British Museum. (*Photo: B. Museum.*)

137 Flying westward to the land of the Hyperboreans, Perseus found the Gorgons asleep. He successfully beheaded Medusa and was astonished to see, springing fully grown from her body, the winged horse Pegasus and the warrior Chrysaor, both of whom had been begotten on her by Poseidon.

138 Though pursued by Stheno and Euryale, Perseus in Hades's helmet escaped to the south. Some say that he petrified the Titan Atlas by showing him the Gorgon's head and then flew over Ethiopia.

139 Here he saw, chained naked to a rock on the sea coast, the lovely Andromeda, and at once fell in love with her. He learned the cause of her plight from her parents, Cepheus, King of Ethiopia, and his wife Cassiopeia. The latter had rashly boasted that Andromeda was more beautiful than the Nereids, and when they had complained of this to Poseidon, the sea-god had sent a monster to lay waste the country. Only by the sacrifice of Andromeda, said the oracle of Ammon, could the land be delivered.

140 Perseus promptly offered to rescue the maiden, provided she would become his wife, but, after he had slain the monster, Cepheus and Cassiopeia were reluctant to keep their promise, for they said Andromeda had already been contracted to another. Their protégé and his followers, arriving at the wedding, attempted to seize the bride, but were easily circumvented by Perseus, who showed them Medusa's head and turned them all to stone. Poseidon set the images of Cepheus and Cassiopeia among the stars, the latter in a humiliating position.

141 Perseus, with Andromeda, now hastened to Seriphos, where he found that Danaë and Dictys had been obliged to take refuge in a temple, but going to Polydectes's palace, he exposed the Gorgon's head and turned the king and all his followers to stone. He then gave the head to Athene, who set it in her aegis, and Hermes restored Perseus' accoutrements to the Stygian nymphs.

142 After making Dictys King of Seriphos, Perseus, taking with him Danaë and Andromeda, returned to Argos, and Acrisius, mindful of the oracle, fled to Larissa, in vain, however, for Perseus, visiting Larissa and taking part in public games, accidentally killed his grandfather by a throw of the discus.

143 Grieved by this mishap, Perseus arranged to exchange kingdoms with his cousin Megapenthes, the son of Proetus, who now moved to Argos while Perseus became King of Tiryns. He also founded Mycenae, which, like Tiryns itself had mighty fortifications built by the Cyclopes.

144 The massive remains of both cities have been investigated by Schliemann and other archaeologists, and remain as some of the most interesting antiquities in all Greece.

(ii) BELLEROPHON

145 The story of Bellerophon is told by William Morris in *The Earthly Paradise*.

146 Bellerophon, the son of Glaucus, King of Corinth, having killed one Bellerus, fled to Proetus, King of Tiryns. Unfortunately Proetus's wife, Anteia, fell in love with the young man, and when he refused her advances falsely accused him to her husband of trying to seduce her. Proetus, reluctant to kill a guest, sent him instead to Anteia's father, Iobates, King of Lycia, carrying a letter which requested that the bearer be put to death.

147 Iobates also shrank from killing a guest and decided to send Bellerophon against the Chimaera, a fire-breathing monster with a lion's head, goat's body, and serpent's tail, said to be the offspring of Echidne and Typhon, which was now ravaging Lycia.

148 Bellerophon was advised to catch the winged horse Pegasus, sprung from Medusa. Pegasus, by striking his hoof on the earth of Mt. Helicon, had created the spring of Hippocrene, sacred to the Muses, and he was found by Bellerophon at another of his fountains, that of Pirene in the Acropolis of Corinth. The hero flung over the horse's head a golden bridle, which Athene had given him, and astride his flying steed he easily shot the Chimaera with his arrows.

149 The frustrated Iobates now sent Bellerophon against the Amazons, and, when the hero again returned victorious, planted an ambush of guards against his arrival. Bellerophon slew them all, and Iobates, convinced at last that there had been some mistake, produced Proetus's letter and learned the truth. He gave his guest his daughter in marriage and made him his heir.

150 Later tradition records that Bellerophon presumptuously tried to soar to Olympus mounted on Pegasus, but that Zeus sent a gadfly which stung the horse and caused him to throw his rider to earth. Bellerophon ended his days in wretchedness, but Pegasus gained Olympus.

(iii) JASON AND THE ARGONAUTS

151 The story of Jason and the Argonauts was already popular in Homer's day, and has more recently been told by Kingsley in *The Heroes,* and by William Morris in *The Life and Death of Jason.*

152 Jason's father Aeson, the rightful King of Iolcus, had been deprived of his kingdom by his two half-brothers, Pelias and Neleus. The mother of all three was Tyro, who, seduced by Poseidon, bore him the twins Pelias and Neleus. She exposed the twins, but they were reared by a horse-herd, and when Tyro later married Cretheus, founder and King of Iolcus, they were adopted by him.

153 Tyro's son by Cretheus was Aeson, but on Cretheus's death Pelias imprisoned Aeson, expelled Neleus, and made himself supreme. The life of Aeson's infant son Jason was saved only because he was smuggled out of Iolcus and entrusted to the care of Cheiron, the Centaur.

154 When a young man, Jason returned to Iolcus, fearlessly demanding his kingdom, and Pelias, to be rid of him, asked him to go to Colchis to fetch the golden fleece. This, the fleece of the ram on which Phrixus had escaped, and which he had given to King Aeëtes of Colchis, was now hanging on an oak-tree in the grove of Ares, guarded night and day by a sleepless dragon.

155 Jason welcomed the enterprise and commanded Argus, the Thespian, to build him a fifty-oared ship called the *Argo*, into whose prow Athene herself fitted an oracular beam. Most of the heroes of the day flocked to join Jason, and his crew included the Dioscuri (Castor and Polydeuces) Heracles, and Orpheus the musician.

156 They met many adventures on the way. After lingering too long with the women of Lemnos, they slipped through the Hellespont and reached Mysia. Here Hylas, the squire of Heracles, while fetching water was stolen away by the Naiads, leaving nothing but an empty pitcher, and Heracles left the *Argo* in a vain search for him.

157 On the island of Bebrycos the Argonauts were met by its king, Amycus, son of Poseidon, and a renowned boxer, who contrived to kill all strangers by challenging them to a boxing match, but Polydeuces met the challenge and killed the bully. In Thrace they freed the blind king and prophet Phineus from a plague of Harpies, and in gratitude he advised Jason how to navigate the Bosphorus. At its entrance were the perilous floating islands, the Symplegades. It is possible that rumours of icebergs gave rise to the fable of these islands, which clashed together and crushed any ship which attempted to pass between them. But Jason, following the advice of Phineus, released a dove, and the *Argo* slipped between the islands as they recoiled. Henceforth they remained fixed. After overcoming other dangers, the Argonauts at last reached the River Phasis and Colchis.

158 Here Aeëtes promised that he would give Jason the fleece if he could yoke together two fire-breathing bulls with brazen feet, the work of Hephaestos, plough the field of Ares, and sow it with the dragon's teeth left over by Cadmus at Thebes. It was Medea who enabled Jason to perform this terrible task. This sorceress princess, the daughter of Aeëtes by his first wife, fell instantly in love with Jason and promised to help him if he would swear by all the gods to marry her and be faithful. She gave him a fire-resisting lotion and he completed the task. Then when Aeëtes failed to keep his promise Medea charmed the dragon to sleep while Jason took down the fleece and they fled together in the *Argo*.

159 The furious Aeëtes pursued them, but Medea ruthlessly murdered the young half-brother Absyrtus she had brought with her, and cut him into pieces which she dropped one by one over the side of the boat. Aeëtes, stopping to collect the fragments for burial, soon lost sight of the fugitives.

160 There are many conflicting accounts of the *Argo*'s return journey, but none of them is feasible, for the Greek knowledge of geography was at that time very limited. Tradition said that the ship reached the western Mediterranean and visited the island of Circe, who purified Jason and Medea of murder.

161 On their return to Iolcus they found that Pelias had forced Aeson to take his life, though one tradition mentioned by Ovid and by Shakespeare in *The Merchant of Venice,* says that he was renewed to youthful vigour by Medea. All agree that Medea took a terrible revenge on Pelias. She persuaded his daughters, with the exception of Alcestis, to cut their father up and boil him in a cauldron, promising falsely that this would rejuvenate him. Pelias's son Acastus, horrified at the murder, then expelled Jason and Medea and they repaired to Corinth.

162 For many years they lived happily until they were involved in the final tragedy, dramatised by Euripides in his *Medea*. Jason deserted Medea for Glauce, also called Creusa, daughter of Creon, and the sorceress sent the young bride a garment which consumed her in flames, set fire to the palace, and involved Creon also in death. Some say that Medea also killed her own children by Jason.

163 Medea then escaped in a chariot drawn by winged serpents and took refuge with Aegeus of Athens, who married her. But on Theseus' arrival in the city, Medea departed and after many wanderings became an immortal. Some say that Jason took his own life; others that he was mercifully killed when the poop of his own ship *Argo* fell upon him.

(iv) HERACLES

164 Heracles, the most famous of the Greek heroes, was the son of Alcmene by Zeus.

165 Alcmene's brothers having been killed by the Taphians, she would not consummate her marriage with her husband Amphitrion, son of Alcaeus, until he had avenged their death. While Amphitrion was away from Thebes fighting the Taphians, Zeus visited Alcmene in her husband's likeness and told her how he had been victorious. The true Amphitrion returned the following day, and the ensuing confusion is the theme of comedies by Plautus, Molière, and Dryden.

166 Nine months later Zeus boasted that he was about to become the father of a son who would be called Heracles, or glory of Hera, and who would be ruler of the house of Perseus. The jealous Hera exacted from him a promise that any son born that day to the house of Perseus should be king. She then hastened the birth of Eurystheus, who was a grandson of Perseus, and delayed that of Heracles. Alcmene bore two children, Heracles, son of Zeus, and Iphicles, Amphitrion's son, who was a night younger. Alcmene, fearing Hera, exposed Heracles, but Hera in error nursed him, thus conferring on him immortality.

167 Returned to Alcmene, Heracles prospered, and when still in his cradle, strangled with either hand two terrible snakes which Hera had sent to destroy him. In his youth he was taught how to drive the chariot by Amphitrion, fighting by Castor, how to sing and play the lyre by Eumolpus, wrestling by Autolycus, and archery by Eurytus. Linus, who was once teaching him to play the lyre, censured him, and Heracles then promptly killed his teacher with his own lyre, so Amphitrion sent him away to keep cattle.

168 In his eighteenth year he set out to attack the lion of Mt. Cithaeron which was destroying the herds of both Amphitrion and his neighbour Thespius. The chase lasted fifty days, and Thespius, who was Heracles's host all this time, rewarded him by giving up his fifty daughters to him.

Heracles killed the lion with a wild-olive club and made himself a garment of the pelt, with the head as helmet, though some say that he wore the skin of the Nemean lion.

169 On his return to Thebes, Heracles challenged the Minyan heralds from Orchomenus, who had come to collect tribute of cattle, and then led a victorious campaign against the Minyans in which his foster-father Amphitrion was killed.

170 Heracles was rewarded by Creon King of Thebes, who gave him his eldest daughter, Megara or Megera, in marriage, and Heracles became by her the father of several children. Creon's youngest daughter was married to Iphicles.

171 But Hera now visited Heracles with madness, so that he killed his own children and two of Iphicles's. When he recovered his reason he went, after purification, to consult the oracle at Delphi. The Pythia, calling him for the first time Heracles, advised him to go to Tiryns and there serve Eurystheus King of Argos for twelve years, doing whatever he was commanded. At the end of that time immortality would be conferred on him.

172 Most reluctantly Heracles set out. The gods gave him gifts of armour, but he relied on his bow and arrows and on the olive clubs which he cut for himself. His nephew Iolaus, oldest son of Iphicles, accompanied him as his faithful charioteer and companion. Thus supported, Heracles embarked on the twelve gigantic tasks imposed on him by Eurystheus.

The Twelve Labours of Heracles

173 The First Labour was to bring back the skin of the Nemean or Cleonaean lion, an enormous creature, said to be the offspring of Typhon and Echidne, which was devastating the valley of Nemea near Cleonae. As the pelt could not be pierced by any weapon, Heracles strangled the lion with his hands. He rededicated the Nemean games to Zeus and took the lion's carcase back to Tiryns, where he flayed it with its own claws. Some say that he wore the pelt as his armour. Eurystheus was so terrified that he now took refuge in a brazen urn whenever Heracles approached.

174 The Second Labour was to kill the Lernean hydra, another monster which was said to be the offspring of Echidne by Typhon, and which Hera brought up. It lived at the sevenfold source of the River Amymone and haunted the neighbouring swamp of Lerna. It had a dog-like body and nine snaky heads, one of them immortal. As soon as Heracles struck off one head with his club, two grew in its place, while an enormous crab seized the hero's foot. He crushed the crab and called on Iolaus to burn the necks of the eight heads as he crushed them. The immortal head was buried and Heracles poisoned his arrows in the monster's gall, so that henceforth any wound they caused was fatal. Hera placed the image of the crab among the signs of the zodiac.

175 The Third Labour was to capture alive the Ceryneian hind. This creature had brazen feet and golden antlers, and was therefore often called

Heracles, wearing the skin of the Nemean lion, captures the Ceryneian hind. Black-figured Attic vase painting. British Museum. (*Photo: Michael Holford.*)

a stag. Heracles pursued it tirelessly for a year, and eventually shot an arrow which pinned the forelegs together without causing bloodshed. He then carried the creature back on his shoulders.

176 The Fourth Labour was to capture alive the Erymanthian boar, which had come down from Mt. Erymanthus to ravage Psophis. During his journey Heracles was entertained by the Centaur Pholus, who had a cask of wine given by Dionysus. When this was opened, other Centaurs besieged the cave. Repulsed by Heracles, some of them fled to the Centaur Cheiron. Heracles accidentally wounded Cheiron, who was an old friend, with one of his poisoned arrows. Cheiron, an immortal, could not die, although he now longed to do so, and was relieved from pain only when he later

143

surrendered his immortality to Prometheus. Heracles continued his pursuit of the boar, drove it into a snow-drift, bound it with chains, and carried it to Eurystheus, but when he heard that the Argonauts were gathering for Colchis he hastened to join them, accompanied by Hylas.

177 The Fifth Labour was to cleanse in one day the stables of Augeias, King of Elis, who had more cattle and sheep than any man on earth. The dung had not been cleared away for years. Heracles swore a bargain with Augeias that he would cleanse the stalls in one day in return for a tenth of the cattle, and Phyleus, son of Augeias, was a witness to their mutual oaths. Heracles then diverted the Rivers Peneius and Alphaeus through the stalls, which were thus cleansed in a day. But Augeias now learned that Heracles had been under Eurystheus's orders, and therefore refused the reward and even denied the bargain. When Phyleus was loyal to the truth Augeias banished him. Heracles later avenged himself on Augeias.

178 The Sixth Labour was to free the marshy lake of Stymphalia in Arcadia of the Stymphalian birds, which were sacred to Ares. These man-eating creatures had brazen beaks, claws, and wings, and used their feathers as arrows. Heracles, helped by Athene, frightened the birds with a rattle and then shot them down, though some say that they flew off to the island of Aretius in the Black Sea, where they were found later by the Argonauts.

179 The Seventh Labour was to capture the Cretan bull. Poseidon had sent the bull to Minos for a sacrifice, but he had substituted another, and it was now raging over the island. Heracles did not avail himself of Minos's offers of help, but captured the bull single-handed and took it to Eurystheus, who set it free again. It roamed through Greece to Marathon, where Theseus captured it and took it to Athens for sacrifice to Athene.

180 The Eighth Labour was to bring back the mares of Diomedes, a savage King of the Bistones in Thrace, who fed his horses on human flesh. On his way Heracles visited Admetus and freed Alcestis from death. Then with a few companions he drove the mares down to the sea, and turning to repel the attacking Bistones, he left them in the charge of his friend Abderus, who was soon eaten by them. Heracles, however, killed Diomedes and threw his body to the mares. He then founded the city of Abdera in honour of his friend and drove the mares back to Eurystheus, who set them free on Mt. Olympus, where they were eaten by wild beasts.

181 The Ninth Labour was to fetch for Admete, daughter of Eurystheus, the golden girdle that Hippolyte, Queen of the Amazons, had received from Ares. After an eventful journey through Europe and Asia, Heracles and his companions reached the land of the Amazons, where Hippolyte, sister of Antiope, received him kindly and promised him the girdle. But Hera roused the Amazons, and they attacked Heracles. In the fight he killed their leaders and Hippolyte herself, from whom he took the girdle. On his way home Heracles came to Troy, where he rescued Laomedan's daughter Hesione from a sea monster sent by Poseidon.

182 The Tenth Labour was to fetch the oxen of Geryon without either demand or payment. Geryon, a powerful monster with three bodies, lived

*Greek votive relief from Piraeus, c. 400 B.C., shows actors holding masks before the god
Dionysus, patron of drama. National Museum, Athens. (Photo: Photoresources.)*

*-century B.C. Greek bronze statuette of the god Zeus hurling
nderbolt. National Museum, Athens. (Photo: Photoresources.)*

*Roman mosaic from a villa near Palermo depicting the sea-
god, Neptune. (Photo: Photoresources.)*

*Greek terracotta from Melia,
475–450 B.C., showing Bellerophon
on Pegasus attacking the Chimera.
British Museum (Photo: Michael
Holford.)*

*Painted Attic vase from Vulci,
c. 550 B.C., shows Heracles
shooting the Stymphalian birds.
British Museum. (Photo: Michael
Holford.)*

on the island of Erythia. Its site was disputed. Some said it was beyond the ocean stream. Others identified it with Gades (Cadiz). Heracles travelled to the frontiers of Libya and Europe, where he set up two pillars, Calpe and Abyla, on the two sides of the Straits of Gibraltar, hence called the 'Pillars of Hercules.' When Helios shone too brightly, Heracles shot at him with an arrow, and Helios, admiring such boldness, gave him a golden cup or boat in which he sailed to Erythia. Geryon's cattle were guarded by the two-headed dog Orthrus, said to be the offspring of Typhon and Echidne, and the herdsmen Eurytion, son of Ares. Heracles felled both of these with his club, and, after overcoming Geryon, he sailed with the cattle to Tartessus in Spain, where he returned the golden boat to Helios. On his adventurous journey back through Gaul, Italy, Illyricum, and Thrace, he resisted many attempts, such as that of Cacus, to steal the cattle and eventually handed them over to Eurystheus, who sacrificed them to Hera.

183 The Eleventh Labour was to fetch the golden apples of the Hesperides. These grew on the tree which Hera had received from Ge at her wedding and which she planted in a garden on Mt. Atlas. It was guarded by the Hesperides and the dragon Ladon, another offspring of Typhon and Echidne. Heracles first consulted Proteus, or as some say Prometheus, and, following the advice he received, he persuaded Atlas to fetch the apples, while he himself upheld the celestial globe. According to some, he also shot Ladon. Atlas, returning with three apples, tried to avoid taking back the burden of the globe, but Heracles, by a ruse, transferred the globe back to the giant's shoulders, took the apples, and hastened away. On his return journey he killed the giant Antaeus, and also persuaded Zeus to free Prometheus, the arrow with which Apollo shot the vulture being placed among the stars as Sagitta. Eurystheus made Heracles a gift of the apples, but the hero dedicated them to Athene, who returned them to their rightful place.

184 The Twelfth Labour was to bring back the dog Cerberus from Tartarus, the most difficult task of all. Heracles descended from Taenarum in Laconia and was guided by Athene and Hermes. After he had crossed the Styx and freed his friend Theseus and Ascalaphus, he obtained Hades's permission to carry away Cerberus, provided he could do so without using any weapon. Heracles seized Cerberus by the throat and dragged him up to show Eurystheus. He then carried the monster back to Tartarus.

His Subsequent Adventures
185 According to most writers Heracles now returned to Thebes and gave his wife Megara to his nephew Iolaus, but Euripides, in his play *Heracles,* uses a different version. He represents the hero first killing the tyrant of Thebes, who had attempted to kill Megara and her children, and then, driven insane by Hera, himself killing his wife and family.

186 Heracles now desired to marry Iole, daughter of his friend Eurytus, King of Oechalia. Eurytus had promised her to the man who could surpass him and his sons in shooting with the bow. Though Heracles surpassed them all, Eurytus still refused to give him Iole because he had murdered his own children, and in this Eurytus was supported by all his sons except Iphitus.

Later when Iphitus appeared suspicious of him, Heracles in a frenzy of rage slew him. Though purified from this murder, he was still troubled in mind, and consulted the Delphic oracle. He was advised to serve as a slave and to give the proceeds to the family of Iphitus.

187 Heracles was purchased by Omphale, Queen of Lydia, and widow of Tmolus, and he served her either for one or for three years. Later writers say that he lived effeminately at this time, and that he used to change garments with Omphale, but others say that he continued to perform heroic deeds.

188 His period of servitude to Omphale completed, Heracles sailed against Troy. On a previous occasion, probably when returning from the land of the Amazons, Heracles and his friend Telamon had come to Troy, where they had found Laomedan's daughter, Hesione, exposed naked to a sea-monster, sent by Poseidon (**104**). Heracles had freed Hesione and killed the monster, but Laomedan had refused to give him the reward he had promised, the white horses given by Zeus in exchange for Ganymede.

189 Heracles and Telamon therefore now sailed to Troy to take their revenge. How they sacked the city is described in para. **275**. Hesione was given to Telamon and bore him the son Teucer. On his return, Heracles faced a terrible storm raised by Hera and perils on the island of Cos. He was then led by Athene to Phlegra, where he helped the gods in their battle with the giants.

190 Heracles now took his revenge on Augeias, who had refused him payment for cleansing the stables. He invaded Elis and eventually killed Augeias, his sons, and their allies, the Moliones, though some say that he spared Augeias. He then founded the Olympic Games, and fetched from the source of the Danube the wild-olive tree whose leaves should crown the victor. Heracles then destroyed the city of Pylos, which had helped Elis. He killed Neleus the king and all his sons except Nestor.

191 Heracles next marched against Hippocoon who had fought against him under Neleus. Hippocoon had driven out his brother Tyndareus and seized the kingdom of Sparta. Heracles killed him and all his sons, and restored Tyndareus. He was helped in this enterprise by Cepheus and his twenty sons, but Cepheus and seventeen sons were killed. It was about this time that Heracles seduced the priestess Auge, daughter of Aleus, King of Tegea, and became by her the father of Telephus.

192 After four years in Arcadia, Heracles left for Aetolia, where Oeneus was King of Calydonia and Pleuron. Heracles wished to marry Oeneus's daughter Deianeira and won her by defeating Achelous, the mighty river-god, son of Oceanos and Tethys. He now sent Iolaus as leader of his sons by the daughters of Thespius to settle in Sardinia.

193 Three years later, while at a feast, Heracles accidentally killed the boy Eunomus, and went into voluntary exile, taking Deianeira and their son Hyllus.

194 They reached the River Evenus, across which the Centaur Nessus carried travellers for a small fee. Heracles let Nessus carry Deianeira, while he himself swam, but the Centaur galloped off with her and would have violated her if Heracles had not shot him through the breast. The dying Centaur then told Deianeira to take his blood as a charm to keep Heracles's love.

195 Heracles now resided at Trachis, and from there invaded Oechalia with an army in order to avenge himself on Eurytus, who had refused to surrender his daughter Iole, even though Heracles had won her in the archery contest. The hero killed Eurytus and all his family, and sent Iole to Deianeira in Trachis while he visited Cenaeum in Euboea and prepared a thanksgiving sacrifice to Zeus.

196 He had sent Lichas to Deianeira to fetch a white shirt to wear at the ceremony. Deianeira, fearful that Iole might win Heracles's love, rubbed the shirt in Nessus' blood, not knowing that Heracles's arrow, steeped in the hydra's blood, had poisoned it. When Heracles put the shirt on, it burned with excruciating agony into his body, and attempts to tear it off took flesh with it. Heracles seized Lichas and flung him into the sea and then commanded his son Hyllus to take him to Trachis. Deianeira, aghast at what she had unintentionally done, hanged herself. Heracles asked Hyllus to promise to marry Iole and to build him a funeral pyre on Mt. Oeta.

197 This tragic climax to Heracles's career has been dramatised by Sophocles in the *Women of Trachis*, or *Trachiniae*, where Deianeira's distress at Iole's arrival and her ill-fated ruse to keep her husband's love are touchingly represented.

198 Heracles finally ascended his funeral pyre to be burned alive. To Philoctetes, who kindled the flame, he gratefully bequeathed his quiver, bow, and arrows. Thunderbolts demolished the pyre, and Heracles was carried by a cloud to Olympus. There he became immortal. Hera was persuaded by Zeus to adopt him as her son, and reconciled to her at last, he married her daughter Hebe.

The Children of Heracles, or Heracleidae

199 Eurystheus now determined to expel from Greece Alcmene and all the children of Heracles. Only in Athens did they find protection, and when Eurystheus attacked the city he was resisted by Theseus (or by his son Demophon), Iolaus, and Hyllus. As an oracle had demanded the sacrifice of one of Heracles's children, his daughter Macaria killed herself. Eurystheus was then defeated, by either Iolaus or Hyllus, and despatched by Alcmene.

200 These events are the theme of Euripides's play, *The Children of Heracles* or *Heracleidae*.

201 Hyllus later, endeavouring to enter Peloponnesus, was slain in single combat by Echemus, King of Tegea. Only Tleopolemus settled in Argos.

202 Some generations later, the descendants of Heracles conquered Peloponnesus in conjunction with the Dorians. This legend indicates the conquest of the Achaeans by the later invaders.

(v) THESEUS

203 Theseus, the great hero of Attica, was the son of Aethra by Aegeus, King of Athens, though he was also reputed to be the son of Poseidon. Aethra was the daughter of Pittheus, King of Troezen, and here she secretly brought up her young son.

204 When he was of age, Aethra showed him the sandals, and a sword which was an heirloom of Cecrops, that Aegeus had left for him under a great rock. Theseus was able to lift the rock, recover the tokens, and proceed to Athens.

205 He insisted on going not by sea, but by the dangerous land route, and, like Heracles, he freed the country of many terrors. He killed Periphetes, whose club he afterwards carried, Sinis, the wild sow of Crommyum, Sciron, Cercyon, and Sinis's father Polypemon, who was surnamed Procrustes.

206 Meanwhile in Athens Aegeus had married Medea, who had fled for safety from Corinth. Medea recognised Theseus, and jealous for Medus, her son by Aegeus, she attempted to poison him. But Aegeus recognised Cecrops's sword in time and welcomed his son with great rejoicing. Medea fled, taking Medus, and Theseus then scattered other rivals, the fifty sons of Pallas, nephews of Aegeus, who had hoped to succeed him to the throne.

ΦΑΙΔΙΜΟΣ   ΒΙΘΟQΑΜΙΑ

ΒΑΣDOLOS

207 Theseus next captured and sacrificed to Athene the Marathonian bull which Heracles had brought from Crete and which had been driven to Marathon.

208 He now, of his own free will, went as one of the seven youths who with seven maidens were chosen by lot to be sent to Crete as yearly tribute, to be devoured there by the Minotaur (233). Ariadne, daughter of Minos, King of Crete, fell in love with Theseus, and gave him a sword and a clue of thread by which he might find his way out of the labyrinth where the Minotaur lived. Theseus slew the monster, released his fellow Athenians, and fled with them and Ariadne, but at Naxos he deserted her and she was consoled by Dionysus, to whom the island was sacred.

209 Theseus forgot on his return to hoist the white sail which was to have been a sign of victory, and Aegeus, seeing the black sail, threw himself in despair into the sea now called Aegean. Theseus then became the King of Athens.

210 He is said to have invaded the country of the Amazons either with Heracles or later, and here he carried off Antiope, who became his wife, though according to another tradition, Theseus took not Antiope but her sister Hippolyte. It is 'Hippolyta' who appears as his bride in *A Midsummer*

Detail from the 'François vase' painted by Cleitas, *c.*570 B.C., shows a ship arriving to collect Theseus and the youths and maidens he rescued from the Minotaur. Archaeological Museum, Florence. (*Photo: Hirmer.*)

149

Red-figured vase painting by Euthymides, *c.* 510 B.C., shows Theseus abducting Helen. Peirithous looks on. Staatliche Antikensammlungen, Munich. (*Photo: Mansell Collection.*)

Night's Dream. In revenge the Amazons invaded Attica, and were eventually defeated by Theseus in the midst of Athens itself.

211 Later Theseus married Ariadne's sister Phaedra, another daughter of Minos, who bore him the sons Acamas and Demophon. But Phaedra fell desperately in love with her step-son Hippolytus (Theseus's son by either Antiope, or Hippolyte), and when the young man rejected her advances she killed herself, after leaving a letter falsely accusing him to Theseus. The enraged Theseus prayed to Poseidon that Hippolytus might die that very day, and the god sent a sea-monster which so terrified the chariot horses of Hippolytus that they dragged him to death. The story is the theme of Euripides's tragedy *Hippolytus*, and the *Phèdre* of Racine.

212 Theseus was a close friend of Peirithous, King of the Lapithae, and attended his wedding to Hippodameia, and when a drunken Centaur attempted to carry off the bride, Theseus joined with the Lapithae in the famous fight against the Centaurs.

213 After Hippodameia's death, Peirithous and Theseus together carried off the girl Helen of Sparta, and she fell by lot to Theseus. As she was too young to marry, he concealed her in the village of Aphidnae, where she was cared for by his mother Aethra.

214 Theseus then, full of misgiving, fulfilled his promise to Peirithous to help carry off another daughter of Zeus, by accompanying him to the Underworld to take away Persephone. But Hades chained them both to a rock, where they languished till Heracles came to the Underworld and released Theseus only (**184**).

215 Meanwhile Helen's brothers, the Dioscuri Castor and Polydeuces, invaded Attica, and being told by Academus where Helen was hidden, they rescued her, taking Aethra as her slave.

216 When Theseus returned from Tartarus he was unable to keep order among his people, who were being stirred up against him by Menestheus. He retired to the island of Scyros, where he was treacherously killed by King Lycomedes. He nevertheless returned in spirit to help the Athenians at the Battle of Marathon, and though Menestheus succeeded Theseus as king, the sons of Theseus were afterwards restored to the throne.

217 Theseus, like Heracles, took part in the heroic enterprises of his age. He joined in the Calydonian hunt and helped Adrastus at Thebes, and he may have been one of the Argonauts.

218 Although Athenians in later times looked on Theseus as an historical figure, ascribing political institutions to him, he was in fact a legendary hero.

Cretan Myths
219–239

219 Recent archaeological discoveries have indicated that many of the ancient legends concerned with Crete have a factual basis, and a very readable book on the subject is *The Bull of Minos*, by Leonard Cottrell.

220 In 1899 Sir Arthur Evans began his excavations at Cnossos and soon unearthed the remains of the magnificent, unfortified and labyrinthine so-called 'Palace of Minos' with its indications of an elegant and highly artistic civilisation.

Bull's head *rhyton* (wine-pourer) from the little palace at Cnossos. Heraklion Museum. (*Photo: Charisiades, Athens.*)

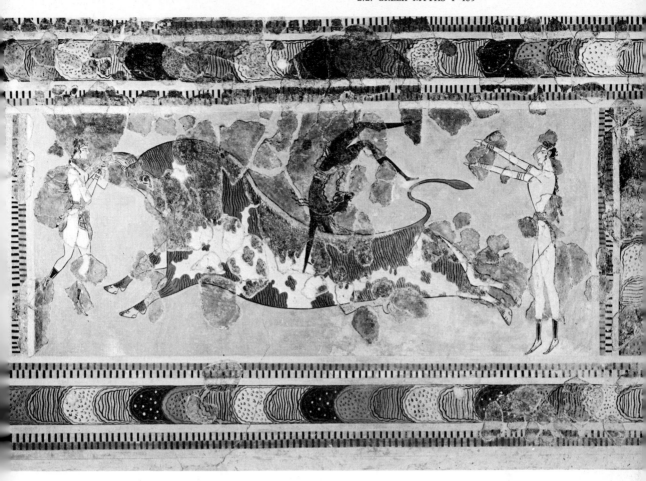

Youths and girl leaping over a bull. Fresco from the palace at Cnossos *c.* 1500 B.C. (*Photo: Charisiades.*)

221 From the architectural evidence available, scholars now consider that there existed in Crete between 2500 and 1400 B.C., a 'Minoan' pre-Hellenic culture which had affinities with that of Egypt. This maritime, commercial culture, its sea-power making fortification unnecessary, spread to the mainland of Greece, where it became known as Mycenaean. It is in fact possible that Crete may have exercised some kind of suzerainty over the mainland. The Cretans probably worshipped a goddess who was served by priestesses. The favourite sport was bull-fighting, in which men and women toreadors showed amazing skill. Cretan architects and engineers were exceptionally ingenious.

222 Discoveries such as these give special significance to such legends as that of Minos's sea power, and of Crete's exaction from Athens of a tribute of men and maidens for the Minotaur. Again the constant appearance of the bull in Cretan legend and Daedalus's building of the labyrinth appear to have foundation in historical fact.

223 It was also to Crete that Zeus, in the form of a bull, brought Europa, said to be the daughter of Agenor, the King of Phoenicia (son of Poseidon) and his wife Telephassa.

(i) EUROPA AND HER SONS

224 As the lovely Europa was playing on the sea-shore with her maidens, Zeus appeared as a white bull and she dared to climb on his back, an incident depicted in the masterly painting by Paul Veronese in the Palace of the Doges in Venice. Suddenly Zeus, plunging into the sea, carried off Europa to Crete, where he fathered on her the three sons, Minos, Rhadamanthus, and Sarpedon. When the reigning king later married Europa he adopted her three sons as his heirs.

225 The brothers quarrelled, however, over the boy Miletus, son of Apollo. As Miletus preferred Sarpedon, they both fled from Minos to Asia Minor. Here Miletus founded the kingdom that bore his name, and Sarpedon, after aiding Cilix, King of Cilicia, against the Lycians, became king of the latter and was permitted by Zeus to live for three generations.

226 Rhadamanthus, though at first ruler of part of Crete, also found it wise to flee. He went to Boeotia, and on Amphitrion's death married Alcmene. So just a ruler did he prove, that he became one of the judges of the Underworld.

(ii) MINOS AND THE MINOTAUR

227 Minos, now sole ruler of Crete, was confirmed in his power by Poseidon, who sent him a magnificent white bull. This so delighted the king that he withheld it from sacrifice, and when it later ran savage it was captured by Heracles as his Seventh Labour, and eventually slain by Theseus.

228 Minos was the law-giver to Crete and was helped in the defence of the island by Talos, a bull-headed, brazen giant and by his powerful fleet.

229 Curious legends are told of Minos's loves. One was Procris, another Britomartis, a Cretan nymph whom he pursued for nine months, until she leaped into the sea and was deified by Artemis, sharing with her the epithet Dictynna.

230 Once when Minos was besieging Nisa, the port of Megara, which belonged to King Nisus, Scylla, Nisus' daughter, fell in love with him, and killed her father by cutting off the hair on which his life depended. Although Scylla let him into the city, Minos was so horrified at her parricide that he left her, and she swam after his ship until her father's soul, changed to a sea-eagle, pounced on her, and she was turned to the bird Ciris. Others say that Minos drowned Scylla, and she was turned into the fish Ciris. She has sometimes been confused with Scylla the daughter of Phorcys.

231 The wife of Minos was Pasiphaë, daughter of Helios and Persë, and several of their children, such as Glaucus, Androgeos, Ariadne, and Phaedra were the subject of legend.

232 Glaucus when a boy was drowned in a cask of honey, and his body found by the seer Polyeidus. Unable to resuscitate Glaucus, Polyeidus was entombed with him, but here a serpent revealed a herb which restored Glaucus to life, and the seer and the boy were released.

Red-figured vase shows the lovesick Phaedra and below Peirithous and Theseus rescuing Hippodameia from the drunken Centaur (212). British Museum. (*Photo: Mansell Collection.*)

233 Androgeos won every contest in the Panathenaic games and was slain at the instigation of Aegeus. Minos in revenge exacted from Athens a yearly tribute of seven youths and maidens to be devoured by the Minotaur.

234 This monster with bull's head and man's body, was the offspring of Pasiphaë and the white bull. Daedalus the craftsman (**237–238**) had enabled her to satisfy her desire, and afterwards built the labyrinth in which her shameful offspring was housed.

235 When Aegeus's son Theseus voluntarily joined the youths destined for the Minotaur, Ariadne fell in love with him, and enabled him to kill the monster by giving him a sword and a clue of thread by means of which he found his way out of the labyrinth. Ariadne then escaped with Theseus, but was deserted by him on Naxos, where she was found by Dionysus, as depicted in Titian's 'Bacchus and Ariadne' in the National Gallery. Tintoretto's picture in the Doges' Palace in Venice shows the marriage of Ariadne to the god.

236 Her sister Phaedra was later married to Theseus, and her unrequited passion for her stepson Hippolytus and its tragic outcome have been described in **211**.

(iii) DAEDALUS AND ICARUS

237 The cunning Daedalus, whose craftsmanship was symbolic of the latest development in sculpture and architecture, had been welcomed by Minos after his flight from Athens. The legend runs that he had been so bitterly jealous of his nephew Talos, or Perdix, inventor of the saw, chisel, and compasses, that he threw him headlong from Athene's temple on the Acropolis. Athene changed Talos into the bird *perdix* or partridge, and the Areopagus banished Daedalus.

238 Welcomed to Crete, he found his skill greatly valued by Minos, until the king discovered how he had aided Pasiphaë. Minos then imprisoned Daedalus with his son Icarus in his own labyrinth. They were released by Pasiphaë, and Daedalus made wings fastened to the shoulders with wax on which they flew away. Icarus mounted too high, the sun melted the wax and he was drowned in the Icarian Sea, but Daedalus reached Cumae near Naples, and fled thence to Sicily. Here Cocalus welcomed him, and when Minos pursued the craftsman, Cocalus's daughters enabled him ingeniously to kill the king.

239 After Minos's death, although his son succeeded him, Cretan civilisation collapsed. Minos himself became a judge in the Underworld.

Theban Myths
240–271

(i) CADMUS

240 The legend concerning the origin of Thebes is that of Cadmus, who according to common tradition was the son of Agenor, the King of Phoenicia (son of Poseidon) and his wife Telephassa.

241 The sister of Cadmus, Europa, was one day carried off by Zeus, who appeared to her in the form of a bull (224) and Agenor sent Cadmus in search of his sister.

242 Unable to find her, Cadmus consulted the Delphic oracle, who advised him to relinquish his search but to follow a cow and build a town where she should sink down with fatigue. Cadmus followed the cow from Phocis to Boeotia, and where she rested he built Cadmea, later the citadel of Thebes.

243 Making sacrifice to Athene, he sent his men for water from a spring of Ares not knowing that it was guarded by a dragon, which killed most of his men. When Cadmus had killed the dragon Athene advised him to sow its teeth, and immediately there sprang up, fully armed, the Sparti, or 'Sown Men', who fought with each other till only five survived—Echion, Udaeus, Chthonius, Hyperenor, and Pelorus. These five were the ancestors of Thebes, and with their help the Cadmea was built.

244 Zeus gave to Cadmus as wife Harmonia, daughter of Ares and Aphrodite, and the Olympian deities attended the wedding. Harmonia received as a gift from Aphrodite the famous necklace made by Hephaestos, which Zeus had originally given Europa, and which conferred irresistible loveliness upon its wearer. From Athene she received a magic robe which conferred divine dignity. The children of Cadmus and Harmonia were Autonoe, Ino, Semele the mother of Dionysus, Agave, Polydorus, and later Illyrius.

245 It is said that Cadmus introduced to Thebes from Phoenicia the use of letters.

246 In old age Cadmus resigned the throne to Pentheus, his grandson, the son of Agave and Echion. But Pentheus, resisting the worship of Dionysus, was destroyed by Agave and her sisters Autonoe and Ino, as is depicted in *The Bacchae* of Euripides (123).

247 Cadmus and Harmonia then left Thebes and were later, in the form of serpents, received in the Islands of the Blessed.

(ii) AMPHION AND ZETHUS

248 Another legend concerning Thebes is that of Amphion and Zethus, the twin sons of Antiope by Zeus.

249 Antiope was divorced by her husband Lycus of Thebes, and cruelly treated by his second wife, Dirce. Meanwhile Amphion and Zethus were brought up by cattle men on Mt. Cithaeron. When they were old enough to know what had happened they took their revenge. They killed Lycus and

157

Dirce, who was tied to the horns of a wild bull and her body thrown into a fountain which henceforth bore her name, and then took possession of Thebes.

250 Amphion and Zethus now built the lower fortifications below the Cadmea, and so skilfully did Amphion play on the lyre given him by Hermes that the stones moved into place of their own accord. The brothers ruled jointly, Zethus married Thebe, who gave her name to the city, and Niobe became the wife of Amphion.

251 Niobe, the proud daughter of Tantalus and sister of Pelops, had seven sons and seven daughters, and boasted that she was superior to Leto, who had only two children. As punishment to her, Apollo killed the boys with his arrows, and Artemis the girls, and Niobe 'all tears' was turned by Zeus into a stone on Mt. Sipylus. The crag of Niobe, being snow-capped, appears to weep when the sun strikes the snow. It is said the Amphion also was either killed by Apollo or that he took his own life.

(iii) OEDIPUS

252 Most famous of Theban kings was Oedipus, who claimed direct descent from Cadmus through Polydorus, Labdacus, and Laius, and all three of the great Greek tragic dramatists were inspired by the fateful story of Oedipus and his children.

253 Oedipus the son of Laius, King of Thebes, and of his wife Jocasta, was as a new-born child exposed on Mt. Cithaeron, his feet tied together and pierced with a nail, for Laius had learned from the oracle at Delphi that he would be killed by his own son. Found by a shepherd of Polybus, King of Corinth, the child was called from his swollen feet Oedipus, and was reared by Polybus as his own son.

254 When Oedipus grew to manhood, he was told by the Delphic oracle that he was destined to kill his own father and marry his mother, and he resolved never to return to Corinth. But going from Delphi, he met Laius riding in a chariot, and in a quarrel killed him.

255 Laius had been on his way to ask the Delphic oracle how he could rid Thebes of the Sphinx, a winged lion with the head and breast of a woman. This monster was said to be the offspring of Typhon and Echidne, or of Orthrus and the Chimaera. Seated on a rock, she challenged each wayfarer with her riddle and strangled him when he failed to solve it.

256 Oedipus, arriving in Thebes, heard the Sphinx's riddle. 'Which being, having only one voice, has sometimes two feet, sometimes three, and sometimes four and is weakest when it has most'. Oedipus answered rightly that the being was a man, who crawls in infancy and supports himself with a staff in old age, and the Sphinx thereupon flung herself to death.

257 As the Thebans had promised that whoever should vanquish the Sphinx should become king and marry Jocasta, Oedipus became King of Thebes and had four children by his own mother, Eteocles, Polyneices, Antigone, and Ismene.

Red-figured vase painting shows Apollo and Artemis killing Niobe's children. Louvre. (*Photo: Mansell Collection.*)

Red-figured painting from
the inside of a cup, c. 470
B.C., shows Oedipus and
the Sphinx. Vatican
Museum. (*Photo: Mansell
Collection.*)

Limestone metope in the archaic Greek style,
c. 550 B.C., from the temple of Selinute, Sicily,
shows Zeus as the bull, carrying off Europa.
(Photo: Photoresources.)

Red-figured kylix, mid-fifth century B.C. *shows the Greek rainbow goddess, Iris. British Museum. (Photo: Michael Holford.)*

Painted Greek amphora from Vulci, c. 440 B.C., *shows the seated muse Terpsichore attended by a youth and maiden. British Museum. (Photo: Michael Holford.)*

258 Thebes, thus defiled by murder and incest, was visited by plague and the blind seer Teiresias said that the city would be saved when one of the 'Sparti' (a title given also to descendants of the 'Sown Men') should give his life. When he learned this, Menoeceus, father of Jocasta, leapt from the walls to his death.

259 The plague still raging, Oedipus consulted Teiresias, and it is at this point that the famous *Oedipus Tyrannus* of Sophocles begins. Oedipus was horrified when at last convinced of his unconscious guilt and, after Jocasta had hanged herself, he blinded himself with a pin taken from her garment and prayed her brother Creon to banish him.

260 Eventually Oedipus went into exile accompanied by Antigone, and followed later by Ismene. At Colonos in Attica he found refuge in a grove of the Eumenides and, protected by Theseus, was received at last by the gods. These last hours of Oedipus are most touchingly presented by Sophocles in his *Oedipus at Colonos*.

(iv) THE THEBAN WARS

261 Angered by his sons' neglect, Oedipus had cursed them, saying that they should divide their inherited land by the sword. They therefore agreed to rule in turn, but when Eteocles's term had expired he refused to abdicate. Polyneices then sought the help of Adrastus, son of Talaus and King of Argos, whose daughter Argia he married, while her sister Deipyle married Tydeus (son of Oeneus of Calydon), who, on account of some murder he had committed, was also a fugitive.

262 When Adrastus prepared to restore Polyneices, his brother-in-law, the seer Amphiaraus, prophesied death for all the leaders save Adrastus. Amphiaraus had married Adrastus' sister Eriphyle, and Polyneices, following the advice of Tydeus, bribed Eriphyle, giving her the famous necklace of Harmonia on the condition that she would persuade her husband to join the expedition.

263 Adrastus, Amphiaraus, Polyneices, and Tydeus were joined by Capaneus, Hippomedon, and Parthenopaeus, the son of Meleager and Atalanta, and these seven marched against Thebes. The war that followed was dramatised by both Aeschylus, in his *Seven against Thebes,* and by Euripides, in *The Phoenician Maidens*.

264 After Thebes had suffered initial reverses, Teiresias prophesied that a royal prince must sacrifice himself, and a second Menoeceus, the son of Creon, now took his own life.

265 The attackers were soon repelled. Capaneus, scaling the walls, was struck by Zeus with lightning. Tydeus, wounded by Melanippus, might have been saved by Athene with an elixir given her by Zeus, but Amphiaraus, who bore him a grudge, persuaded him to drink the brains of the dead Melanippus. This so disgusted Athene that she left him to his fate. Hippomedon and Parthenopaeus also having been killed, Polyneices offered to settle the dispute in single combat with Eteocles, but both were mortally wounded. Amphiaraus fled in his chariot and the earth opened and swallowed him. As the seer had prophesied, Adrastus was the only one of the seven left alive.

266 Thebes was not unscathed. The *Antigone* of Sophocles opens at the point where Creon refused to allow burial to Polyneices. The courageous Antigone dared to disobey him and he ordered that she should be imprisoned alive in a cave. Here she hanged herself, and Creon's son Haemon, to whom she was betrothed, took his own life in despair.

267 Euripides, in *The Suppliants,* dramatises the next phase of the story. Since the Thebans had refused burial to their fallen enemies, Adrastus and the mothers of the slain went to Eleusis and secured the help of Theseus. He defeated the Thebans, and the bodies of the Argives received burial rites, but Evadne, daughter of Iphis and wife of Capaneus, threw herself on to the flaming pyre and perished.

268 Thebes was again attacked ten years later, when Adrastus assembled the 'Epigoni', the descendants of the 'Seven'. His own son Aegialeus made one, and also Diomedes, son of Tydeus, with his faithful companion Stheneleus, son of Capaneus and Evadne.

269 Since Alcmaeon, like his father Amphiaraus, was unwilling to join the Epigoni, Thersander followed the example of his father Polyneices in once more bribing Eriphyle, this time with the magic robe of Harmonia. She then persuaded Alcmaeon to join the expedition along with his brother the seer Amphilochus.

270 Aegialeus was killed before the walls of Thebes, and Teiresias then advised the Thebans to evacuate the city and himself accompanied them, though he died next dawn on drinking from the well of Tilphussa. That day Adrastus, hearing of Aegialeus's death, also died of grief, and in accordance with Teiresias' prophecy the Argives took the empty city.

271 Alcmaeon, on return, slew his mother Eriphyle, in revenge for her vanity and deceit towards his father and himself. Pursued by the Erinnyes, he fled to Phlegeus, King of Psophis, who purified him and gave him his daughter Arsinoë in marriage. Alcmaeon gave his wife Harmonia's necklace and robe, but was soon forced by the Erinnyes to flee once more. He was next purified by the river-god Achelous and married his daughter Callirrhoë, who soon demanded the necklace and robe. Alcmaeon, daring to revisit Psophis, obtained them from Phlegeus on the pretext of taking them to Delphi, but when Phlegeus discovered that they were destined for Callirrhoë he ordered his sons to slay Alcmaeon. Finally, Phlegeus himself sent the ill-fated treasures to Delphi.

Legends of Troy
272–352

272 One of the most romantic discoveries of modern times is that of the German Schliemann, who, trusting the descriptions of Homer, excavated a site on the coast of Asia Minor, near the entrance to the Dardanelles. Between 1871 and 1873 he unearthed the foundations not of one Troy but of seven, his most spectacular find being a hoard of exquisite gold ornaments. His work proved that Troy belonged not only to legend but also to history.

(i) THE FOUNDING OF TROY

273 It is now considered that in the Bronze Age Troy was an important centre for trade. Frequently attacked, it was many times rebuilt, and Greeks, Cretans, and Phrygians all claimed to have had a hand in establishing it. In Homer's time, when the sixth Troy was standing, it had probably absorbed three small towns, Dardania, Tros or Troy, and Ilium, and was probably inhabited by three tribes, Dardanians, Trojans, and Ilians, whose names are all represented in the early legends of Troy's foundation.

274 One of these tells how Scamander of Crete founded a colony in Phrygia, and how, jumping into the River Xanthus, he changed its name to his own. The nymph Idaea bore him a son Teucer (whence the Trojans are called Teucri), and Teucer gave a piece of land to Dardanus, the son of Zeus by the Pleiad Electra, who built there the town of Dardania. The grandson of Dardanus was Tros, who became the father of Ilus and also of Ganymede, whom he relinquished to Zeus for a gift of horses. The son of Ilus was Laomedon.

275 It was to Laomedon that Zeus assigned Apollo and Poseidon as labourers. They built for him the walls of Troy, and when Laomedon refused payment, Poseidon sent the sea-monster, which would have devoured his daughter Hesione had not she been rescued by Heracles. But again Laomedon refused the agreed reward—the white horses given by Zeus in exchange for Ganymede—and Heracles returned later to sack Troy. He gave Hesione to his fellow-warrior Telamon, and killed Laomedon and all his sons save Podarces, who was ransomed by his sister Hesione, and his name changed to Priam, which means 'redeemed'.

276 After a few years Priam sent Antenor to demand that Telamon should send back Hesione, and the Greeks' scornful refusal was one of the causes of the Trojan War.

277 Priam had fifty sons, nineteen of them by his second wife Hecabe, or Hecuba, who bore him many famous children, including Hector, Paris, Deiphobus and the prophetic twins Helenus and Cassandra. Troilus may have been her son by Apollo.

(ii) PARIS AND HELEN

278 Before the birth of her second son, Hecuba dreamed that she had brought forth a blazing firebrand, and that the new-born child was therefore exposed on Mt. Ida. Brought up by a shepherd, he was called Paris, and later, by his courage earned the name Alexander or 'defender of men'. Paris was beloved by the nymph Oenone, but he deserted her as a result of a tempting suggestion of Aphrodite's.

279 The occasion of this was the famous 'Judgment of Paris', of which a Renaissance version can be seen in Rubens's picture in the National Gallery.

280 The story goes that alone of all the gods, Eris was not invited to the marriage of Peleus and Thetis, and in revenge she flung in the golden apple of discord with 'to the fairest' inscribed upon it. Immediately Hera, Athene, and Aphrodite disputed its possession, and Zeus commanded Hermes to lead the goddesses to Mt. Ida for Paris to judge the dispute.

281 Although Hera promised him rule in Asia, and Athene fame in war, Paris gave the apple to Aphrodite, who promised him as his wife the loveliest of all women.

282 Paris now discovered his parentage and was joyfully welcomed by Priam, and under Aphrodite's protection sailed to Sparta.

283 His sister Cassandra foretold doom, but was as usual disregarded. In her youth she had been loved by Apollo, who had taught her the art of prophecy on condition that she became his lover. But she had disappointed him, and Apollo had then ordained that her prophecy should never be believed.

284 Welcomed to Sparta by King Menelaus, Paris fell in love with his beautiful queen, Helen, and in Menelaus's absence he succeeded in carrying her off to Troy with much treasure, thus precipitating the Trojan War, now inevitable by reason of an oath sworn by the leading chieftains of Greece to defend Helen's husband.

285 Helen, the daughter of Leda by Zeus, had been brought up in the court of Leda's husband, Tyndareus of Sparta. So lovely was she that even as a young girl she had been carried off by Theseus and Pirithous, to be rescued and brought back by her brothers, the Dioscuri. All the noblest in Greece then became rivals for her hand, and at the instigation of Tyndareus swore an oath to defend her chosen husband.

286 Helen married Menelaus, and when the Dioscuri were immortalised, he succeeded Tyndareus as King of Sparta.

(iii) THE TROJAN WAR

287 After Helen had fled with Paris, leaving her husband and daughter Hermione, Menelaus summoned the chieftains to war. His powerful brother Agamemnon, King of Mycenae, who had married Helen's half-sister, Clytemnestra, was leader, and from the Peloponnese came also old Nestor of Pylos. Nestor was the only one of Neleus's twelve sons spared by Heracles (**190**). Renowned for wisdom and eloquence, he had been a courageous

Sculptured frieze showing Helen and Paris being drawn into love by Aphrodite and Eros. National Museum, Naples. (*Photo: Mansell Collection.*)

ΑΦΡΟΔΙΤΗ

ΑΛΕΞΑΝΔΡΟΣ

6680

fighter. He had defeated the Arcadians and Eleans and had taken part in the Calydonian hunt and the fight between Centaurs and Lapithae. Although he had ruled over three generations, he gladly joined the expedition to Troy.

288 The courageous Diomedes, son of Tydeus, and King of Argos, also came from the Peloponnese with eighty ships. He had been one of the Epigoni who had taken Thebes, and two fellow Epigoni came with him—Sthenelus, son of Capaneus, and Euryalus, the Argonaut. Tleopolemus, son of Heracles, the Argive who had settled in Rhodes, brought nine ships, and Palamedes, son of Nauplius, joined the muster from Euboea.

289 But Agamemnon needed more distant allies, and together with Menelaus and Palamedes, he went to Ithaca to persuade Odysseus to join them.

290 Odysseus was the son of Anticleia, a daughter of the wily thief Autolycus, and of Laertes, King of Ithaca, though some say that his father was really Sisyphus. He had won his wife Penelope, daughter of King Icarius of Sparta, in a foot race, and when Icarius had tried to persuade Penelope to remain with him, Odysseus had told her she might do as she wished. Penelope had veiled her face to hide her blushes and had followed her husband to Ithaca.

291 An oracle had warned Odysseus not to join the expedition to Troy, and when the envoys arrived they found him ploughing and sowing salt. But the far-sighted Palmedes placed Odysseus' infant son Telemachus in front of the plough, and Odysseus was tricked into revealing his sanity and joining the expedition.

292 Agamemnon also welcomed allies from Salamis and Locris. From Salamis, bringing twelve ships, came Great Ajax, son of King Telamon, a courageous fighter, who boasted that he needed not the help of the gods. His half-brother, Teucer, son of Telamon by Hesione and the best archer in Greece, fought behind Great Ajax's shield. Little Ajax also fought with them. Son of Oileus, King of the Locrians, he was small in stature but swift of foot, and skilled in throwing the spear. He brought forty ships.

293 An important contingent from southern Thessaly also sailed to Troy, for Calchas, a renegade prophet from Troy, foretold that the city could not be taken without the help of Achilles, son of Peleus, King of the Myrmidones at Phthia in Thessaly, and of the Nereid, Thetis.

294 By dipping her son into the Styx, Thetis had made him invulnerable, except for the heel which she was holding. Achilles had been taught by Cheiron and by his tutor Phoenix, and was renowned for strength, speed, and high courage.

295 Thetis, knowing that if Achilles went to Troy he would never return alive, sent him disguised as a girl to the court of Lycomedes, King of Scyros, and here Lycomedes's daughter Deidamia bore him the son Neoptolemus, or Pyrrhus. When Odysseus, accompanied by Nestor and Ajax, visited Scyros, he left a spear and shield among a pile of gifts for the maidens, and Achilles, seizing these, revealed his identity.

296 Achilles joined the Greeks together with his tutor Phoenix and Patroclus, his cousin, who had come as a boy to Peleus's court after an accidental murder and had become the inseparable friend of Achilles.

297 The Greeks were further strengthened by Idomeneus, King of Crete, who brought 100 ships and shared the command with Agamemnon. Meriones accompanied Idomeneus.

298 The fleet was fortunate in being abundantly supplied with provisions, by Anius, son and priest of Apollo in Delos, for his three daughters who had been dedicated to Dionysus received from the god power to produce at will corn, oil, and wine.

299 The expedition set out from Aulis, but first made a false landing and ravaged the country of Telephus, son of Heracles and Auge, and now King of Mysia. When he repelled the Greeks, Dionysus caused him to stumble over a vine, and he was wounded by Achilles. Told by an oracle that his wound could be cured only by him who had inflicted it, he visited the Greeks, who likewise knew through an oracle that they could not take Troy without the aid of Telephus. Achilles therefore gladly cured him with rust from the spear which had injured him, and Telephus showed the Greeks the route they should take.

300 Assembled a second time at Aulis, the Greeks were delayed by unfavourable winds, for Agamemnon, by killing a hart, had vexed Artemis. Calchas foretold that only the sacrifice of Agamemnon's daughter Iphigeneia would appease the goddess, and Agamemnon reluctantly gave his consent, though some say that Artemis snatched Iphigeneia from the altar and bore her off to Tauris (**396**). Certainly the winds changed and the fleet set sail.

301 When they had landed on the island of Tenedos, in sight of Troy, Achilles killed King Tenes and his father Cycnus, and here Philoctetes, son of Poeas suffered misfortune. Most famous of the Greek archers, he had been the friend of Heracles, and had received from him the famous bow and poisoned arrows when he set fire to the hero's funeral pyre on Mt. Oeta. He was now injured in the foot by one of these arrows or, as some say, by the bite of a snake, and the smell of the wound became so offensive that, on the advice of Odysseus, Philoctetes was left behind on the island of Lemnos.

302 It was probably from Tenedos that the envoys Menelaus, Odysseus and Palamedes were sent to Priam to request the return of Helen. They were courteously entertained by Antenor, the wisest of the Trojans, who advised that Helen should be sent back, but the Trojans were obdurate.

303 The Greeks then attacked the mainland, and Protesilaus of Thessaly, who was an uncle of Philoctetes, was the first to leap ashore, though he knew through an oracle that it meant death. Wordsworth, in his poem *Laodamia*, tells how Laodamia his wife, the daughter of Acastus, desolate with grief, begged the gods to let her husband return for only three hours. Hermes led Protesilaus to her, and when he died the second time she died with him.

304 Achilles, the second to land on Trojan soil, soon distinguished himself as the most courageous and formidable of all the Greeks.

305 It was through Achilles that Aeneas entered the war. At first he took no part, although he was the son of Priam's cousin Anchises. But when Achilles raided his herds on Mt. Ida, he led his Dardanians against the Greeks, and distinguished himself in battle. His mother, Aphrodite, frequently helped him, and once carried him away when wounded by Diomedes, while the god Poseidon, though hostile to Troy, saved him from Achilles.

306 Many cities allied to Troy were raided by Achilles. In Thebes, in Cilicia, he killed King Eëton, father of Hector's wife Andromache, while Great Ajax raided the Thracian Chersonesus and in Teuthrania killed the King Teuthras and took his daughter Tecmessa.

307 In the tenth year of the war the Greeks at last concentrated their armies before Troy itself, which was defended by the mighty Hector, by Aeneas, and by many allies, including Sarpedon, a son of Zeus, who was in command of the Lycians.

308 The Greeks were hampered by rivalries between the chiefs. Odysseus took a cruel revenge on Palamedes, who had tricked him into joining the forces. He bribed one of Palamedes's servants to hide under his master's bed a letter written in the name of Priam, and then accused Palamedes of treachery. Palamedes's tent was searched, the letter was found, and he was stoned to death by the whole army. Thus perished the sage, who was said to have invented lighthouses, scales, measures, the discus, certain letters of the alphabet, and dice.

309 Then in the tenth year there broke out the notorious quarrel between Achilles and Agamemnon with which the *Iliad* opens. Chryseis, the daughter of the Trojan priest, Chryses, had been taken prisoner and assigned to Agamemnon, and when Chryses came to ransom her, Agamemnon roughly repulsed him. Apollo, in revenge, sent a plague among the Greeks, and on Calchas's advice, Agamemnon unwillingly sent Chryseis back. He recompensed himself, however, by seizing Briseis, who had been given to Achilles, and Achilles then stubbornly refused to take any further part in the fighting, though some say that his motive in this was to curry favour with Priam, for he had fallen deeply in love with Priam's daughter Polyxena.

310 The Trojans quickly seized this opportunity to attack, and Agamemnon was glad to grant a truce so that Paris and Menelaus might settle the quarrel by a duel. But when Paris was losing, Aphrodite carried him away and fighting broke out again.

311 Diomedes wounded Aeneas and Aphrodite and then strove with Glaucus, a Lycian prince second in command to Sarpedon, but when they remembered the friendship between their forefathers they desisted and exchanged gifts. Hector and Ajax fought in single combat till nightfall, when they also exchanged gifts, Hector giving Ajax a sword and receiving a purple baldric.

312 The Greeks, hard-pushed, were now forced to build a wall and trench, and when they were driven back even farther, Agamemnon in alarm offered to return Briseis to Achilles, but he courteously and firmly refused.

313 Diomedes and Odysseus then made a night-raid on the Trojan lines. After killing the spy, Dolon, they slew Rhesus the Thracian and drove off his snow-white horses, for an oracle had declared that once they had drunk of Scamander, and eaten the grass of the Trojan plain, the city would not be taken. The play *Rhesus*, attributed to Euripides, dramatises these incidents from the *Iliad*.

314 Next day, however, the Trojans victoriously set fire to a Greek ship, and Achilles went so far as to lend Patroclus his own armour and let him lead the Myrmidones. After killing Sarpedon, Patroclus drove the Trojans back to their very walls, until he was at last himself wounded by Euphorbus, son of Panthous, and slain by Hector, who at once stripped him of his borrowed armour, though Menelaus, who had killed Euphorbus, now joined with Ajax in rescuing the body.

315 Achilles was prostrate with grief, but Thetis visited him with new armour made by Hephaestos, and he made peace with Agamemnon, who

Roman frieze showing Hephaestos (Vulcan) and the Cyclopes forging the armour of Achilles. Aphrodite watches from the left. Museo nuovo nel Palazzo dei Conservatori, Rome. (*Photo: Mansell Collection.*)

at last sent Briseis back. Achilles then drove the terrified Trojans back to the city. The noble Hector alone withstood him, though Priam and Hecuba, implored him to come in. Thrice did Achilles chase Hector round the walls of Troy, and then finally killed him, stripped him of his armour, and, tying him by the ankles to his chariot, dragged him ignominiously back to the ships, though some say that Achilles dragged Hector three times round the walls of Troy by the purple baldric that Great Ajax had given him.

316 Each day at dawn Achilles, crazed with grief, pulled the corpse three times round the tomb of Patroclus until at last, in one of the most touching scenes of the *Iliad,* Priam, led by Hermes, went to Achilles's tent and begged to ransom his son's body for burial.

317 The lovely Penthesilea now came to the Trojans' aid. She was the daughter of Otrere and Ares, and Queen of the Amazons. But Achilles killed her, and as he mourned over her, he was ridiculed by Thersites, the ugliest and most scurrilous of the Greeks, and Achilles felled him with a blow. This angered Diomedes, a kinsman of Thersites, and he flung the body of Penthesilea into the Scamander, but it was rescued and honourably buried, some say by Achilles himself.

318 Memnon, the black-skinned handsome King of Ethiopia, son of Eos and Priam's half-brother Tithonus, now reinforced the Trojans. He killed several Greeks, including Antilochus, the gallant son of Nestor, who, too young to sail from Aulis, had later joined his father.

319 The vengeful Achilles then engaged Memnon in fierce single combat while Zeus weighed their fates in the balance. Memnon was slain and, at the request of Eos, Zeus honoured him by causing birds, called Memnonides, to rise from his funeral pyre and fight above it till they fell as a sacrifice. They were said to visit yearly the hero's tomb on the Hellespont.

320 Many great monuments, called Memnonia, were supposed by the Greeks to have been erected in Memnon's honour, the most famous being the colossal statue behind the temple of Egyptian Thebes, which gave forth each sunrise a sound like the breaking of a lyre-string.

321 Achille's own course was now run, and in a battle near the Scaean Gate Paris, aided by Apollo, shot him through the vulnerable ankle.

322 Great Ajax then killed Glaucus, and he and Odysseus rescued the body of Achilles. But they quarrelled violently over the possession of the armour. Homer, in the *Odyssey,* says that Odysseus killed Ajax, and that when he summoned the spirits of the dead, Ajax held sullenly aloof. Sophocles, however, in his tragedy *Ajax,* represents Ajax thrown into madness by defeat and slaying the sheep of the Greeks, believing them to be his rivals, and finally falling on the very sword that Hector had given him.

323 So many heroes dead, the Greeks lost heart, and Calchas said they must fetch the bow and arrows of Heracles. Odysseus and Diomedes therefore sailed to the island of Lemnos, where Philoctetes had been left to languish, and Sophocles, in his play *Philoctetes,* shows how he was persuaded to return.

Painting on a black-figured amphora by Exekias, *c.* 540 B.C., shows Achilles killing Penthesilea, Queen of the Amazons. British Museum. (*Photo: B. Museum.*)

324 Cured of his wound by one of the sons of Asclepios, either Machaon or Podalirius, Philoctetes challenged Paris to an archery contest. Mortally wounded, Paris besought his former lover Oenone to cure him, but she refused, and then in remorse at his death took her own life, events described by Tennyson in his *Death of Oenone*.

325 Helenus and Deiphobus then quarrelled for the possession of Helen, now homesick for Sparta, and when Deiphobus forcibly married her, Helenus, as some say, fled to Mt. Ida, where either he freely joined the Greeks, or was captured or ensnared by Odysseus, for Calchas had said that only Helenus knew the secret oracles which protected Troy. Helenus said it would fall that summer, if a bone of Pelops were brought to the Greeks, if Achilles's son Neoptolemus, or Pyrrhus, joined them, and if Athene's Palladium were stolen from the citadel.

326 Agamemnon at once sent for the shoulder-blade of Pelops, while Odysseus, Phoenix, and Diomedes went to Scyros and persuaded Lycomedes to let Neoptolemus join them. Odysseus then gave Neoptolemus his father's armour.

327 It is said that Priam now sent Antenor to Agamemnon to sue for peace, but Atenor, out of hatred for Deiphobus, conspired with the Greek leader as to how they might secure the Palladium. They arranged that Odysseus, disguised as a filthy runaway slave, should gain entrance to Troy. Recognised by Helen alone, he gained much useful information, including the confession that she longed to return home. It was either on this occasion that he stole the Palladium, or later when he was accompanied by Diomedes.

328 Odysseus is said to have devised the stratagem of the wooden horse. This was built by the cowardly Epeius, son of Panopeus, under the supervision of Athene, and it bore an inscription saying that it was dedicated to the goddess. Then twenty-three or more of the bravest Greeks, including Neoptolemus, Odysseus, Sthenelus, and Thoas of Calydon, climbed into the hollow belly.

329 At nightfall, Agamemnon and the remaining Greeks burnt their camp and sailed to the island of Tenedos, leaving behind only Sinon, a cousin of Odysseus and grandson of the cunning Autolycus.

330 At dawn Priam and his sons found the wooden horse on the shore, and believing it to be sacred to Athene, in spite of opposition had it hauled up to the citadel. Cassandra declared that warriors were within it, and she was supported by Laocoön, son of Antenor, and priest to both Apollo and Poseidon, who flung a spear at the horse's flank and caused a clatter of arms. Their warning was, however, neglected, partly because Sinon, who had let himself be taken prisoner, said that the horse was the Greeks' atonement for stealing the Palladium, partly because the fate which now befell Laocoön was misinterpreted.

331 Laocoön had offended Apollo by marrying in spite of vows of celibacy, and the god now punished him by sending two enormous serpents, which crushed to death both the priest and his two sons—a disaster represented

in the magnificent sculpture probably dating from the first century B.C. and now in the Vatican. Priam wrongly supposed this to be a punishment for smiting the horse, and it was now welcomed with feasting and revelry.

332 In the evening Helen with Deiphobus strolled round the horse and, imitating in turn the voice of each man's wife, she called to the heroes, who stifled their replies.

333 At night Agamemnon, warned by a beacon lit by Sinon, sailed to the shore, and as Antenor gave the word the warriors within the horse leapt down to slaughter and pillage.

334 Priam had been persuaded by Hecuba to take refuge with her and her daughters before an altar to Zeus, but their son Polites was slain before their very eyes by Neoptolemus, and when the old king feebly tried to attack the slayer, Neoptolemus butchered him also. Odysseus and Menelaus meanwhile killed and mangled Deiphobus, but Menelaus pardoned Helen, and led her safely to the ships.

Neck of a late seventh-century B.C. clay vase from Mykonos shows the Trojan horse with the Greeks inside it. Mykonos Museum, Athens. (*Photo: German Archaeological Institute, Athens.*)

173

Painting on a black-figured amphora shows Neoptolemus killing Priam. Hecuba looks helplessly on. British Museum. (*Photo: Michael Holford.*)

335 Cassandra fled to the sanctuary of Athene, but Little Ajax roughly dragged her away, and she was claimed as booty by Agamemnon. Her sister Laodice, the wife of Helicaon, was mercifully swallowed up by the earth.

336 Hector's widow Andromache was given to Neoptolemus, and the Greeks, eager to exterminate the whole family of Priam, even killed her infant son Astyanax, by hurling him to death from the city walls, fearful lest he should one day avenge his parents.

337 At the demand of Achilles's ghost Polyxena was sacrificed to him by Neoptolemus, to ensure favourable winds. Some say this happened at Troy, others only when the Greek fleet had reached Thrace.

338 Hecuba fell to the share of Odysseus, who took her to Thracian Chersonesus, and there she avenged the death of one of her sons. Polydorus, the youngest of Priam's sons, had, according to Homer, been slain by Achilles, but later accounts speak of another son of the same name. Just before the fall of Troy Priam had entrusted him, together with much gold, to Polymester, King of Thracian Chersonesus, and when Troy fell Polymester murdered Polydorus for his gold and cast him into the sea. Hecuba discovered the body. She contrived to kill Polymester and his two sons, and she then evaded the angry Thracians by turning herself into a bitch named Maera.

339 Euripides combined this story of Hecuba's revenge with that of the sacrifice of her daughter Polyxena in his tragedy *Hecuba*.

340 Few of the inhabitants of Troy escaped death or slavery. The wise Antenor, his wife Theano, and their children were all spared, and were said to have sailed to the west coast of the Adriatic and there to have founded Venice and Padua.

341 Aeneas carried on his back his blind father Anchises through the Dardanian gate and so to safety. The Romans said that he took with him the Palladium, that stolen by Odysseus being only a replica, and after seven years' wandering, reached Italy (**428**).

342 Aethra, the mother of Theseus, who had served Helen as a slave, was rescued by her grandsons, Acamas and Demophon, the sons of Theseus and Phaedra.

(iv) THE RETURNS FROM TROY

343 Part of the ancient *Epic Cycle* of the Greeks was the cycle known as *The Returns,* which was used by both Homer and Aeschylus. It told of the adventures of the Greeks on their way home. Most suffered misfortune.

344 The fate of Agamemnon is described in **386–388**, and that of Odysseus in **353–369**.

345 Menelaus, who failed to sacrifice to Athene, took eight years, and only by seizing Proteus learned how to reach Sparta, where he married Hermione to Neoptolemus.

346 Neoptolemus had been accompanied by Andromache and by Helenus, who prophesied a safe route. He had abandoned his kingdom in Thessaly and settled in Epirus, part of which he gave to Helenus, who married Andromache. Neoptolemus then claimed Hermione, although her grandfather, Tyndareus, had betrothed her to Orestes, and as a result he was murdered, either by Orestes himself or at his instigation.

347 Many Greeks settled in Italy. Diomedes, hated by Aphrodite, finding on his return to Argos that his wife had been unfaithful, left for Aetolia to help his grandfather Oeneus, and later settled in Daunia in Italy, where he married Euippe, daughter of King Daunus. He was buried in one of the islands since called Diomedans, and his companions were turned into gentle birds. Philoctetes also settled in Italy.

348 Idomeneus, caught by tempest on his return to Crete, vowed to sacrifice to Poseidon the first person he met on return. As this was his own son, Crete was punished by pestilence, and Idomeneus exiled. He settled in Calabria in Italy.

349 Demophon, son of Theseus visited Thrace and gained the love of the king's daughter, Phyllis, but when he left her to visit Athens, she killed herself in despair of his return and was turned into a tree.

350 Many sailors were shipwrecked on the dangerous promontory of Caphareus, where Nauplius, King of Euboea, eager to avenge the death of his son Palamedes, lighted misleading fires.

351 The seer Calchas, like Amphilochus, went safely overland to Colophon. Here he contended in prophecy with Mopsus, a son of Apollo and Manto, the daughter of Teiresias, and being surpassed, he died of grief. Amphilochus joined with Mopsus in founding the city of Mallus, but they killed each other in a fight for its possession.

352 Nestor alone returned home without mishap and enjoyed a happy old age.

The Wanderings of Odysseus
353–369

353 Odysseus' journey home, lasting ten years, and his final arrival in Ithaca are the theme of Homer's epic, the *Odyssey*. E. V. Rieu says that this may be thought of as a novel, and Samuel Butler argued that it might well have been written by a woman! The incidents of the *Odyssey* form the background of reference to the *Ulysses* of James Joyce.

354 After leaving Troy, Odysseus and his men visited the Cicones, where he obtained several jars of sweet wine, and then they landed on the Libyan promontory of the Lotophagi. Here lived the Lotus-eaters, who gave his men some of the fruit, inducing the enervating dreaminess described by Tennyson in *The Lotus-eaters*.

355 Next, landing on the west coast of Sicily, Odysseus, with twelve companions, entered the cave of a giant, but when the owner, the one-eyed Cyclops, Polyphemus, son of Poseidon, came in with his flocks, he blocked the entrance with a gigantic stone, and devoured two of Odysseus' companions. Next evening, by which time only six of his men survived, Odysseus made Polyphemus drunk with his sweet wine and then blinded him. At dawn the Greeks escaped by clinging under the bodies of the sheep as they went out to graze, and so reached their ship, but henceforth they had to reckon with the vengeful hostility of Poseidon.

Mid-seventh-century B.C. painting on a vase from Argos shows Odysseus and a companion blinding Polyphemus. Argos Museum. (*Photo: Photoresources.*)

356 Odysseus was next entertained by Aeolus, who gave him a bag of winds, but when his foolish crew untied this, they were blown back to Aeolus, who now refused further help.

357 In Telepylos, city of Lamus, King of the cannibal Laestrygones, Odysseus lost all his ships except one, but in this he reached Aeaea, the island of the enchantress Circe, daughter of Helios and Perse. Men sent by Odysseus to explore were turned by her to swine, and only Eurylochus returned to tell the news. Odysseus, hastening to their rescue, was given, by Hermes, the plant Moly, which vanquished Circe's charms. She restored his companions and lavishly entertained them all for a year.

358 Then, on Circe's advice, Odysseus sought the counsel of the dead seer Teiresias. He sailed to the River Oceanos, and in the land of the Cimmerians summoned the spirits of the dead, who thronged to lap the blood of a libation he had prepared. First appeared Elpenor, one of his crew, who while drunk had fallen to death from Circe's roof. Later came Teiresias, who gave him prophetic advice, and then Anticleia, the mother of Odysseus, the men and women of antiquity, and his former comrades.

359 He again visited Circe, who advised him how to circumvent the Sirens and Scylla and Charybdis. Odysseus nullified the Sirens' spell by having himself lashed to the mast, and by filling the sailors' ears with wax, and he just avoided the whirlpool Charybdis, though Scylla's six mouths snatched and devoured as many of his seamen.

360 At the island of Thrinacia, against the warnings both of Teiresias and Circe, Odysseus' companions slaughtered the cattle of Helios, and when they put to sea Zeus destroyed all save Odysseus himself.

361 Clinging to wreckage, he drifted ten days until he reached the island of Ogygia. Here the nymph Calypso lovingly kept him for eight years, until at Athene's request Zeus sent Hermes to command his release.

362 On a raft that Calypso had taught him to make, Odysseus sailed for eighteen days, till it was wrecked by vengeful Poseidon. Then helped by Leucothea and Athene, Odysseus landed on the island of Scheria. Here he was led by the beautiful Nausicaa to the court of her father Alcinous, who was the prosperous ruler of the Phaeacians. Alcinous gave Odysseus a ship, and after an absence of ten years he at last landed on Ithaca. Athene disguised him as a beggar and he was hospitably welcomed by his swineherd Eumaeus.

363 Odysseus' mother Anticleia had died of grief, Laertes his father had withdrawn to the country, and his wife Penelope had been keeping at bay a crowd of unruly suitors led by Antinous. She had promised to wed one of them when she had finished a robe for Laertes, but each night she unpicked the work of the day, until her servants betrayed her ruse, and she was now hard-pressed. Her son Telemachus had gone in search of Odysseus, and after visiting Nestor and Menelaus, he now returned to Ithaca and also visited the hut of Eumaeus.

Red-figured vase painting shows Odysseus, lashed to the mast, resisting the Sirens' sons. Königs-museum, Berlin. (*Photo: Mansell Collection*.)

364 Here Odysseus made himself known to Telemachus and they planned revenge. First the son set out for home, followed later by Odysseus still in beggar's disguise. He was recognised only by his aged hound Argus, which at once expired, and by his nurse Eurycleia.

365 Next day Penelope announced that she would accept the suitor who could shoot with the great bow of Eurytus which only Odysseus had been able to wield. No one could bend it till Odysseus seized it and shot Antinous. Supported by Telemachus, he killed the suitors, and at last made himself known to Penelope. He then visited Laertes, but the kinsmen of the suitors rose against him and battle ensued until Athene, disguised as Mentor, effected a reconciliation.

366 At this point the *Odyssey* ends, though Teiresias had prophesied that Odysseus must again set out on a journey and propitiate Poseidon and then return to an honourable old age till death came to him from the sea.

367 Tennyson, in his poem *Ulysses,* imagines him, even in age, hungry still for travel.

368 Another tradition says that Telegonus, son of Odysseus by Circe, while searching for his father, landed on Ithaca and began to plunder for food. When opposed by Odysseus and Telemachus, all unknowing he killed his father. He then took Telemachus and Penelope back to Aeaea, and there married Penelope, while Telemachus married Circe.

369 Although Homer represents Penelope as a faithful wife, other writers say that she became the mother of Pan, either by Hermes or by all the suitors. It is a tradition such as this that Joyce evidently follows in his *Ulysses.*

Legends of the House of Pelops
370–398

370 Some of the most dramatic of all Greek stories have their setting in Mycenae, city of the legendary hero Agamemnon. In 1876 Schliemann began excavation on this ancient site, and here he unearthed the famous shaft-graves with their precious treasures, which probably date from 1600 B.C., four centuries before the era of Agamemnon and the siege of Troy. Schliemann thus proved to the learned world that the city at all events was historical, and scholars now believe that it was the centre of a Late Bronze Age culture.

(i) TANTALUS
371 According to legend, Agamemnon was a descendant of Tantalus, son of Zeus and the nymph Pluto, and father of Pelops, Broteas, and Niobe. Tantalus was said to be a wealthy king, but whether of Lydia, Argos or Corinth, is uncertain.

Gold death mask, the so-called 'mask of Agamemnon', *c.* 1550 B.C., from the tombs of
Mycenae. National Museum, Athens. (*Photo: Charisiades.*)

372 Highly favoured by his father Zeus, Tantalus was even invited to Olympian banquets, but he proved unworthy of such honours, divulging Zeus's secrets and stealing nectar and ambrosia from Olympus.

373 Tantalus was also said to have received from Pandareus a dog made of gold, and then to have sworn by Zeus that he had never seen or heard of it. As this dog was the one which Hephaestos had made for Rhea, and which she had set to watch the cradle of the infant Zeus, the gods were naturally incensed. Pandareus perished miserably, his orphan daughters were carried off by Harpies, and Tantalus suffered agonising punishment for this and other crimes, the most ghastly of which was his murder of his son Pelops. Having invited the gods to a banquet, he cut Pelops into pieces and served them in a stew. Demeter, still grieving for Persephone, was the only divinity who did not notice what she was eating, and she consumed the shoulder.

374 Tantalus's punishment became proverbial. Tortured with thirst, he was placed in a lake whose waters receded whenever he attempted to drink, while above his head were laden fruit boughs which flew upwards as soon as he reached for them. Thus 'tantalised', he also saw suspended above his head a huge rock which threatened to fall and crush him.

(ii) PELOPS

375 After punishing Tantalus, Zeus ordered Hermes to put the limbs of Pelops into a cauldron and boil them. Clotho took him from the cauldron, Demeter gave him an ivory shoulder, which became a kind of birthmark for his descendants, and Pelops was restored to life.

376 Pelops was later expelled from his kingdom of Phrygia and came with his followers to Pisa in Elis. Here Oenomaus, son of Ares, was king, and as an oracle had said that he would be killed by his son-in-law, he challenged to a chariot race all who came to woo his daughter, Hippodameia. If the young man won, he would marry Hippodameia, if not he would be killed by the spear of Oenomaus, which, like his wind-begotten horses, was a gift of his father Ares.

377 Many suitors had lost their lives when Pelops arrived in Pisa. He was already possessed of a winged chariot, the gift of Poseidon, but he also bribed Oenomaus's charioteer Myrtilus, the son of Hermes, with the promise of half the kingdom, to remove the lynch-pin from the chariot of his master and substitute one of wax. Oenomaus was flung out and killed, and Pelops married Hippodameia.

378 Pelops refused to keep faith with Myrtilus and flung him into the sea. Myrtilus, as he died, cursed the whole race of Pelops, and his image was set among the stars as the charioteer by his father Hermes. Pelops soon became master of Olympia and revived the Olympic Games. His wealth and power in the peninsula were so great that it was called the Peloponnesus, or 'Island of Pelops'.

Frieze on a Roman sarcophagus depicting the chariot race between Oenomaus and Pelops. Vatican Museum. (*Photo: Mansell Collection.*)

(iii) ATREUS AND THYESTES

379 The eldest sons of Pelops, Atreus and Thyestes, with the connivance of their mother, killed Chrysippus, their half-brother, and were obliged to flee their home.

380 They were kindly received at Mycenae, and after the death of King Eurystheus, Atreus seized the kingdom in spite of the bitter rivalry of Thyestes, whom he forthwith banished.

381 Thyestes, however, who had already succeeded in seducing Atreus's second wife Aerope, now tricked his brother into killing Pleisthenes, his own son by his first wife. Atreus, planning grisly reprisals, lured Thyestes to Mycenae by promising him half the kingdom. He then killed the sons of Thyestes and served him their flesh at a banquet. When the horror-stricken father realised what he had eaten, he laid a curse on the house of Atreus and fled once more.

382 Thyestes, seeking revenge, was advised by the Delphic oracle to beget a son by his own daughter, and going to King Threspotus at Sicyon, where his daughter Pelopia was a priestess, he ravished her and fled.

383 Atreus now visited Sicyon, and, believing Pelopia to be a daughter of Threspotus, married her as his third wife. When she gave birth to Thyestes' son, Aegisthus, she exposed the baby, but Atreus, believing Aegisthus to be his own child, took him in and reared him.

384 When later Thyestes was seized and brought back to Mycenae, Atreus commanded Aegisthus to slay him, but Thyestes disarmed the boy, and recognising him as his own son, ordered him to kill Atreus. Then, at last, Thyestes ruled in Mycenae.

385 According to Homer, Atreus had two sons by Aerope, Agamemnon and Menelaus, and these two now took refuge with King Tyndareus of Sparta. Here Menelaus married Helen, daughter by Zeus of Tyndareus's wife, Leda, and some say that Agamemnon was helped by Tyndareus to expel Thyestes and gain his father's throne.

(iv) THE HOUSE OF AGAMEMNON

386 Agamemnon's wife was Clytemnestra (the daughter of Tyndareus and Leda), whom he forcibly married after killing her first husband in battle. But when his brother's wife, Helen, was stolen away by Paris, and the Trojan War broke out, Agamemnon was away fighting for ten years, and it was not difficult then for Aegisthus to seduce Clytemnestra.

387 Not only had Agamemnon forcibly married Clytemnestra, but he had also agreed to the sacrifice of their daughter, Iphigeneia at Aulis, and Clytemnestra's cup of bitterness was full when she learned that he was returning from Troy, bringing with him Priam's daughter, the prophetess Cassandra, as his mistress.

388 It is at this point that Aeschylus's great trilogy of the *Oresteia* begins. Clytemnestrâ conspired with Aegisthus to kill both Agamemnon and Cassandra. She welcomed her husband royally on his return, but while he was in his bath entangled him in a net, and after Aegisthus had twice struck him, she beheaded him with an axe. She then went out to kill Cassandra, who had refused to enter the palace because, in visionary trance, she was horrified to smell the ancient shedding of blood and the curse of Thyestes (**381**).

389 It was not difficult now for Clytemnestra to seize power, for Orestes, her young son, had been smuggled out of Mycenae by his sister Electra, and for many years Clytemnestra and her paramour ruled in Mycenae.

390 Aegisthus, however, lived in constant fear of vengeance. He would have killed Electra had Clytemnestra allowed. He married her to a peasant, who was fearful of consummating their union. Orestes meanwhile had taken refuge with Strophius, King of Phocis, who had married Agamemnon's sister, and here he formed that friendship with the king's son, Pylades, which became proverbial.

391 The intensely dramatic situation at this point has inspired all three of the great Greek tragedians, and it is most interesting to compare the various interpretations given by Aeschylus, in *The Libation Bearers,* the second play of his trilogy, by Sophocles, in *Electra*, and by Euripides, in *Electra*.

392 Electra, burning for revenge, sent constant messages to Orestes, and when he and Pylades were of age they came secretly to Mycenae, and with Electra's help killed both Aegisthus and Clytemnestra.

393 The agonising punishment that Orestes now endured is portrayed in the *Eumenides,* the last play of Aeschylus's trilogy, and in the *Orestes* of Euripides. Although the Delphic oracle had encouraged Orestes to avenge his father, she was powerless to prevent his being pursued by the Erinnyes, the avengers of matricide, who drove him mad and hounded him from land

to land. At length, on the further advice of the Pythian priestess, he reached Athens and embraced the image of Athene in her temple on the Acropolis. The goddess then summoned the Areopagus to judge his case. Apollo defended him against the Erinnyes on the grounds that motherhood is less important than fatherhood, and he was acquitted by the casting vote of Athene, the verdict being a triumph for the patriarchal principle.

394 The furious Erinnyes were then pacified by Athene, who persuaded them to accept a grotto in Athens, where they would be offered sacrifices, libations, and first fruits. Their name henceforward was Eumenides, or the 'well-meaning'.

395 According to another tradition, followed by Euripides, in his *Iphigeneia among the Taurians*, Orestes was told by Apollo that he would be freed from madness by fetching the statue of Artemis from the Tauric Chersonese.

396 When Orestes and Pylades reached Tauris they were seized by the barbarous natives, who sacrificed all strangers to Artemis, but they found to their amazement that the priestess was none other than Orestes' own sister Iphigeneia. Orestes believed that she had lost her life when sacrificed to Artemis at Aulis (**300**), but she had in fact been rescued by the goddess and brought to Tauris as her priestess.

Red-figured vase painting, *c.* 370 B.C., shows the naked Oedipus seeking refuge at Delphi. The Pythian priestess flees from the omphalos in terror while Apollo and Artemis protect Oedipus from the Erinnyes (*Photo: Mansell Collection.*)

397 Iphigeneia, by her ready wit, rescued Orestes and Pylades from sacrifice, and all three returned to Greece, carrying with them the image of the goddess. Here they were reunited with Electra, and returned to Mycenae, where Orestes, by killing Aegisthus' son and becoming king, finally ended the strife between the sons of Atreus.

398 Orestes, after killing his rival Neoptolemus, married his cousin Hermione, and Electra was married to Pylades.

The Underworld
399–409

399 The Greeks expected to enter after death into the cheerless nether world, the domain of Hades, known to the Romans as Orcus, or Dis, but as Hades was possessor of all the rich metals and gems of the earth, the ancients usually preferred the euphemism 'Pluto', 'the wealth', when speaking of one so dreaded.

400 The word 'Hades' was used too of his actual domain, which was also called Tartarus, although in the *Iliad,* the word 'Tartarus' had been reserved for the very lowest region of the Underworld, where the rebel Titans had been thrust.

401 Hades, son of Cronos and Rhea, won the lordship of the nether world when his brother Zeus won the sky, and Poseidon the sea. His most treasured possessions were the helmet of darkness, given him by the Cyclopes, and the staff with which he drove the ghosts.

402 He ruled with his queen, Persephone, whom he had forcibly abducted from the upper world, but he was not always faithful to her, and she once changed the nymph Minthe, whom he was pursuing, into the plant mint, and the nymph Leuce, whom he loved, was afterwards changed into the white poplar.

403 The companion to Persephone was Hecate, who had once aided Demeter in her search for the lost maiden. Hecate was a mysterious divinity, a triple goddess, mighty in heaven, on earth, and in the Underworld, honoured by Zeus and all the immortal gods. She came to be regarded by the Hellenes as primarily a dread divinity of the Underworld, as one who kept company with the dead and who fostered sorcery and witchcraft. She figures as such in *Macbeth*. Worshipped where three roads met, she was represented with three bodies and three heads.

404 Also dwelling in the Underworld were the Erinnyes, winged daughters of earth or of night, with serpent hair, who punished unnatural crime. They were later known euphemistically, as the 'Eumenides', or 'well-meaning', and this name was said to have been given them after the acquittal of Orestes, as is portrayed in the *Eumenides* of Aeschylus (**393–394**). Later writers named three Erinnyes, Alecto, Megaera, and Tisiphone.

405 Ghosts conducted to Hades's realm by Hermes had first to cross the Styx, the 'hated' river, and supplied by relatives with a coin laid under the tongue of the corpse, they paid the surly ferryman Charon. Without this coin they were unable to cross the Styx. Arrived on the farther bank, they propitiated Cerberus, represented by later writers as a fierce dog with three heads, said to be another of the monsters born to Echidne.

Attic vase painting *c.* 400 B.C. shows Charon receiving a soul. National Museum, Athens. (*Photo: Mansell Collection.*)

406 Styx was not the only river ghosts encountered. There was also Acheron, river of woe, Phlegethon, river of flames, Cocytus, river of wailing, and Lethe, the river of forgetfulness, where ghosts drank and forgot their past.

407 The three judges of the Underworld were Aeacus, Rhadamanthus, and Minos. Wicked spirits were sent by them to the place of punishment, those who had led an indifferent life to the cheerless asphodel fields, and the virtuous to Elysium.

408 Although Elysium was said to be near the Underworld, it formed no part of Hades's dominion, and Homer placed it far away to the west of the earth, near Oceanos. It was a blessed abode, without cold or snow. Later writers also spoke of the 'Fortunate Isles', located by Greek geographers as beyond the pillars of Heracles, and eventually identified with the Canary and Madeira islands.

409 In their picture of life after death the Greeks combined contradictory ideas. Broadly speaking, the figures of Persephone and Hecate represent the hopes of pre-Hellenic people for an after-life, while Hades personifies the Hellenic fear of the finality of death.

ROME

Aeneas
410–430

410 The belief that Greek survivors of the Trojan War, notably Epeius, Diomedes, Philoctetes and Odysseus, had later emigrated to Italy was probably current before 300 B.C. How the tradition of Aeneas's arrival grew up is unknown, though the *Iliad* makes it clear that he escaped the sack of Troy (**341**) and there are hints that Greek epics and plays, now lost, told of his travels to a westerly country. One tradition strong in Rome at least as early as the fourth century and later recorded by Q. Lutatius Catulus (*Origin of The Roman Nation*) said that Aeneas betrayed Troy to the Greeks out of hatred for Paris and was later given a safe-conduct.

411 According to Virgil's *Aeneid* during the sack of the city Aeneas, helped by Venus (Greek Aphrodite, q.v.), his mother, rescued the Penates of the city and carrying his old father Anchises on his back, leading his son Ascanius, escaped the holocaust.

412 Together with a small band of refugees Aeneas set sail to find a new home. He consulted Apollo's oracle at Delos and was told to seek the country of his ancestors. He therefore set out for Crete since Dardanus, founder of the Trojan royal house, was said to have originated there, but advised by the Penates that Dardanus's first home had been in Italy, Aeneas changed course for that land.

413 He put in at Epirus, now ruled by Helenus (**277, 325, 346**) who further advised him that on reaching Italy he should seek for a white sow and thirty piglets and establish a city in that place. Further counsel could be had from the Sibyl of Cumae.

414 Arriving in Sicily Aeneas was welcomed by Acestes at Drepanum. Here his aged father Anchises died. After a year's stay, Aeneas and his men again set sail and, owing to the hostility of the goddess Juno (Hera, q.v.), were driven ashore near Carthage, city of Queen Dido.

415 Dido fell passionately in love with Aeneas, and Venus, the hero's mother, persuaded Juno to agree to their marriage. Dido regarded their illicit union in a cave as marriage, thus breaking her vow, made on the death of her husband Sychaeus, when she swore that she would never again take a husband. Retribution ensued, for Jupiter (Zeus, q.v.) now told Aeneas he must depart. The hero planned to leave secretly but Dido discovered his intention and, failing to dissuade him, committed suicide. As Aeneas put out to sea, the smoke rose from her funeral pyre.

416 Returning to Drepanum Aeneas honoured his father's death with funeral games. Meanwhile Juno led some of his followers' women to fire four of their ships. Undaunted, Aeneas again set sail, though leaving some of his company behind.

417 Although his pilot Palinurus fell asleep at the helm and was washed overboard, Aeneas at length succeeded in landing in Italy. He went to Cumae, where the Sibyl told him to arm himself with the Golden Bough from a wood near Lake Avernus. She then led him down to the Underworld to consult his father's spirit.

418 On the way, they encountered Dido, who silently turned her back. From Anchises Aeneas learned of the future glory of the city he was to found and its ultimate splendour under the great Augustus.

419 Returning to the upper world Aeneas reboarded his ship and sailed on to the estuary of the Tiber, where the god of the river appeared to him in a dream telling him that Helenus's prophecy was about to be fulfilled. Thus forewarned, Aeneas set out next day and came upon the white sow and her thirty piglets at the site of the city of Alba Longa, which his son would found thirty years later.

420 Latinus, the old Aborigine King of the neighbouring Laurentum, who had been told by the oracle that his daughter Lavinia would marry a foreigner, agreed to her marriage with Aeneas but Juno incited the Rutulian Prince Turnus of Ardea to claim that since he was of Mycenaean ancestry the oracle clearly referred to him not Aeneas.

421 The great Trojan's suit was also opposed by Latinus's queen Amata. When Aeneas's son Ascanius accidentally shot a pet stag nothing could avert war between the rival factions.

422 Following the earlier advice of Father Tiber, Aeneas now sought the aid of the Arcadian Greek King Evander, who ruled the Palatine Hill. Evander told him of Hercules's (Heracles) visit to the hill and his slaughter of the terrible man-eating ogre, Cacus, son of Vulcan, who had stolen the great hero's cattle (**182**). Evander promised to support Aeneas's cause and the king's son Pallas joined the Trojan's forces.

423 As the two heroes descended from the Palatine Hill Venus appeared and presented Aeneas with wonderful armour made by the great Vulcan.

Scene from the Emperor Augustus Caesar's Altar of Peace, 13–9 B.C., shows Aeneas sacrificing the white sow (419) to the deities of Lavinium. (*Photo: Mansell Collection.*)

It included a magnificent shield depicting the future history of Rome including Augustus' great victory at the Battle of Actium.

424 Turnus now opened hostilities by attacking the Trojan camp and burning its ships. These had been made of wood from Mt. Ida, sacred to the goddess Cybele, who now persuaded Neptune (Poseidon, q.v.) to transform them into sea nymphs and so save them from utter destruction.

425 Jupiter, unable to reconcile Venus and Juno, who supported the opposing sides, concluded that the outcome of the battle must be decided by Fate.

426 Many heroes were killed. Aeneas's great friend, Pallas, was slain by Turnus himself, but Aeneas and his men inflicted great casualties on the Rutulian forces, killing many of their most able leaders. Turnus now therefore decided to meet Aeneas in single combat, though both Latinus and Amata tried to convince him of his folly.

427 Jupiter pacified Juno by agreeing that the Trojans and Latins should unite to form a single nation, and so the stage was set for Aeneas's victory. Amata, believing Turnus already dead, hanged herself. In the fight Turnus, mortally wounded, asked Aeneas to allow his old father to have his body. About to concede this request Aeneas suddenly noticed that Turnus was wearing the golden belt of his dead friend Pallas and, enraged, despatched the Rutulian with a single thrust of his sword.

428 Aeneas now married Lavinia and so united the Latins and Trojans. To please Juno, Jupiter decreed that the Trojans should forget their own language and customs and adopt Italian manners.

429 Aeneas founded a new city at the spot where he had landed, and named it Lavinium. Here temples were established to his mother Venus, to Vesta and to the Trojan Penates.

430 It was said that, towards the end of his life, Aeneas met Dido's sister Anna beside the River Numicius. Having been purified in the river's waters he was received into the company of the gods.

Romulus and Remus
431–445

(i) THE ETRUSCAN STORY
431 The early Etruscan myth, probably much influenced by Greek stories such as that of Neleus and Pelias, was preserved by Plutarch in his *Romulus*.

432 Tarchetius, wicked King of Alba Longa, saw on several consecutive days a vision of a penis rising from the flames of his household hearth. He consulted the oracle of Tethys, which told him a virgin should give herself to the apparition. She would bear a splendid son.

433 Tarchetius ordered his daughter to unite with the mysterious penis, but she, feeling insulted, sent her servant girl to take the part. Tarchetius imprisoned them both but Vesta prevented him from executing them.

434 The servant girl bore twin boys whom Tarchetius gave to Teratius ordering him to kill them, but Teratius laid them on a river bank, where they were fed by a wolf and birds until the creatures' strange behaviour caught the attention of a cowherd, who found the children and adopted them. When they reached manhood the boys assassinated Tarchetius.

(ii) THE ROMAN STORIES OF ROMULUS AND REMUS
435 After the city of Alba Longa had been founded by Ascanius, Aeneas's son, it was ruled by his descendants for nearly three hundred years. Then Amulius usurped the throne of his brother Numitor, whom he exiled. Numitor's daughter, Rhea Silvia, was forced to become a Vestal Virgin, but, raped by Mars (Ares, q.v.), she bore twin sons, Romulus and Remus.

The wolf suckling Romulus and Remus. Capitoline Museum, Rome. (*Photo: Angela Hornak.*)

436 Amulius imprisoned her and ordered the children to be drowned, but servants instead left them in a basket on the river bank underneath the Ruminalis fig tree. There they were suckled by a wolf and later found by the shepherd Faustulus who took them home to his wife Acca Larentia.

437 As they grew up, the twins took to attacking bandits and relieving them of their stolen booty. This they divided among the shepherds. The brigands retaliated by laying a trap for the twins during the Lupercal festival and captured Remus, whom they took prisoner to Amulius, complaining that he and his brother had been raiding the lands of the exiled Numitor. Remus was therefore handed over to Numitor. The secret of the twins' identity became known. They assassinated Amulius and replaced Numitor on the throne.

438 As the population of Alba Longa had grown, the twins now resolved to found a new settlement at the place where they had been left and later given a home. Since they could not agree as to which of them should give his name to the new city, they consulted the auguries. Romulus stood on the Palatine Hill, Remus on the Aventine. Soon Remus saw six vultures. No sooner was this reported than Romulus saw twelve. Each was acclaimed king. A fight ensued and Remus was killed.

439 Another story recorded by Livy said that Remus mocked Romulus and sacrilegiously leaped the half-built wall of his new city. Infuriated, Romulus slew him, vowing that all who leaped his walls should meet a similar fate.

440 Having become king, Romulus made a sanctuary on the Capitoline Hill where any fugitive might take refuge and so increase the population of the new settlement. However this seemed likely to dwindle for lack of women and though Romulus sought marriage alliances with various neighbouring states all rejected his overtures. At the time of the annual harvest festival in honour of the god Consus, when Sabine visitors had flocked to Rome, Romulus therefore ordered that all the young women among them should be seized.

441 Titus Tatius, King of the Sabines, led his army on Rome and was circling the Capitoline Hill when Tarpeia, daughter of the garrison's commander, looking down upon the enemy was much impressed by their gold bracelets and rings. She secretly sent a messenger to Tatius suggesting that in return for all the Sabines wore on their left arms, she should let them into the citadel by night. This she did, whether from greed or from the cunning intention of depriving them of their shields is a matter of dispute. However when the time came for her payment the Sabines hurled their shields at her and she was killed, in order, says Livy, to show that even the Sabines felt a traitor should never be trusted.

442 Led by their champion Mettius Curtius, the Sabines now attacked Romulus, but Mettius was overconfident and his horse foundered in the swamps on the site of the later Forum. Some say it was from this incident that the Lacus Curtius in the Forum derived its name.

443 Meanwhile, the Romans' Sabine wives, distraught with grief, interposed themselves between the two armies, so winning a truce. It was agreed that the two peoples should unite under a single government led by Romulus and Tatius, thus creating a precedent for the later dual consulship of the Republic.

444 Titus Tatius, who, some said, was the ancestor of the great Titurian and Vetian families, died before Romulus, who then ruled once more alone until his father Mars descended and swept him up into the air to become the god Quirinus (q.v.).

445 Later, it was said that after Romulus's disappearance his friend Julius Proculus was out riding when he was met by an apparition of Romulus in shining armour. When Julius asked the reason for his desertion of the city, Romulus explained that the gods had decided that those who like Julius and himself were of divine descent should ultimately return to the heavens. This tale was almost certainly an invention of the Julian family to glorify their own origins.

Tarquinius Superbus (Tarquin the Proud)
446–453

446 It is generally agreed that Rome was for a considerable time under Etruscan government. According to tradition the last of these kings was the tyrant Tarquinius Superbus, sixth successor to the throne of Romulus.

447 Prompted by Tullia his sister-in-law, Tarquinius murdered his brother Arruns Tarquinius and married Tullia. He then threw her aged father, the King Servius Tullius, down the senate house steps into the street, where he was murdered by hired assassins. Returning from acclaiming Tarquinius's usurpation, Tullia drove over the old man's corpse and was splattered with blood from head to toe.

448 When his son Sextus Tarquinius asked his advice about the people of Gabii, Superbus silently decapitated the tallest poppies in the garden. Sextus took the hint and executed the Gabian leaders so his father took the town.

449 Soon afterwards, Tarquinius's sons, accompanied by Lucius Junius Brutus, went to consult the Delphic oracle as to which of them would succeed their father Superbus. The oracle replied it would be he who first kissed his mother. Pretending to stumble, Brutus fell and kissed the earth.

450 Meanwhile Tarquinius's brutality was alienating all his subjects. Rebellion was already in the air when Sextus his son precipitated the crisis by raping Lucretia, wife of Lucius Tarquinius Collatinus. Summoning her husband and her father Spurius Lucretius Tricipitinus, she told them of the outrage, adjured them to avenge her and stabbed herself to death before their eyes, in the presence of Lucius Junius Brutus and Publius Valerius Poplicola.

451 This famous story is recounted by Diodorus the Sicilian and by Ovid in his *Fasti*. Shakespeare took it as the subject of his memorable poem *The Rape of Lucrece*.

452 The people of Collatia, city of Lucretia's husband Collatinus, were outraged and, led by Brutus, marched on Rome, roused the city and persuaded its people to shut the gates against Tarquinius, who was away besieging Ardea. Tarquinius and his sons fled into exile. Rome now became a republic governed by consuls, of whom in this early period Brutus was the most renowned.

453 There were three abortive attempts to restore the hated monarchy. In the first of these Brutus's own sons were implicated. He executed them. Later he himself died in single combat with Arruns Tarquinius.

Horatius
454–456

454 The Tarquinians' final attempted coup was made with the aid of Lars Porsenna (Porsena) of Clusium, who besieged Rome and made a concerted attack upon the Pons Sublicius (the wooden bridge over the Tiber, giving access to the heart of the city).

455 The Romans fled before Porsenna's troops, and Publius Horatius Cocles, who was guarding the bridge, called for help to hold off the enemy while the bridge was demolished. Spurius Lartius and Titius Herminius responded. As the bridge was about to fall Horatius ordered them back to safety and single-handed kept the enemy at bay until the bridge's final collapse. Then, with a prayer to Father Tiber, he leaped fully armed into the raging stream and swam to safety beneath a cloud of Etruscan missiles.

456 The story is dramatically related by Thomas Babington Macaulay in his *Lays of Ancient Rome* (1842).

Gaius Mucius Scaevola
457–460

457 Though prevented by Horatius's heroic stand from taking Rome, Lars Porsenna yet beseiged it. Disguised as an Etruscan, Gaius Mucius Scaevola entered the enemy camp intending to assassinate its leader, but being ignorant of Porsenna's appearance could only guess who he was and mistook his man.

458 Brought before Porsenna himself Gaius Mucius placed his right hand into a flaming pan of coals and held it there unflinching, arousing such admiration in Porsenna that the Etruscan freed him and returned his sword, which Gaius Mucius received in his undamaged left hand, thus earning his cognomen Scaevola (left-handed).

459 Moved by the king's generosity, Scaevola warned him that there were three hundred other disguised Romans in his camp waiting their chance to murder him. Scaevola ventured to suggest that so great a king might rather be a friend than an enemy of Rome and such was Porsenna's admiration for the hero that he agreed to call a truce.

460 Parts of this story are Greek in origin and derive from the tale of the mythical King Codrus of Athens who in order to save his country from the Dorians, disguised himself in Dorian costume and penetrated the enemy camp. Dionysius of Halicarnassus says that Scaevola's own surname was Cordus, which would seem to have been prompted by that of Codrus.

Camillus and the Siege of Veii
461–466

461 At the turn of the fifth and fourth centuries B.C. the Romans attacked Veii, an Etruscan city commanding the Tiber at Fidenae. For ten years they lay siege to it with fluctuating fortunes until in 396 B.C. Marcus Furius Camillus was appointed dictator (sole governor of Rome for the duration of the war).

462 The Romans captured a Veientine soothsayer, whose tale that the city would fall only when the Alban Lake was drained received confirmation from the Delphic oracle. Camillus therefore had it drained. He then ordered troops to tunnel under the city. They had reached a point below the temple when above them they heard the Veientine king, about to sacrifice to Juno, say that whoever made this sacrifice should win the war. Bursting through the floor the Romans offered it and their troops stormed the city. Watching from a high tower Camillus wept at the sight.

463 The Veientine Juno was then taken to Rome and booty sent to Apollo at Delphi but Camillus, charged with retaining spoils for himself and with an excessively ostentatious Triumph, was forced into exile.

464 Grant points out that many details of this story derive from the tale of Troy, also besieged for ten years and taken when the Greeks gained secret entry in the Wooden Horse. The story of the soothsayer is Etruscan in origin, while Camillus's pity for the sacked town is paralleled by Publius Scipio Africanus the Younger's reaction to the siege of Carthage.

465 Later, it was said, while Rome was besieged by Brennus the Gaul, and the Capitoline Hill saved from capture only by the cackling of Juno's sacred geese, Camillus returned from exile and, attacking the Gauls in the rear, decimated their forces.

466 So far as it is known this tale is a complete fabrication, for the Gauls having successfully sacked Rome later departed from it unharmed. They almost certainly captured the Capitoline Hill as well as the rest of the city, but later this fact became unacceptable and a more fitting conclusion to the siege was therefore invented.

PART 3
Index and Glossary

The following abbreviations are used:
E: Etruscan; G: Greek; R: Roman.

Abas (G) (i) son of Celeus and Metanira, turned by Demeter into a lizard because he mocked her when she drank too eagerly. See also 113.

(ii) the grandson of Danaus and twelfth King of Argolis, was renowned for his sacred shield, the very sight of which subdued revolt. He was father of the twins Acrisius and Proetus.

Abderus 180.

Aborigines (R) a tribe of allegedly Greek origin who, with the similar Pelasgians, were the first founders of Rome, according to some early myths.

Absyrtus (or **Apsyrtus**) 159.

Abyla 182.

Academus 215.

Acamas (G) a son of Theseus and Phaedra, went with Diomedes to Troy to demand the surrender of Helen. See also 211, 342.

Acastus (G) son of Pelias, King of Iolcos. He joined the Argonauts, but after Medea had caused the death of Pelias, Acastus banished her and Jason. He later received Peleus kindly, but when he falsely suspected his guest of making love to his wife, he treacherously deserted him. Acastus and his wife were later slain by Peleus. The daughter of Acastus was Laodamia.

Acca Larentia 436.

Acestes 414.

Achelous 192, 271.

Acheron 406.

Achilles 293, 294, 295, 296, 299, 301, 304, 305, 306, 309, 312, 314, 315, 316, 317, 319, 321, 322, 337, 338.

Acrisius 129, 130, 131, 132, 142.

Actaeon 83.

Actium, Battle of 423.

Admete 181.

Admetus (G) King of Pherae in Thessaly, was helped by Apollo to marry Alcestis, the beautiful daughter of Pelias. Apollo also ensured that Admetus should escape death, provided that one of his family would die in his place (73). When the time came and Hermes summoned Admetus to Tartarus, only Alcestis was willing to die in his stead, but when she descended to Tartarus,

Persephone refused the sacrifice. A later version says that Heracles arrived with an olive club just in time to prevent Hades, who had arrived in person, from carrying off Alcestis. The earlier version represents a matriarchal point of view. The later was dramatised by Euripides in his *Alcestis*, translated by Browning.

Adonis 62.

Adrastus 261, 262, 263, 265, 267, 268, 270.

Aeacides (G) descendants of Aeacus.

Aeacus (G) son of Zeus and Aegina, was King of the Myrmidones. He helped Poseidon and Apollo to build the walls of Troy. By his wife Endeis he had two sons, Peleus and Telamon, while Phocus was his son by a Nereid. So virtuous was the life of Aeacus that he became one of the three judges of the underworld. See also 407.

Aeaea 357, 368.

Aedon (G) the daughter of Pandareus and wife of Zethus, King of Thebes. Her son was Itylus. Aedon was jealous of Niobe, the wife of Zethus's brother, Amphion, and in an attempt to kill Niobe's eldest son she killed her own son Itylus in mistake. Zeus, in pity, turned her into a nightingale whose song still mourns for Itylus.

Aeëtes 154, 158, 159.

Aegaeon another name for Briareus.

Aegeus 203, 204, 206, 209, 233.

Aegialeus 268, 270.

Aegina (G) daughter of Asopus, mother, by Zeus, of Aeacus.

Aegisthus 383, 384, 386, 388, 390, 392.

Aegyptus see Danaides.

Aemilii p. 111

Aeneas 62, 305, 307, 311, 341, 410–430.

Aeneid 93, 411.

Aeolus (G) (i) son of Hellen and ruler of Thessaly, was ancestor of the Aeolic Greeks.

(ii) son of Poseidon, was ruler of the seven Aeolian isles. Zeus gave him control of the winds. See also 356.

Aerope wife to Atreus, 381, 385.

Aeschylus 19, 263, 343, 388, 391, 393, 404.

Aesculapius see Asclepios.

Aeson 152, 153, 161.

Aethra 203, 204, 213, 215, 342.

Aetolus (G) son of Endymion, was King of Elis. Having accidentally killed Apis in a chariot race, he was banished across the Gulf of Corinth and conquered the country called Aetolia after him. His two sons were Pleuron and Calydon. Both these names are also names of cities in Aetolia.

Africanus, Publius Scipio, the Younger 464.

Agamedes see Trophonius.

Agamemnon 287, 289, 291, 292, 297, 300, 309, 310, 312, 315, 326, 327, 329, 333, 335, 344, 370, 371, 385, 386, 387, 388, 390.

Aganippe (G) a fountain at the foot of Mt. Helicon in Boeotia. It was sacred to the Muses, hence called Aganippides, and was thought to inspire those who drank it. The epithet Aganippis is also applied to the fountain of Hippocrene, also sacred to the Muses.

Agave 123, 244, 246.

Agenor (G) (i) King of Phoenicia, 223, 240, 241.

(ii) son of the Trojan Antenor and Theano.

Aglaia (G) 'the bright one', one of the Charities or Graces.

Aglauros (G) (i) wife of Cecrops.

(ii) daughter of Cecrops. To her and her sisters, Erichthonius was entrusted.

Aides or **Aidoneus** (G) Hades.

Ajax (G) (i) Great Ajax, son of Telamon, 292, 306, 311, 314, 315, 322.

(ii) Little Ajax, son of Oileus, 292, 335.

Ajax of Sophocles 322.

Alba Longa pp. 110, 111, 419, 432, 435, 438.

Alban Lake 462.

Alban Mount p. 110

Alcaeus 165.

Alcestis see Admetus and 161.

Alcides (G) a name of Heracles, a reputed grandson of Alcaeus.

Alcinous 362.

Alcippe 67.

Alcmaeon 269, 271.

Alcmene 164–167, 199, 226.

Alcyone or **Halcyone** (G) (i) daughter of Atlas and Pleione, and leader of the Pleiades.

(ii) daughter of Aeolus and wife of Ceyx. When her

son, Parthenopaeus, to Meleager. Reconciled to her father, she refused to marry unless a suitor should conquer her in a foot race, those who failed in the attempt being killed by her. Eventually Milanion outstripped Atalanta by dropping in her way one after the other, three golden apples given him by Aphrodite. Atalanta stopped to gather these and lost the race. See also **263**.

(ii) The Boeotian Atalanta was said to be daughter of Schoeneus and to have married Hippomenes, but the same tales are told of her. See Swinburne's play *Atalanta in Calydon* and the poem *Atalanta's Race*, by William Morris.

Ate (G) daughter of Eris or of Zeus, who, angered by her mischief, cast her from Olympus. She represents infatuation.

Athamas (G) the son of Aeolus and King of Orchomenus in Boeotia. At Hera's command he married Nephele, and had children Phrixus and Helle. But Athamas secretly loved Ino, daughter of Cadmus and Harmonia, who bore him Learchus and Melicertes. Deceived by Ino's intrigues, Athamas would have sacrificed Phrixus, had not a ram with a golden fleece, sent by Hermes, rescued the boy and flown through the air with him and his sister Helle. Between Europe and Asia, Helle fell into the straits since called Hellespont, but Phrixus reached Colchis, where he sacrificed the ram to Zeus and gave the fleece to Aeëtes, from whom it was later carried off by Jason. Meanwhile Athamas, driven mad by Hera because he had sheltered Dionysus, killed his son Learchus, and Ino flung herself into the sea with Melicertes, where both were transformed into marine deities. Ino became Leucothea, and Melicertes changed to Palaemon. Athamas, forced to flee, settled in Thessaly. See also **120**.

Athene see especially **38–45** and also **14, 15, 48, 66, 77, 102, 105, 134, 135, 141, 148, 155, 178, 184, 189, 243, 244, 265, 280, 281, 325, 328, 330, 335, 345, 361, 362, 393, 394.**

Athens **42, 48, 86, 97, 102, 105, 112, 114, 117, 118, 128.**

Atlantiades **91.**

Atlantis (G) a legendary island, west of the Pillars of Hercules. Its virtuous and powerful inhabitants, becoming degenerate, were defeated by the Athenians, and the island was swallowed up by the ocean in a day and night. See the *Timaeus* of Plato.

Atlas (G) the son of Iapetus and Clymene, was father of the Pleiades, Hyades, and Hesperides. See also **7, 9, 16, 91, 138, 183** and **1.2.94.**

Atlas, Mt. **136, 183.**

Atreus **379, 380, 381, 383, 384, 385, 397.**

Atropos (G) one of the Fates.

Auge **191.**

Augeias, stables of **177, 190.**

Augustus **418, 423.**

Aulis **299, 300, 318, 387.**

Aulus Vibenna (E) brother of Caeles Vibenna and possibly to be identified with that Olus whose head was discovered when the foundations of the Capitoline temple were being dug and who is said to have been a local king.

Auster see Notus.

Autolycus **96, 167, 290, 329.**

Autonoe **244, 246.**

Aventine Hill **438.**

Avernus, Lake **417.**

Bacchae **117, 123.** Also called Bacchantes, Maenads, or Thyiads.

Bacchae, The **123, 246.**

Bacchoi **117.**

Bacchus a name for Dionysus, **117–128.**

Bassareus (G) an epithet of Dionysus. 'Bassaris' was a fox-skin which was worn by the god and also by the Maenads in Thrace. Hence Bassaris means Maenad or Bacchante.

Bathos **12.**

Baucis see Philemon.

Bebrycos **157.**

Begoe see Egeria.

Bellerophon **145–150.**

Bellerus **146.**

Belus (G) son of Poseidon and father of Aegyptus, Danaus, and Cepheus.

Bias (G) brother of Melampus.

Biton and Cleobis (G) sons of a priestess of Hera at Argos, in their filial devotion once dragged their mother's chariot to the temple. Their mother prayed Hera to grant them the best gift for mortals, and they both died while asleep in the temple.

Boeotia **117, 120, 123.**

Boreas (G) the North wind, was the son of Astraeus and Eos, and brother to the other beneficent winds—Notus, Eurus and Zephyrus. He carried off Oreithyia, daughter of Erectheus, who bore him twin sons, Zetes and Calais, and the daughters Chione and Cleopatra (the wife of Phineus). Boreas was friendly to the Athenians and destroyed the ships of Xerxes.

Bosphorus **157.**

Brauron **86.**

Brennus, the Gaul **465.**

Briareus one of the Hecatoncheires, **1, 32.**

Briseis **309, 312, 315.**

Britomartis **81, 229.**

Bromius **117.**

Brontes **1.**

Broteas **371.**

Brutus, Lucius Junius **449–453.**

Butes (G) son of Panion, King of Athens, was a priest of Pallas Athene.

Cabiri (G) two early fertility gods of Phrygia and Thebes. On Lemnos, where their father was said to have been Hephaestos (q.v.) they were regarded as smiths. Elsewhere they were referred to either as sons of Uranos who had assisted at the birth of Zeus or of Proteus and so guardians of sailors. In this last capacity they were identified with the Dioscuri (q.v.). Other stories give them as the children of Zeus and Calliope. The phallic *herms* were said to have been brought to Athens as part of the Cabiri's cult. It is probable that the Cabiri represent the Phrygian version of the twin agricultural deities known elsewhere among the Indo-Europeans; cf. the Vedic Ashvins (vol. 3: 5.3.).

Cacus (i) (E) an extraordinarily beautiful youth, seer and singer killed by Hercules. He was later identified with Caeculus, legendary ancestor of the powerful Caecilii family of the Roman Republic.

(ii) (R) ancient fire-god of the Palatine Hill, later described as the half-human son of Vulcan. A man-eating giant he lived in a cave on the hill and terrorised the Arcadians (q.v.) until slain by Hercules whose cattle he had stolen. One story says he was a wicked slave of Evander (q.v.). See also **182, 422.**

Cadmea **242, 243, 250.**

Cadmus **158, 240, 241, 242, 243, 244, 245, 246, 247, 252.**

Caduceus **98.**

Caeles Vibenna (E) Etruscan leader whose faithful companion Mastarna (q.v.) rescued him from captivity. He is said to have given his name to the Caelian Hill in Rome. His brother was Aulus Vibenna (q.v.) with whom he attacked Cacus (q.v.).

Caeneus (G) offspring of Elatus, was originally the nymph Caenis, beloved by Poseidon, who had consented to change her to a man. Caeneus accompanied the Argonauts and helped to hunt the Calydonian Boar. Although invulnerable, he was killed by the Centaurs in the battle with the Lapithae, for they buried him under a mass of trees. His soul flew out as a

A Centaur. The Capitoline Museum, Rome. (*Photo: Mansell Collection.*)

bird, and in the Underworld he regained female form.

Caere p. 111.

Calais see Zetes.

Calchas 293, 300, 309, 323, 325, 351.

Calipe (G) one of the pillars of Heracles, 182.

Calliope (G) the Muse of epic poetry, is represented with a tablet and stylus and sometimes with a roll of paper or a book.

Callirrhoë 271.

Callisto (G) daughter of Lycaon, was one of Artemis's huntresses. She was seduced by Zeus, who tried to deceive Hera by turning her into a bear. Hera, discovering the ruse, contrived that Artemis should hunt Callisto down, but Zeus caught her up and set her image among the stars as Arctos. Some say that Artemis herself in anger turned Callisto into a bear; others that she was pursued by her own son Arcas and that Zeus snatched both to heaven, Callisto becoming the Great Bear and Arcas the Little Bear.

Calypso 361, 362.

Camilla (R) Amazonian leader of the Volscians, allied with Turnus against Aeneas (421–427). She was slain by Arruns.

Camillus, Marcus Furius 461–466.

Capaneus 263, 265, 267, 268.

Capitoline Hill 440, 441, 465–466.

Capricorn 6.

Carmentia (R) a goddess of water, childbirth and prophecy, sometimes credited with having taught the Romans to write. She is said to have been the mother of Evander (q.v.).

Carthage 414–415, 464.

Cassandra 277, 283, 330, 335, 387, 388.

Cassiopeia 139, 140.

Castalian Spring 69.

Castalides (G) the Muses.

Castor one of Dioscuri, 155, 167, 215, 285, 286.

Catulus, Q. Lutatius 410.

Caucasus 17.

Cecrops (G) said to be the first king of Attica, and to have founded Athens. See also 204, 206.

Celeus 113.

Centaurs (G) in Homer appear as savage creatures, but in later accounts are described as having the upper part of the body human, the lower part equine. They were said to be the offspring of Ixion and a cloud. They lived on Mt. Pelion in Thessaly, a district famous for hunting the bull on horseback. On one occasion they fought with Heracles (176), but their most celebrated fight was that with the Lapithae (212). Wisest of the Centaurs was Cheiron.

Centimani 1.

Cephalus (G) married Procris, but Eos, who fell in love with him, revealed that Procris was easily seduced by gold. Procris then fled in shame to Crete, where she was seduced by Minos. She later returned to Athens, disguised as a youth and bringing a hound and spear, the gifts of Artemis, that never missed their quarry. Cephalus so coveted these, that husband and wife became reconciled. Procris, however, suspected him of loving Eos, and jealously watched him while hunting. One day Cephalus accidentally killed her with the unerring spear.

Cepheus (G) (i) son of Aleus, and one of the Argonauts, was King of Tegea in Arcadia, but he and most of his sons were killed while helping Heracles against Hippocoon. See also 191.

(ii) King of Ethiopia, 139, 140.

Cerberus (and Heracles) 184, 405.

Cercyon (G) the son of Poseidon or Hephaestos. He lived near Eleusis, where he killed all travellers by challenging them to a wrestling match, but was himself overcome and killed by Theseus. See also 205.

Ceres see Demeter, 110–116.

Ceryneian Hind 175.

Ceto 134.

Ceyx see Alcyone.

Chaos 1.

Charis 55.

Charities or Graces (G) were called Gratiae by the Romans. At first the Greeks personified one Grace only, Charis, who in the Iliad appears as the wife of Hephaestos. Later the Greeks spoke of three Graces, Euphrosyne, Aglaia, and Thalia, daughters of Zeus. They were especially the friends of the Muses, living with them on Mt. Olympus.

Charon 405.

Charybdis see Scylla and 359.

Cheiron or Chiron (G) the wisest and best of all the Centaurs. He was the son of Cronos and Philyra, and was hence called Philyrides and lived on Mt. Pelion. Taught by Apollo and Artemis, he was skilled in music, medicine, prophecy, hunting and gymnastics, and taught many of the heroes of antiquity, such as Jason, Castor and Pollux, Peleus, and Achilles. Heracles accidentally caused his death (176), and Zeus placed his image among the stars as Sagittarius.

Chimaera 147, 148, 255.

Chione (G) (i) daughter of Oreithyia and Boreas and mother of Poseidon of Eumolpus, hence called Chionides.

(ii) mother of Autolycus by Hermes. She was killed by Artemis.

Chiron see Cheiron.

Chrysaor 108, 137.

Chryseis 309.

Chrysippus 379.

Chthonius one of the Sparti, 243.

Cicones 354.

Cilix 225.

Cimmerians 358.

Circe 160, 357, 358, 359, 360, 368.

Ciris 230.

Cithaeron (G) a lofty range of mountains between Boeotia and Attica, sacred to Dionysus and the Muses. Pentheus and Actaeon were killed there. See also 168.

Claudii p. 111.

Cleobis see Biton.

Cleonaean (or Nemean) Lion 173.

Clio (G) the Muse of History, represented with a roll of paper or a chest of books.

Cloelia (R) When Porsenna agreed to a truce with Rome (459) he demanded hostages. Among them was Cloelia. She asked to be allowed to swim in the river and while the guards' backs were turned swam back to Rome with her companions. Porsenna was so impressed he allowed them to remain free.

Clotho (G) one of the Fates, 375.

Clusium p. 111, 454.

Clymene (G) (i) mother of Phaeton by Helios.

(ii) wife of Iapetus.

Clytemnestra 287, 386, 387, 388, 389, 390, 392.

Cnidos 116.

Cnossos p. 108 and 30, 220.

Cocalus 238.

Cocles, Publius Horatius see Horatius.

Cocytus 406.

Codrus, King of Athens 460.

Colchis 154, 157.

Collatia 452.

Collatinus, Lucius Tarquinius 450, 452.

Colonos 260.

Consuls, the 444, 452.

Consus p. 109 and 440.

Cordus 460.

Core (Kore), the Maiden 39, 111.

Corinth 45, 58, 102, 105, 118, 146, 148, 161.

Coriolanus (R) probably originally the mythical ancestor of the Coriolian family but the main part of his legend developed during the fourth century B.C. at the time of Gaius Marcius Rutilus the consul. Born Cnaeus Marcius, the soldier Coriolanus received his cognomen after capturing the town of Corioli (Monte Giove) from the Volscians in 493 B.C. Later, as consul, he was accused of having denied grain to starving plebians and generally behaving like a tyrant. He was forced into exile. Joining forces with the Volscians he attacked Rome but withdrew his men after his mother Volumnia and his wife Vergilia came with his two young sons to plead with him. Shakespeare makes the story the basis of his play *Coriolanus*.

Cornelii p. 111.

Cornucopia 6.

Coronis 74.

Corybantes (G) priests of Rhea in Phrygia noted for their dances to drums and cymbals.

Cottus (G) one of the Hecatoncheires.

Creon (i) of Corinth, 162.
(ii) of Thebes, 259, 266.

Cretan Bull 179, 227.

Crete 68, 81, 90, 128, 219–239, 412.

Cretheus 152, 153.

Creusa (G) (i) daughter of Creon of Corinth, 162.
(ii) wife of Xuthus.

Crommyum, Sow of 205.

Cronos (G) son of Uranos and Ge and father, by his sister Rhea, of Hestia, Demeter, Hera, Poseidon, Hades, and Zeus. See also 1–9.

Cumae p. 111 and 12, 417.

Cumae, Sibyl of 413, 417.

Curetes 6.

Curiatii see Horatii.

Curtius, Mettius 442.

Cybele (G and R) name for the Mother Goddess worshipped in Asia Minor. See 424 and 1.3: Kubaba.

Cyclades 132.

Cyclopes (G) different accounts are given of the Cyclopes. Hesiod describes them as Titans (1, 3, 4, 8, 9). Homer speaks of them as one-eyed giant shepherds in Sicily, the chief being Polyphemus (355). Later tradition describes them as helpers of Hephaestos living in Mt. Etna (54). The walls of unhewn stone in Mycenae and other ancient sites are known as Cyclopean (130, 143).

Cycnus 301.

Cyllene, Mt. 92.

Cyllenius 92.

Cynthus (G) a mountain in Delos where Leto bore Apollo and Artemis, hence called Cynthus and Cynthia.

Cyprus 58, 59.

Cyrene (G) daughter of Hypseus, was beloved by Apollo and became the mother of Aristaeus. She was carried by Apollo from Mt. Pelion to Libya, where the city Cyrene was named after her.

Cythera 58, 59.

Dactyli (G) beings who were supposed to have discovered iron and the art of

working it by fire. Mt. Ida in Phrygia was their original abode.

Daedalus 222, 234, 237, 238.

Danae 130, 131, 132, 133, 141, 142.

Danai used in Homer of the Greeks.

Danaides (G) the fifty daughters of Danaus, son of Belus and King of Libya. Danaus's brother Aegyptus, the father of fifty sons, suggested a mass marriage, and Danaus in fear fled with his daughters to Argos, where he was elected king in place of Gelanor. The fifty sons of Aegyptus followed Danaus and asked for his daughters as wives. Danaus agreed, but gave each daughter a weapon with which to kill her bridegroom on the bridal night. All complied save Hypermestra, who spared her husband Lynceus. Lynceus, after killing Danaus, became King of Argos. The story is the theme of Aeschylus's play *The Suppliants*. In Hades the Danaides were condemned continually to carry water in sieves.

Danaus see Danaides.

Daphne (G) a daughter of the river god Peneus in Thessaly, was pursued by Apollo in the vale of Tempe, but when she cried for help she was turned into a laurel-tree, which became the favourite tree of Apollo. The myth probably refers to the Hellenes' capture of Tempe, where the goddess Daphoene was worshipped by Maenads who chewed the laurel and thus intoxicated themselves. Afterwards only Apollo's Pythoness might chew laurel.

Daphnis (G) a son of Hermes and a nymph, who exposed him in a laurel grove. He was adopted by Sicilian shepherds, taught by Pan to play the pipes, and was looked on as the inventor of bucolic poetry. He was blinded by a nymph to whom he was faithless, and Hermes caused the fountain Daphnis at Syracuse to spring up in his honour.

Dardania 273, 274.

Dardanus 274, 411.

Daulia or **Daulis** (G) an ancient town in Phocis. It was the residence of Tereus and the scene of the story of Philomela and Procne, who are hence called Daulias.

Daunus 347.

Deianeira 192, 193, 194, 195, 196, 197.

Deidamia 295.

Deiphobus 277, 325, 327, 332, 334.

Deipyle 261.

Delian Homeric Hymn 71.

Delos 69, 70, 412.

Delphi 69, 71, 72, 76, 117, 118, 171, 186, 242, 253, 254, 271, 382, 393, 463.

Delphi, oracle of see Delphi and **449**, **462**.

Delphinos 106.

Demeter 7, 10, 25, 99, 103, 110–116, 373, 375.

Demodocus 60.

Demophon (G) (i) son of Celeus and Metaneira who received Demeter hospitably. In return the goddess tried to make their son immortal by holding him over the fire, but the scream of Metaneira broke the spell and Demophon died. Cf. 1.2.155.
(ii) son of Theseus, 199, 211, 342, 349.

Despoena 103.

Deucalion 20, 21.

Diana 81, 89.

Dictaean Cave 6.

Dicte (G) a mountain in the east of Crete, where Zeus was brought up, and hence called Dictaeus.

Dictynna 81, 229.

Dictys 132, 141, 142.

Dido, Queen of Carthage 414–418, 430.

Diodorus the Sicilian p. 112 and 451.

Diomedes, Mares of 180.

Diomedes son of Tydeus, 268, 288, 305, 311, 313, 317, 323, 326, 327, 347, 410.

Dione 24, 60.

Dionysia 118.

Dionysius of Halicarnassus p. 112 and 460.

Dionysus 10, 14, 26, 37, 61, 95, 114, 117–128, 298, 299.

Dioscuri (G and R) the twin heroes, Castor and Polydeuces (called by the Romans Pollux). According to Homer they were sons of Leda and King Tyndareus of Sparta, but some said that they were, like Helen, children of Leda and Zeus, and that all three were born at the same time out of an egg. Another tradition held that only Helen and Polydeuces were children of Zeus and that Castor was son to Tyndareus and therefore mortal. Polydeuces, famous as a boxer, and Castor, as tamer of horses, were inseparable. They were noted for their rescue of Helen from Aphidnae (215), for their part in the Calydonian hunt and the expedition of the Argonauts (155, 157), and for their final battle with another pair of inseparable twins, their cousins and rivals, Idas and Lynceus, sons of Aphareus. Accounts of the battle vary, but it is usually said that Idas killed Castor, that Polydeuces killed Lynceus, and that Zeus intervened by slaying Idas with a thunderbolt. Polydeuces, the only survivor, implored Zeus to let him die with Castor, but Zeus decreed that the twins should spend their days alternately under the earth and among the gods. He also set their image among the stars as Gemini. The worship of the Dioscuri as divine spread from Sparta.

Black-figured amphora painting by Exekias, *c.* 540 B.C., shows the Dioscuri welcomed home by Leda and King Tyndareus. Vatican Museum. (*Photo: Mansell Collection.*)

Poseidon giving them power over wind and wave, they were worshipped especially as protectors of sailors. They were regarded as inventors of the war-dance and patrons of bards, and they presided at the Spartan Games. In art each is represented as mounted on a magnificent white horse, carrying a spear, and wearing an egg-shaped helmet crowned with a star. Dumézil suggests they should be regarded as the equivalents of the Vedic Ashvins (vol. 3: 5.3.).

Dirce 249.

Dis 399.

Dius Fidius (R) ancient god of contracts whom Dumézil believes to have been a Roman equivalent of Mitra (vol. 3: 5.3.) though later texts present him as an aspect of Jupiter.

Diva Angerona (R) goddess whose festival was celebrated at the winter solstice, possibly analogous to the Vedic Aditi (vol. 3: 5.3.).

Dodona 24, 27, 28.

Dolon 313.

Dorians 68.

Doris (G) daughter of Oceanos and Thetis, wife of her brother Nereus, and mother of the Nereides.

Dorus (G) son of Hellen, was the mythical ancestor of the Dorians.

Drepanum 414, 416.

Dryads (G) nymphs of trees.

Dryope (G) the daughter of King Dryops, was seduced by Apollo. She was afterwards carried away by the Hamadryads or tree-nymphs. See also **74**.

Echemus 201.

Echidne (G) a monster half woman, half serpent, said to be the mother of many monsters, such as: Chimaera, **147**; Nemean Lion, **173**; Lernean Hydra, **174**; Orthrus, **182**; Ladon, **183**; Sphinx, **255**; Cerberus, **184, 405**. Her mate was Typhon. She was killed by Argus.

Echion (G) (i) son of Hermes, took part in the Calydonian hunt and was herald to the Argonauts.

(ii) one of the Sparti, **243**, **246**.

Echo (G) a nymph who diverted Hera's attention with incessant talking while Zeus amused himself with the nymphs. When Hera discovered the trick she took from Echo all use of her voice except in repetition of another's speech. Echo then fell in love with Narcissus, a beautiful youth, who repulsed her, and she pined away in grief until only her voice remained. Artemis, in anger at Narcissus' coldness, caused him to fall in love with his own reflection in a fountain. In despair he took his own life and was turned into the flower.

Edones 122.

Eëtion 306.

Egeria (R) goddess or nymph credited with prophetic foresight, who became the consort of King Numa Pompilius. She may derive from the Etruscan Begoe (Vegoia) who was said to have advised Arruns Veltumnus, King of Clusium. Egeria's cult was brought to Rome from Aricia and Ovid says that on Numa's death she went to mourn for him there.

Elatus (G) one of the Lapithae, and father of Caeneus.

Electra (G) (i) the Pleiad, **274**.

(ii) daughter of Agamemnon and Clytemnestra, **389**, **390**, **392**, **397**, **398**.

Electra of Euripides **391**.

Electra of Sophocles **391**.

Electryon, King of Mycenae (G) the son of Perseus and Andromeda. His daughter Alcmene married Amphitryon.

Eleusis (G) in Attica, had a splendid temple of Demeter, **112**, **113**, **114**.

Elpenor 358.

Elysium 407, **408**.

Empusae (G) daughters of Hecate, were horrible demons, with the haunches of asses and wearing brazen slippers. They could disguise themselves as bitches, cows, or maidens, and in the latter shape they would lie with men asleep and suck their strength till they died. The idea of Empusae was probably brought from Palestine, where the Lilim, or daughters of Lilith, had similar characteristics.

Enceladus 11, **12**.

Endymion, King of Elis (G) a beautiful Aeolian youth, who, while sleeping in a cave on Carian Mt. Latmus, was seen by Selene the moon, who came down and kissed him. He afterwards returned to the cave and fell into a dreamless sleep. By his wife he had four sons, one of them being Aetolus, who conquered the land now called Aetolia. The myth probably indicates the fate of one who marries the moon goddess. See Keats's *Endymion*.

Enipeus (G) the river god loved by Tyro.

Enna 112.

Eos (G), in Latin Aurora. She was the Dawn, daughter of Hyperion and Theia. She drove her chariot each morning to announce the approach of her brother Helios, and as Hemera, accompanied his across the sky to arrive with him in the West in the evening as Hespera. Her husband was Astraeus, said by some to be father by her of the stars and all winds save the East. Eos carried off several beautiful youths, including Orion, Cephalus, and Tithonus. Her son by Tithonus was Memnon. Eos asked Zeus to grant Tithonus immortality, but omitted to ask also for perpetual youth. Tithonus therefore shrank away until he became a cicada. Among Greeks in Asia Minor the golden cicada was an emblem of Apollo the sun-god.

Epaphus (G) son of Zeus and Io, reigned over Egypt, and was rumoured to be the sacred bull, Apis (see 1.3.).

Epeius 328, **410**.

Ephesia (Artemis Ephesia) **81**.

Ephesus 87, **88**.

Ephialtes 11, **13**.

Epigoni 268, **269**.

Epimetheus 16, **17**, **20**.

Epirus 413.

Erato (G) the Muse of erotic poetry and mime, sometimes carries a lyre.

Erebus (G) or darkness, son of Chaos, begot Aether and Hemera by his sister Night. See also **25**.

Erichthonius (G) (i) son of Hephaestos. Athene entrusted to the daughters of King Cecrops of Athens a chest which they were forbidden to open. It concealed the infant Erichthonius. According to one version, the daughters (Aglauros, Pandrosos, and Herse) were overcome with curiosity and opened the chest. Seeing a serpent within it, they leapt in madness from the Acropolis to their death. Erichthonius succeeded Cecrops as King of Athens, and was himself succeeded by Padion.

(ii) Erechtheus the second was grandson of Erechtheus, son of Hephaestos, and the son of Pandion, whom he succeeded as King of Athens. He was father by Praxithea of four sons, including Cecrops, and seven daughters, Protogonia, Pandora, Procnis wife of Cephalus, Creusa, Oreithyia, Chthonia, and Otionia. When the Eleusinians under Eumolpus son of Poseidon attacked Athens, Erechtheus was told to sacrifice Otionia, whereupon her two eldest sisters, Protogonia and Pandora, also sacrificed themselves. Erechtheus slew Eumolpus, whereupon Poseidon demanded vengeance, and either he or Zeus slew Erechtheus.

Eridanus (G) a deified river. Phaethon fell to his death here. Because amber was found here Eridanus was later supposed to be the Po.

Erigone see Icarius.

Erinnyes or **Eumenides 3**, **260**, **271**, **393**, **394**, **404**.

Eriphyle 262, **269**, **271**.

Eris 65, **280**.

Eros (G) in Latin Amor or Cupid. He was said to be the son of Aphrodite by either Ares, Hermes, or her own father Zeus. The early Greeks thought of him as a winged 'sprite', but by the fifth century B.C. he was represented as a boy, irresponsible but lovely, flying on golden wings and carrying torches and in his golden quiver arrows which could wound both men and gods. He was sometimes portrayed as blindfolded. He usually accompanied his mother Aphrodite. See also Psyche.

Erymanthian Boar 176.

Erysichthon (G) son of Triopas, dared to cut down trees in a grove sacred to Demeter, and when he ignored protests she punished him with an insatiable hunger.

Eryx, Mt. **58**.

Eteocles 257, **261**, **265**.

Etna, Mt. **12**, **14**.

Euippe (G) (i) the daughter of Cheiron, being with child by Aeolus, son of Hellen, was changed into a horse. Their child was Melanippe.

(ii) the daughter of Daunus, **347**.

Eumaeus 362, **363**.

Eumenides or **Erinnyes 3**, **260**, **271**, **393**, **394**, **404**.

Eumenides **393**, **404**.

Eumolpus (G) 'the good singer', the son of Poseidon and Chione, daughter of Boreas and Oreithyia. His mother threw him into the sea as soon as he was born, but his father Poseidon cared for him. He was brought up in Ethiopia, and lived later at the Court of King Tegyrius of Thrace, and then came to Eleusis in Attica. Here he became the priest of the mysteries of Demeter and Persephone. He initiated Heracles into the mysteries and taught him to sing and play the lyre. Eumolpus led an expedition against Erectheus of Athens, three of whose daughters sacrificed themselves to ensure victory. Eumolpus was killed by Erectheus, who was then himself slain by either Poseidon or Zeus. Eumolpus's descendants became hereditary priests of Demeter at Eleusis.

Eunomus 193.

Euphorbus 314.

Euphrosyne (G) one of the Charities or Graces.

Euridice see Orpheus.

Euripides 123, 161, 185, 200, 211, 246, 263, 267, 313, 339, 391, 393, 395.

Europa 223–224, 244.

Eurus (G) son of Astraeus and Eos, was the South-east wind.

Euryale 134, 138.

Euryalus 288.

Eurycleia 364.

Eurylochus 357.

Eurynome 25, 51.

Eurystheus 166, 171–184, 199, 380.

Eurytion 182.

Eurytus 167, 186, 195, 365.

Euterpe (G) the Muse of lyric poetry, or of music, represented with a flute.

Evadne 267, 268.

Evander (i) (G) minor Arcadian deity associated with Pan.

(ii) (R) leader of expedition of Arcadian Greeks who were said to have founded Rome before Aeneas arrived in Italy. His father was Hermes, his mother the nymph Carmenta (Themis). The Arcadians settled on the Palatine Hill, whose name according to this myth derives from Pallanteum, the Arcadian city from which the immigrants had come. Evander is sometimes identified with Faunus (q.v.). See also **422.**

Evenus (G) father of Marpessa, who was carried off by Idas. Evenus then drowned himself in the river thenceforth called after him.

Fasti, of Ovid 451.

Fates or **Moerae** or **Moirae** (G) known to the Romans as Parcae, were the white-robed Clotho, Lachesis, and Atropos. Clotho spun the thread, Lachesis measured it, and Atropos cut it with her shears. At Delphi only Clotho and Atropos were worshipped. It has been suggested that the Fates originally represented phases of the moon. See also 25, 94, and cf. Norns, vol. 2: 3.2.149.

Faunus (R) Aborigine leader who welcomed Evander's (q.v.) Arcadians. He was descended from Mars. Sometimes he and Evander were identified. Faunus was the Roman equivalent of Pan (q.v.). It is said that Numa Pompilius trapped him and Picus by mixing wine and honey in their drinking water, and persuading them to tell him their secrets, including a charm against thunderstorms.

Faustulus 436.

Flora (R) early Roman goddess of flowers.

Fortuna (R) counterpart of Tyche (q.v.).

Bronze mirror case showing Zeus in the form of an eagle carrying off Ganymede. British Museum. (*Photo: Mansell Collection.*)

Fortunate Isles 408.

Furies see Eumenides and 3.

Gabii 448.

Gaea see Ge.

Gaia Caecilia see Tanaquil.

Galatea (G) a sea-nymph loved by Polyphemus; but Galatea loved Acis. See also Pygmalion.

Galinthias (G) daughter of Proetus of Thebes and friend of Alcmene.

Ganymede (G) the most beautiful youth alive, was, according to the Homeric account, the son of King Tros and Callirrhoë. He was carried off by the gods to be cupbearer to Zeus, in place of Hebe. Later writers say that Zeus himself, in love with Ganymede, disguised himself as an eagle and carried him off. Zeus sent Tros as compensation a pair of horses. Other traditions do not agree as to Ganymede's parentage.

The myth was very popular in Greece and Rome, as it gave a religious sanction to a man's passion for a youth (see Plato's *Phaedrus*, 79). See also **274, 275.**

Ge or **Gaea**, the Earth 1, 3, 5, 8, 25, 30.

Geryon 182.

Glauce (G) daughter of Creon, King of Corinth, also called Creusa, **162.**

Glaucus (G) (i) King of Corinth, the son of Sisyphus and Merope, and father of Bellerophon, was torn to pieces by his own mares because he scorned the power of Aphrodite.

(ii) grandson of Bellerophon, **311, 322.**

(iii) son of Minos, **231, 232.**

Golden Bough, the **417.**

Gordius, King of Phrygia (G) was originally a peasant. An oracle had informed the people of Phrygia that their new king would appear in a wagon, and when Gordius arrived riding in this way they acclaimed him king. He gratefully dedicated his cart to Zeus in the acropolis of Gordium. The pole was tied to the yoke by a curious knot and an oracle decreed that whoever should untie the knot would rule all Asia. Alexander severed it with his sword.

Gorge (G) daughter of Althaea, who with her sister Deianeira, kept her human form when their other sisters were changed by Artemis to birds. She was wife to Andraemon, mother of Thoas.

Gorgons 134, 136, 138.

Graeae 136.

Gyes or **Gyges** one of Hecatoncheires, 1.

Hades (i) the god, see especially **399–402, 409**, and also 7, 9, 10, 65, 93, 98, 101, 106, 111, 135, 184, 214.
  (ii) the Underworld, 399–409, 417–418.

Silver-gilt disc showing the Greek sun-god Helios. British Museum. (*Photo: Mansell Collection.*)

Roman frieze depicting the labours of Hercules (Heracles). Vatican Museum.
(*Photo: Mansell Collection.*)

Haemon 266.

Halirrhothius 67.

Hamadryads (G) nymphs of trees.

Harmonia 244, 247.

Harmonia, Necklace of 244, 262, 271.

Harmonia, Robe of 269, 271.

Harpy (G) a monster with a woman's head and a bird's wings and claws, used by the gods to torment mortals, 373.

Hebe (G) cup-bearer to the gods till Ganymede replaced her. Her Roman counterpart was Juventas. See also 25, 33, 198.

Hecabe see Hecuba.

Hecale (G) a poor old woman who hospitably entertained Theseus when he was out hunting the Bull of Marathon.

Hecate 403, 409.

Hecatoncheires (G) hundred-handed giants, 1.

Hector 277, 307, 311, 314, 315, 322, 336.

Hecuba 277, 278, 315, 334, 338, 339.

Hecuba of Euripides 339.

Helen 213, 215, 284, 285, 286, 287, 302, 325, 327, 332, 334, 385.

Helenus son of Priam, 277, 325, 346, 413, 419.

Helicaon 335.

Helicon (G) a range of lofty mountains in Boeotia sacred to Apollo and the Muses, hence called Heliconiades and Heliconides. The fountains of the Muses Aganippe and Hippocrene spring from Mt. Helicon. See also 148.

Helios or Helius (G) the Roman Sol, was the son of Hyperion and Theia, and brother of Selene and Eos. In Homer he was god of the sun. All-seeing, he reported such incidents as Aphrodite's faithlessness and the rape of Persephone, but failed to notice the theft of his own sacred cattle by Odysseus' companions. His wife Rhode bore him seven sons and one daughter, and his worship flourished in Rhodes, where the famous Colossus was an image of him. Sacred to Helios was the cock, and his sacrifices included white horses and rams, and honey. See also 79, 105, 111, 182, 231, 357, 360, and Phaethon.

Helle (G) daughter of Athamas and Nephele.

Hellen (G) the son of Deucalion and Pyrrha, was mythical ancestor of all the Hellenes. His sons were Aeolus, who succeeded him, Dorus, and Xuthus.

Hellenes p. 107–108, 22, 40, 94.

Hellespont 156.

Hephaestos 10, 17, 25, 41, 46, 47, 48, 49, 50, 51, 52, 55, 56, 60, 65, 82, 158, 373.

Hera see especially 29–35 and also 7, 10, 13, 14, 24, 25, 26, 48, 50–53, 65, 70, 72, 73, 104, 106, 119–121, 166, 167, 171, 174, 181, 189, 198, 280–281.

Heracleidae or Children of Heracles 199–202.

Heracles see especially 164–202 and also 11, 12, 18, 66, 95, 104, 155, 156, 323.

Heracles or Hercules, Pillars of 182.

Herce (E) Heracles, here a most popular deity, regarded as god of merchants and patron of military raids as well as a cthonic fertility god and water deity.

Hercules (R) the Greek Heracles (q.v.), patron of merchants and soldiers, known as 'The Unconquerable'. The great Roman cult of Hercules was possibly Phoenician in origin and later influenced by the Etruscans, who possibly introduced the Greek rites for his worship. Their introduction was however attributed to Romulus. See also 422.

Hermaphroditus 61.

Hermes see especially 90–98 and also 13, 14, 17, 26, 41, 61, 66, 77, 111, 120, 135, 136, 141, 184, 250, 280, 303, 357, 361, 369, 375, 377, 378.

Herminius, Titius 455–456.

Hermione 287, 345, 346, 398.

Hero see Leander.

Herse (G) daughter of Cecrops, beloved by Hermes. To Herse and her sisters the infant Erichthonius was entrusted.

Hesiod 2, 59.

Hesione 188, 189, 275, 276.

Hesperides 30, 183.

Hesperus (G) the evening star.

Hestia 7, 10, 32, 36, 37, 118, 126.

there was peace throughout the Roman domain his temple was closed—an event which happened for only the third time when Octavian Augustus finally came to power. Janus is sometimes described as an early king of Latium who welcomed Saturn(us) (q.v.) after Jupiter had expelled him from Crete. Janus's wife was Camise; their son Tiberinus gave his name to the River Tiber, in which he was drowned.

Jason 151–163.

Jocasta 253, 257, 258, 259.

Julian Family 445.

Juno (R) see Hera, 29–35 and 414, 415, 416, 420, 425, 427–428, 462–463, 465.

Juno Sororia (R) goddess guardian of pubescent girls.

Jupiter (R) see Zeus, 23–28 and, 415, 425, 427–428.

Juturna (R) daughter of King Daunus of Ardea and sister to Turnus whom she helped in his fight with Aeneas (421–427). At length, compelled to abandon all hope of saving him, she sank weeping into the spring at Lanuvium. Jupiter, who seduced her, made her a water nymph.

Juventas see Hebe.

Kore see Core.

Labdacus 252.

Lachesis one of the Fates.

Lacus Curtius 442.

Ladon 183.

Laelaps (G) the swift dog which Procris gave to Cephalus.

Laertes 290, 363, 365.

Laestrygones 357.

Laius 252, 253, 254, 255, 258.

Lamia (G) daughter of Belus, loved by Zeus. She became one of the Empusae.

Lamus 257.

Laocoön 330, 331.

Laodamia wife of Protesilaus, 303.

Laodice (G) (i) daughter of Priam, 335.
(ii) Homeric name for Electra, daughter of Agamemnon.

Laomedon 274, 275.

Lapithae (G) a mythical people living in Thessaly and governed by Pirithous, who, being a son of Ixion, was half-brother to the Centaurs. Rivalry between the Centaurs and Lapithae reached its climax at the celebrated struggle at the wedding of Pirithous. See also 212.

Lara (R) daughter of Tiber (q.v.), she not only refused to help Jupiter seduce Juturna (q.v.) but hampered him by warning both Juturna and Hera of his

intentions. Jupiter tore out her tongue and sent her to the Underworld in Mercurius's care. He seduced her and she bore the Lares (q.v.).

Larentia see Acca Larentia.

Lares (R) sons of Mercurius by the nymph Lara (q.v.) they were honoured as household gods.

Larissa 142.

Lartius, Spurius 455–456.

Latinus (i) (G) the son of Odysseus and Circe, who, with Agrius his brother ruled the famous Tyrrhenians in the far-off 'sacred isles'.
(ii) (R) King of Laurentum sometimes described as Hercules's son, at others as Faunus's. Early writers now described him as Aeneas's ally, now as among his enemies. See also 420–421, 426.

Lavinia (R) daughter of Evander, sometimes said to have been the wife of Hercules, but more often of Aeneas. See 420, 428.

Lavinium p. 110, 429.

Leander (G) a youth of Abydos, swam across the Hellespont every night to visit Hero, priestess of Aphrodite in Sestos. One night he was drowned, and Hero then flung herself into the sea. Marlowe tells the story in his poem *Hero and Leander*.

Leda (G) the daughter of Thestius and the wife of Tyndareus, King of Sparta. Her children were Helen, Polydeuces, Castor, and Clytemnestra. According to the usual tradition, Zeus visited Leda in the form of a swan, and she laid an egg, from which were hatched Helen, Polydeuces, and Castor, while Clytemnestra was the daughter of Tyndareus. Others say that only Helen and Polydeuces were Zeus's offspring; others, including Homer, that Helen alone was child to Zeus. The rape of Leda is the subject of Yeats's fine poem, *Leda and the Swan*.

Lemnos 47, 52, 56, 156, 301, 323.

Lerna, Hydra of 174, 196.

Lethe 406.

Leto (G) called Latona, was the daughter of the Titans, Coeus and Phoebe, and mother by Zeus of Apollo and Artemis. See also 26, 70, 72, 251.

Leuce 402.

Leucippus (G) son of Oenomaus, was in love with Daphne, and disguised as a woman joined her nymphs. When Apollo advised them to bathe naked, his disguise was discovered and the nymphs tore him to pieces.

Leucothea (G) a sea-goddess, formerly Ino, beloved by Athamas, 362.

Libation Bearers 391.

Lichas 196.

Linus (G) (i) according to the Argive story, Linus was the son of the princess Psamathe by Apollo. Psamathe exposed her son, who was reared by shepherds, but later torn to pieces by her father's dogs. Her distress at this revealed her predicament to her father, who condemned her to death. Apollo, in anger, visited Argos with a plague, until the Argives propitiated Linus and Psamathe by dirges called *linoi*.
(ii) another tradition told of a Linus, son of a Muse, who was gifted in music and killed by jealous Apollo.
(iii) the Thebans also told of Linus the instructor of Heracles, who was killed by the hero with a lyre. See also 167.

The ancient *linoi* dirges were widespread, and they have been described by Frazer in *The Golden Bough*. They are most probably lamentations for Linus as a vegetation spirit, perhaps of flax.

Lipara 56.

Livy p. 112, **439**, 441.

Lotophagi 354.

Lotus Eaters 354.

Loxias 69.

Lua (R) goddess wife of Saturnus (q.v.), Livy refers to her being invoked to destroy enemy arms.

Lucifer (G) 'bringer of light' is the name of the planet Venus when seen before sunrise. The planet was called Hesperus when seen in the evening sky.

Lucretia 450–451.

Lupercalia (R) popular festival of unknown origin held on 15 February. Two teams of aristocratic youths, the *Lupercii*, sacrificed goats and a dog in the Lupercal cave on the Palatine Hill. After a feast, dressed in skins of the sacrificed goats, they raced to the foot of the hill, whipping anyone in their path with thongs of goatskin. This was believed to promote fertility. See also 437.

Lycaon (G) angered Zeus by serving him with human flesh. He and all his sons, save Nyctinus, were either killed by lightning or turned into wolves.

Lycia 47, 68, 146, 147.

Lycius 68, 69.

Lycomedes 216, 295, 326.

Lycurgus, King of Edones 122.

Lycus (G) (i) son of Pandion, expelled by his brother Aegeus, took refuge in Lycia, so called after him.
(ii) of Thebes, 249.

Lynceus (G) (i) son of Aphareus, and devoted twin brother of Idas, was noted for his keen sight. The twins took part in the Calydonian hunt and the Argonauts' expedition, and were

Sculpture from the Parthenon shows Centaur and Lapith fighting. British Museum. (*Photo: Mansell Collection.*)

finally killed in a battle with the Dioscuri.

(ii) son of Aegyptus, see Danaides.

Lystra 93.

Macareus (G) son of Aeolus committed incest with his sister Canace. Their daughter, Issa, was beloved by Apollo.

Macaria 199.

Macedonia 10, 117.

Machaon 324.

Maenads 117, 121, 123, 127.

Maera 338.

Maia (G and R) daughter of Atlas and Pleione, was the eldest and most beautiful of the Pleiades. She bore Hermes to Zeus. She was identified by the Romans with a goddess of spring (see Keats's *Ode to Maia*). See also **26, 91**.

Mamercus (R) legendary founder of the great Aemilian family, who claimed he was the son of Numa Pompilius (q.v.) or possibly even of the Greek philosopher Pythagoras. cf. Pinus and Pompo.

manes (R) generic term for the spirits of the dead, who were believed to linger in or near their tombs and required regular feeding. They were provided with a funeral meal and subsequently fed annually during the Parentalia festival. Neglected, they might grow dangerously restive.

Manto 351.

Marathonian Bull, the Cretan Bull **179, 227**.

Marpessa (G) daughter of Euenus the river-god, was loved by Apollo, but Idas carried her off in a winged chariot which Poseidon had given him. Apollo fought with Idas for the possession of Marpessa until Zeus intervened, saying that Marpessa must choose. She chose to marry Idas.

Mars 64, 435.

Marsyas 77.

Mastarna (E) famous hero whom the Romans later identified with Servius Tullius (q.v.). He and his friend Vibenna are depicted in the wall paintings on the François Tomb at Vulci.

Matralia (R) festival of Mater Matuta, celebrated on 11 April. It involved a servant woman being forced into the temple's sanctuary and then being forcibly ejected, while, for the duration of the ceremonies, women treated their sisters' children as if they were their own. Dumézil suggests that Matuta is a goddess analogous to the Vedic Ushas (vol. 3: 5.3.) and the ritual a symbolic

enactment of driving out the 'bad' night by her sister, dawn. It may also have associations with the driving out of winter by spring.

Medea 158–163, 206.

Medus (G) son of Aegus and Medea, **206**.

Medusa 40, 108, 133, 134, 135, 137, 138, 141, 148.

Megaera (G) one of the Eumenides, 3, 404.

Megapenthes 143.

Megara or **Megera** 170, 185.

Melampus (G) son of Amythaon, was the prophet and seer who first introduced into Greece the worship of Dionysus. Having cured the three daughters of Proetus and other Argive women of madness, he and his brother Bias received from Proetus two-thirds of the kingdom.

Melanippe (G) the child of Aeolus, son of Hellen and Euippe.

Melanippus 265.

Meleager (G) the son of Oeneus and Althaea. When he was seven days old the Fates declared he would die when a certain brand on the hearth should be consumed, but Althaea quickly extinguished the brand and hid it. Meleager accompanied the Argonauts and successfully led the heroes against the Calydonian Boar. When he gave the hide to Atalanta, Althaea's brothers took it from her, and Meleager slew them. Althaea then flung the fateful branch into the fire and Meleager expired. Althaea now killed herself, and her daughters (excepting Gorge and Deianeira) were turned by Artemis into guinea-hens. See also **263**.

Melicertes (G) son of Athamas and Ino.

Melpomene the Muse of tragedy.

Memnon 318, 319, 320.

Memnonia 321.

Memnonides 319.

Menelaus 284, 286, 287, 289, 291, 302, 310, 314, 334, 345, 363, 385.

Menestheus 216.

Menoeceus (G) (i) father of Jocasta, 258. (ii) son of Creon, 264.

Mentor (G) Odysseus' faithful friend, 365.

Mercurius 90.

Mercury see Mercurius.

Meriones 297.

Merope (G) one of the Pleiades, and wife of Sisyphus.

Metaneira wife of Celeus of Eleusis, and mother of Abas, Demophon, and Triptolemus.

Metis 7, 25, 41.

Mezentius, King of Caere (R) an arrogant blasphemer and brutal ruler, exiled from his own city, who allied with Turnus against Aeneas. Aeneas

killed him. A variant story says that, defeated by Ascanius in single combat, he went over to the Trojan side.

Midas (G) the son, or adopted son, of Gordius, King of Phrygia. He kindly entertained Silenus, and when Dionysus asked him what reward he would like, Midas requested that all he touched should be turned to gold. When he was unable to eat, Midas begged to be freed of his golden touch and was told by the god to bathe in the source of the Pactolus, near Mt. Tmolus. The sands of this river then became rich with gold.

Once when Apollo engaged in a musical contest with Pan, Midas declared in favour of Pan and was cursed by revengeful Apollo with a pair of ass's ears. These he hid under a Phrygian cap so that only his barber knew of the disgrace, until the barber, unable any longer to keep the secret, whispered it to a hole in the ground. Then a reed growing in that spot whispered the secret abroad.

Milanion husband of Atalanta.

Miletus 74, 225.

Mimas 11.

Minerva (R) see Athene.

Minoan tradition 6.

Minos 220, 222, 224, 225, 227, 228, 229, 230, 231, 233, 237, 238, 239, 407.

Minotaur 222, 233, 234, 235.

Minthe 402.

Minyans 99, 100, 110, 169.

Mnemosyne (G) 'Memory', daughter of Uranos, 25.

Moerae or **Moirae** see Fates and 25.

Moly 357.

Mopsus 351.

Mulciber see Vulcan.

Musae or **Musagetes** (G) The Muses were divinities presiding over the arts and sciences. They were daughters of Zeus and Mnemosyne, and were born at Pieria near Mt. Olympus. Their worship spread from Thracia and Pieria into Boeotia, where they dwelt on Mt. Helicon, with its sacred fountains of Aganippe and Hippocrene. Mt. Parnassus and its Castalian Spring were also sacred to them. Libations of water or milk and honey were offered to the Muses. Originally three in number, they were afterwards spoken of as nine, Clio of history, Euterpe of lyric poetry, Thalia of comedy, Melpomene of tragedy, Terpsichore of choral dance and song, Erato of erotic poetry and mime, Polymnia, or Polyhymnia, of the sublime hymn, Calliope of epic poetry, and Urania of astronomy.

Mycenaé p. 105, **143, 144, 370, 380, 381, 384, 389, 392, 397**.

Myrmidones 293, 314.
Myrtilus 377, 378.
Mysia 156.

Naiades or **Naiads** (G) the nymphs of
fresh water, 156.
Narcissus see Echo.
Nauplius 350.
Nausicaa 362.
Naxos 13, 124.
Neleus (G) twin brother of Pelias (108,
152, 153). Driven from Iolcus by Pelias,
he went with Melampus and Bias to
Pylus, where he became king. He had
twelve sons. See also 190, 191.
Nemean Lion 173.
Nemean Games 173.
Nemesis (G) said to be a daughter of
Oceanos, a goddess who originally
measured out to men happiness and
misery, chastening those who were
over-fortunate. Later she came to be
thought of as one who punished crime.
She had a shrine at Rhamnus in Attica.
The wheel which she habitually
carried was probably in origin a
symbol of a solar year, according to
whose seasons the sacred king was

fated to rise to the height of his
fortune or to die.
Neoptolemus or **Pyrrhus** 295, 325, 326,
328, 334, 336, 337, 345, 346, 398.
Nephele (G) a phantom created by Zeus
to deceive Ixion, became the wife of
Athamas.
Neptune see Poseidon and 424.
Nereides or **Nereids** (G) daughters of
Nereus, nymphs of the Mediterranean,
109, 139.
Nereus 106.
Nessus 194, 196.
Nestor p. 105, 190, 287, 295, 318, 352, 363.
Niobe 82, 250, 251, 371.
Nisus 230.
Nisyrus 12.
Nomius (G) the Pasturer, a name given
to gods, such as Apollo, Hermes, Pan,
who protect pastures.
Notus (G) called Auster by the Romans,
was the south-west wind. He was a son
of Astraeus and Eos.
Numa Pompilius (R) By tradition
Numa's remarkable piety so impressed
his contemporaries that they invited
him to become Romulus's successor as
king. He taught the Romans their
sacred rituals and instructed them in
the worship of all the gods. He estab-

lished the various ranks of the priesthood, invented a calendar, gave Rome
its sacred shields and the Palladium
(q.v.) as well as the Janus symbol of
peace and war. He entrusted the hearth
of Vesta to the Vestal Virgins so that
the sacred flame might guard the city.
According to Livy he only pretended
all these innovations had been suggested to him by the goddess Egeria
(q.v.) in order to induce the super-
stitious the more easily to accept them;
but according to some stories, possibly
of Etruscan origin, the goddess was his
wife. Numa later came to be regarded
as a disciple of Pythagoras, though
Cato and Cicero scorned this impossible
conjunction. See also Faunus and
p. 110.
Numicius, River 430.
numina (R) spirits of creatures and
plants, and, in men, the breath,
(*numen*, Gk: *pneuma*) spirit of the body
which, on its death, became reincarnate
in plants, etc., unlike the more personal
manes (q.v.).
Numitor, King 435–437.
Nymphae or **Nymphs** (G) were lesser
deities which peopled all parts of
nature.

Frieze on a Roman sarcophagus depicting the Nine Muses. (*Photo: Mansell Collection.*)

Nysa, Mt. **120, 128**.

Oceanides (G) nymphs of the ocean, daughters of Oceanos.

Oceanos 1, 3, 7, 25, 358.

Ocresia (R) mother of Servius Tullius (q.v.) whom according to one tradition, probably of Etruscan origin, she conceived from the household fire, from which the penis of Vulcan rose. See also **432–434**.

Odyssey, The **60, 322, 353–366**.

Odysseus 289, 290, 291, 295, 301, 302, 308, 313, 322, 323, 325, 326, 327, 328, 329, 334, 338, 344, 353–369, 410.

Oebalus (G) King of Sparta and father of Tyndareus, Hippocoon, and Icarius.

Oedipus 252–261.

Oedipus at Colonos **260**.

Oedipus Tyrannus **260**.

Oeneus (G) king of Pleuron and Calydon in Aetolia, married Althaea and was father of Tydeus, Meleager, Gorge and Deianeira. His realm was ravaged by the Calydonian Boar, and was later seized by his nephews, but his grandson Diomedes, son of Tydeus, avenged him and put Gorge's husband

Andraemon on the throne. Oeneus accompanied Diomedes to the Peloponnesus, where he was eventually killed by two nephews who had escaped Diomedes's vengeance. See also **192, 261**.

Oenomaus 376, 377.

Oenone 278, 324.

Ogygia 361.

Oileus (G) king of the Locrians, was one of the Argonauts, **292**.

Olympia 27.

Olympian (G) a name for the Muses and all the gods who were supposed to live on Olympus and not in the lower world. The twelve great Olympian gods in some places worshipped as a body were Zeus, Poseidon, Apollo, Ares, Hermes, Hephaestos, Hestia, Demeter, Hera, Athene, Aphrodite, and Artemis (qq.v.). At a later date Dionysus (q.v.) became one of the great twelve, in place of Hestia.

Olympic Games founded by Heracles, **190, 378**.

Olympus, Mt. **14, 27, 47, 51, 52, 53, 54, 66, 118, 150, 372**.

Omphale 95, 187, 188.

Omphalos 76.

Opheltes (G) the son of King Lycurgus of

Nemea. The Nemean games were founded in his honour, but Heracles re-dedicated them to Zeus.

Ops (R) early goddess of plenty, later identified with Greek Rhea and so sometimes regarded as wife of Saturn(us), but more usually as consort of Consus (q.v.). See also Quirinus.

Orchomenus (G) the capital of the Minyans of Boeotia, **169**.

Orcus 399.

Oreades (G) the nymphs of mountains and grottoes.

Oreithyia (G) daughter of Erectheus, carried away by Boreas.

Oresteia of Aeschylus **388**.

Orestes 346, 389, 390, 392, 393, 395, 396, 398, 404.

Orestes of Euripides **393**.

Origin of the Roman Nation p. 112 and **410**.

Orion (G) a son of Poseidon, was a giant hunter and exceedingly handsome. He fell in love with Merope, the daughter of Oenopion of Chios. Oenopion promised Merope to Orion if he would free the island of wild beasts. When he failed to keep his promise Orion seduced Merope, and was blinded by Oenopion, who was helped by his

213

father Dionysus. An oracle told Orion that he would regain his sight if he travelled east and exposed his eyeballs to the rising sun. He went to Lemnos, where Hephaestos lent him a guide to the East. There Eos fell in love with him, and her brother Helios restored his sight. Orion later joined Artemis as a hunter, boasting that he would kill all wild animals. Apollo, hearing this and fearing that Artemis also might fall in love with Orion, cunningly contrived that the goddess should accidentally kill him. After his death Orion's image was set among the stars, where he appears as a giant with 'belt and sworded hip'. The story of his blindness cured in the East is a myth of the sun, on whose rising the animals retire to their dens.

Orpheus (G) the son of King Oeagrus and Calliope, received a lyre from Apollo and was taught to play by the Muses, so that he was able to enchant beasts, trees, and rocks to follow his music. On returning from his voyage with the Argonauts (155), he married Eurydice, and when she died from a snake bite, he followed her to the underworld. Here his music delighted even Hades, so that he allowed Eurydice to follow her husband back to life, provided only that he did not look round. On the very threshold of life Orpheus anxiously looked back, and so lost Eurydice. He was so desolate with grief that the jealous Thracian women tore him to pieces in an orgy of Dionysus, a god whom he had neglected to honour. The Muses collected the fragments of his body, which were buried at the foot of Olympus, but his head, thrown into the River Hebrus, was carried still singing down to sea and on to Lesbos, whither his lyre also drifted, to be placed later as a constellation in the heavens at the intercession of Apollo and the Muses.

The Greeks considered Orpheus to be the greatest poet before Homer, and fragments of poetry extant were ascribed to him.

The religion 'Orphism' was characterised by a sense of sin and the need for atonement, the idea of a suffering man-god, and a belief in immortality. It had an influence on such philosophers as Pythagoras and Plato, and formed a link between the worship of Dionysus and Christianity.

Orthrus 182, 255.

Palaemon (G) a sea-god, originally Melicertes, son of Athamas and Ino.
Palamedes son of Nauplius, 288, 289, 291, 302, 350.
Palatine Hill p. 111, 423, 438.
Palinurus 417.
Palladium (R) an image of Pallas Athene (Minerva) said to have been brought to Italy by Diomedes after the Trojan War. According to some stories it was given to Aeneas by Diomedes; other accounts suggest it was brought to Rome by Numa Pompilius (q.v.). 325, 327, 330, 341.
Pallas (G) (i) a giant, 11.
(ii) a father of fifty sons, 206.
(iii) a name for Athene, 39, 40.
Pallas (R) 426–427.
Pan (G) the mis-shapen god with goat feet, horns, and tail, was said by some to be an ancient divinity coeval with Zeus, though most reported him to be the son of Hermes. He was the god of shepherds and flocks, living in rural Arcadia, hunting and dancing with the nymphs. He would also lurk in forests, startling travellers with a sudden shout and filling them with 'panic'. Pan loved many nymphs, including Syrinx, who fled in terror and was metamorphosed into a reed, from which Pan made the syrinx (or Pan's pipe) that he was said to have invented, for his love of music was well known. He was also said to have seduced Selene. The Olympians looked down on Pan as a rustic, uncontrolled divinity. He is the only god whose death was reported. The worship of Pan began in Arcadia, which was despised by the Greeks for its backwardness. It did not reach Athens till early in the fifth century B.C. The Romans later identified Pan with Faunus (q.v.). See also 14, 77–97, 369.
Panathenaic 44, 118, 233.
Pandareus 373.
Pandion, King of Athens (G) son of Erichthonius and father of Procne, and Philomela, and of Erechtheus, who succeeded him.
Pandora 17.
Pandrosos (G) daughter of Cecrops. To her and her sisters, Erichthonius was entrusted.

Parentalia (R) important annual festival held 13–14 February in honour of dead parents, whose *manes* (q.v.) were feasted to ensure their continued well-being and placidity. Virgil describes such ceremonies in the *Aenead* Bk. V 49 ff.
Paris 35, 277–282, 284, 287, 310, 321, 324, 410.
Parnassus, Mt. (G) a lofty mountain range north-west of the Gulf of Corinth. The name was usually limited to the two-peaked summit north of Delphi, above which the Castalian spring issued. The mountain was one of the chief seats of Apollo and the Muses, and was also sacred to Dionysus. See also 20, 69, 71.
Parthenon 44, 48, 118.
Parthenopaeus 263, 265.
Parthenos a name of Athene, 39.
Pasiphae 231, 234, 238.
Patroclus 296, 314, 316.
Pax see Irene.
Pegasus 108, 137, 148, 150.
Peirithous (G) the son of Ixion and Dia, was King of the Lapithae in Thessaly. He became a close friend of Theseus. See also 212, 213, 214.
Pelasgians 47. See also Aborigines.
Peleus (G) son of Aeacus, King of Aegina, joined with his brother Telamon in killing their half-brother Phocus. Expelled by Aeacus, he went to Phthia in Thessaly, where he was purified by the king's son Eurytion, but accompanying Eurytion to hunt the Calydonian Boar, he accidentally killed his benefactor. Peleus now fled to Acastus, King of Iolcos, who purified him, but here he was falsely accused by Acastus's wife. Acastus then took Peleus on a hunting expedition on Mt. Pelion, and while his guest was asleep secreted his sword and deserted him. Peleus would have been killed by Centaurs had not Cheiron rescued him. Zeus now decided to give to Peleus the Nereid Thetis as wife. Zeus himself would have married her had he not been warned by Themis that she would bear a son more illustrious than his father. Cheiron told Peleus how to master Thetis by holding her fast whatever form she might assume, and all the divinities save Eris came to the wedding. She in revenge cast in the

Roman mosaic from Palermo shows birds and beasts enchanted by the music of Orpheus's Lyre. National Museum, Palermo. (*Photo: Mansell Collection.*)

Greek bronze mirror cover, fourth century B.C., shows Eros prompting as
Aphrodite gambles with Pan. British Museum. (*Photo: Mansell Collection.*)

golden apple, which caused, eventually, the Trojan War. Thetis bore to Peleus the hero Achilles, whose death he survived. See also **280, 293, 296.**

Pelias (G) **108, 152, 153, 154, 161.**

Pelides (G) the son of Peleus, that is Achilles.

Pelion, Mt. **13.**

Pelopia 382, 383.

Peloponnesus 58, 378.

Pelops 251, 325, 326, 371, 373, 375, 376, 377, 378, 379.

Pelorus one of the Sparti, **243.**

Penates (R) early gods of the family store cupboard (*penus*). Later the two Penates were looked on as the guardians of the nation. Supposed to have been brought by Aeneas from Troy (**411–412**) they were kept in the temple of Vesta (q.v.) and depicted as two seated soldiers armed with spears. Sometimes they were identified with the Dioscuri or Cabiri (qq.v.). See also **429.**

Penelope 290, 363, 365, 368, 369.

Peneus (G) a god of the River Peneus in Thessaly, son of Oceanos and Tethys and father of Daphne and Cyrene.

Penthesilea 317.

Pentheus 123, 246.

Perdix nephew of Daedalus, **237.**

Periclymenus the Argonaut (G) the son of Neleus and brother of Nestor. Though he could assume what shape he chose, he was killed by Heracles.

Periphetes (G) a monster at Epidaurus who used to kill passers-by with an iron club. He was killed by Theseus.

Pero (G) daughter of Neleus and Chloris and wife of Bias.

Perse (G) daughter of Oceanos and wife of Helios, by whom she became the mother of Aeëtes, Circe, Pasiphaë, and Perses.

Persephone 25, 103, 106, 111–115, 214, 373, 402, 403, 409.

Perses (G) son of Helios and Persë and father of Hecate.

Perseus 129–144, 166.

Pesistratus 44, 114, 118.

Petasus 98.

Phaeacians 362.

Phaedra 211.

Phaethon (G) 'the shining', a son of Helios by Clymene. He gained his father's permission to drive the chariot of the sun, but his incompetence provoked Zeus to kill him with a thunderbolt, and he fell into the River Po. His mourning sisters were turned into alder- or poplar-trees, which wept tears of amber. Phaethon's fate may represent the ritual death of the boy interred for the sacred king, who ruled for one day and was then killed, usually by horses.

During the Bronze Age amber, sacred to the king, was carried from Baltic to Mediterranean via the Po valley.

Phalanthus (G) a mythical Spartan said to have founded Tarentum in Italy about 700 B.C.

Phasis, River **157.**

Pherae (G) an ancient town in Thessaly, the home of Admetus.

Pheres (G) son of Cretheus and Tyro, the father of Admetus and Lycurgus and the founder of Pherae in Thessaly.

Philemon (G) an old man of Phrygia who, with his wife Baucis, hospitably received Zeus and Hermes.

Philoctetes 198, 301, 303, 323, 324, 347, 410.

Philoctetes of Sophocles **323.**

Philomela see Tereus.

Phineus (G) the son of Agenor, ruled in Salmydessus in Thrace. He imprisoned his sons by his first wife, Cleopatra, because of a false accusation made by their stepmother, Idaea. For this, or some other fault, he was punished with blindness, and two Harpies tormented him. When the Argonauts reached Thrace, Zetes and Calais, brothers of Cleopatra, killed the Harpies and were also said to have vindicated and freed their nephews, the sons of Phineus. In return, he advised Jason what course to take (**157**). Milton compares himself to Phineus (*Paradise Lost*, Book III, 35–36).

Phlegethon 406.

Phlegeus 271.

Phocis (G) a country in northern Greece, its chief mountain Parnassus and its chief river Cephissus, **390.**

Phocus (G) son of Aeacus, killed by his half-brothers Telamon and Peleus.

Phoebe (G) a name of Artemis as goddess of the moon.

Phoebus 69.

Phoenician Maidens, The **263.**

Phoenix 294, 296, 361.

Pholus (G) a Centaur, **176.**

Phorcys (G) a sea-deity, was, by Ceto, the father of Ladon, Echidne, the three Gorgons, and the three Graeae.

Phoroneus (G) son of Inachus and the nymph Melia, was an early mythical King of Argos.

Phrixus (G) son of Athamas and Nephele.

Phrygia 121.

Phylachus father of Iphiclus.

Phyleus son of Augeias, **177.**

Phyllis beloved of Demophon, **349.**

Picus (R) a god famous for his amorous adventures and penchant for shape-changing. See also Faunus.

Pieria (G) on the south-east coast of Macedonia, was inhabited by Thracian

people, who in early times worshipped the Muses, hence called Pierides. See also **92.**

Pierides (G) (i) The Muses.

(ii) the nine daughters of Pierus, a king in Macedonia, named after the Muses. They were conquered in a contest with the Muses and turned into birds.

Pinus (R) legendary founder of the Pinarian family, said to have been a son of Numa Pompilius. Cf. Mamercus and Pompo.

Pirene 148.

Pisa, in Elis **376, 377.**

Pittheus, King of Troezen son to Pelops and father of Aethra, **203.**

Pleiades (G) daughters of Atlas and Pleione were companions of Artemis (q.v.). They were changed into doves and placed among the stars.

Pleione mother by Atlas of the Pleiades.

Pleisthenes 381.

Pluto (G) (i) a name for Hades, **399.**

(ii) the nymph, **371.**

Podalirius 324.

Podarces (G) (i) original name of Priam, **275.**

(ii) son of Iphiclus, who led the Thessalians against Troy.

Poeas 301.

Polites 334.

Pollux see Polydeuces and the Dioscuri.

Polybus 253.

Polybutes 11, 12.

Polydectes 132, 133, 141.

Polydeuces (G) one of Dioscuri, **155, 157, 215, 285, 286.**

Polydorus (G) (i) son of Cadmus and Harmonia, **244, 252.**

(ii) son of Priam, **338.**

Polyeidus 232.

Polymester 338.

Polymnia or **Polyhymnia** (G) the Muse of the sublime hymn.

Polyneices 257, 261, 262, 263, 265, 266, 269.

Polypemon see Procrustes and **205.**

Polyphemus 355.

Polyxena 309, 337, 339.

Pomona (R) goddess of fruit and its cultivation. Vertumnus (the shape-changer) fell in love with her. Rejected, he changed himself into an old woman and pleaded his cause so eloquently that Pomona changed her mind. See p. 109.

Pompo (R) brother of Mamercus and Pinus. The legendary founder of the great Pomponian family, he was regarded as the son of Numa Pompilius (q.v.).

Pons Sublicius 454–456.

Pontus 1.

Poplicola, Publius Valerius **450.**

Porphyrion 11.

217

Porsenna (Porsena), Lars, of Clusium 454, 457–459.

Poseidon see especially **99–109** and also 7, 9, 10, 13, 32, 36, 42, 44, 60, 67, 73, 110, 134, 137, 139, 140, 152, 157, 211, 223, 227, 305, 330, 348, 362, 366, 377.

Postumius, Aulus (R) It was said that after Lars Porsenna had made peace with Rome (**459**), either Tarquinius Superbus or his son Sextus Tarquinius (qq.v.) allied with the Latins and again attacked Rome. Diodorus describes how they were defeated at the legendary Battle of Lake Regillus when the Romans, led by Aulus Postumius were helped by the Dioscuri (q.v.). To celebrate the victory Postumius founded the temple of Castor and Pollux in the Forum in honour of the Dioscuri. He is also said to have built the temple of Ceres.

Praxitiles 63.

Priam 275, 276, 277, 282, 302, 309, 315, 316, 318, 327, 330, 331, 334, 336, 338.

Priapus (G) son of Dionysus and Aphrodite, a god of fruitfulness.

Procne see Tereus.

Procris (G) daughter of the second Erectheus to be King of Athens. She married Cephalus. See also **229**.

Procrustes (G) the 'Stretcher', the surname given to the robber Poly- pemon. He used to tie travellers to a bed, and if they were too short he would rack them, and if too tall, he would hack off their legs. He was served in the same way by Theseus. See also **205**.

Proetus (G) son of Abas, King of Argolis, inherited the kingdom jointly with his twin brother Acrisius. Soon expelled, he fled to Iobates, King of Lydia, whose daughter Anteia, also called Stheneboea, he married. Returning to Argolis, he forced his brother to divide the king- dom and became ruler of Tiryns, whose massive walls he built by aid of the Cyclopes. See also Melampus, Bellerophon.

Prometheus 16–20, 41, 176, 183.

Protesilaus 303.

Proteus (G) the prophetic old man of the sea, subject to Poseidon, whose flocks of seals he tended. By assuming any shape he chose, he could avoid the need of prophesying, unless gripped fast, when he would at last resume his usual shape and tell the truth. He could be found at midday in the island of Pharos. See also **183, 345**.

Psamathe see Linus (i).

Psyche (G) appears in late Greek literature as a personification of the soul, purified by suffering to enjoy true love. The beauty of the maiden

Psyche excited the envy of Aphrodite who sent Eros to persecute her, but he fell in love with her and secretly visited her nightly. When Psyche, urged by her two sisters, sought to discover his identity, he left her. Searching for Eros, she endured further persecution, but he secretly helped her, and she finally overcame Aphrodite's hatred, to become immortal and united with Eros for ever. The story is told in *The Golden Ass* of Apuleius.

Pygmalion (i) (G) King of Cyprus. According to Ovid he had a lifelike statue of a woman made for him from ivory because no living woman met his ideal. He fell in love with the image and taking pity on him Aphrodite brought it to life. Pygmalion married the woman who bore him a daughter Paphos or Metharme. The name Galatea, some- times given to Pygmalion's wife, is not found in classical authors. The myth forms the basis of Shaw's amusing *Pygmalion* and is also recounted by William Morris in *Earthly Paradise*. Possibly its origins lie in a cult of Aphrodite (q.v.) in which a priest guarded her image at Paphos and obtained power from his association with it.

(ii) (R) King of Tyre. He murdered his sister Dido's husband, Sychaeus or Sicharbus, his own uncle, and so obtained sole rule of the city. Dido fled and founded Carthage (414– 418).

Pylades 390, 392, 396, 397, 398.

Pylos 92.

Pyramus and Thisbe (G ?) Immortalised in the 'rude mechanicals'' play in *A Midsummer Night's Dream,* the story of Pyramus and Thisbe appears in Ovid's *Metamorphoses*. Its origin is unknown and it may have been invented to explain the names of the two adjacent rivers, Pyramus and Thisbe, in Cicilia, Asia Minor. Pyramus and Thisbe lived in Babylon where their parents were neighbours. The young couple fell in love and forbidden to associate whis- pered to each other through a hole in the garden wall. They decided on an assignation at Ninnus's tomb outside the city. Thisbe arrived first but was frightened by a lioness and ran to hide, dropping her veil, which the creature mauled. Finding this, Pyramus, imagining Thisbe to have been killed, stabbed himself and fell dying beneath a mulberry tree, whose fruit, hitherto pure white, was stained with his blood. Thisbe returning, found his body, took his sword and stabbed herself also.

Their parents buried their ashes in a single urn.

Pyrrha 20, 21.

Pyrrhus see Neoptolemus.

Pythia 76, 118, 171.

Pythian or **Pythius** 69.

Python 71, 76.

Quirinus (R) Dumézil believes Quirinus to have been an ancient Roman god representing the third 'function' of the Indo-European triad (see vol. 3: 5.1.). Ops, who is sometimes associated with him, is also an image of this function and together their rôles resemble those of the Vedic Ashvins (vol. 3: 5.3.). Before the beginning of the historical period, Quirinus had become an obscure deity regarded as an aspect of Mars (q.v.), possibly a development arising from the fact that the farming *quirites* class, with whom he was associated, could quickly become *milites* when the need arose. Romulus, who, with Remus, was first a youthful shepherd also began as a third function figure, hence his association with Quirinus and Mars. Some scholars regard Quirinus as originating in a Sabine deity later adopted by the Romans.

Regillus, Battle of Lake. See Postumius Aulus.

Remus 431–439.

Rhadamanthus 224, 225, 226, 407.

Rhea 1, 5, 6, 7, 30, 101, 111, 122, 373.

Rhea Silvia 435.

Rhesus 313.

Rhesus, attributed to Euripides 313.

Rhode or **Rhodos** (G) said to be the daughter of Poseidon. She was the wife of Helios.

Romulus p. 110, 431–445.

Romulus of Plutarch 431.

Ruminalis fig tree 436.

Sabine women, the rape of the p. 110, **440**.

Salmoneus (G) son of Aeolus and brother of Sisyphus, emigrated from Thessaly and built Salmone. In his presumption he emulated Zeus, who destroyed him and his city with a thunderbolt.

Samos 30, 34.

Sarpedon 224, 225, 307, 311, 314.

Saturn(us) (R) ancient Italian god later identified with Greek Cronos (q.v.) but believed to have been an early king of Latium, to which he fled for refuge from Jupiter. His festival, the Saturnalia, was celebrated in December. His wife was Lua, although he was later associated with Ops (q.v.).

Satyrs (G) beings who embodied the fertile power of nature. They were

Statue of the Roman goddess Pomona. Uffizi, Florence. (*Photo: Mansell Collection.*)

Roman terracotta from Cerveteri, second century A.D., shows Maenad and Satyr in a Bacchic dance. British Museum. (*Photo: Michael Holford.*)

represented as men wearing skins and crowned with vine, fir, or ivy, with pointed ears, small horns, and a tail. They were said to be sons of Hermes, and were always connected with the worship of Dionysus. Older Satyrs were called Sileni. See also **121, 127**.

Scaean Gate 321.

Scaevola, Gaius Mucius **457–460.**

Scamander, River **274, 313, 317.**

Scheria 362.

Sciron (G) a robber living on the frontier between Megaris and Attica. He robbed travellers and compelled them to wash his feet on the Scironian rock. He then kicked them into the sea, where a giant turtle devoured them. He was killed by Theseus. See also **205**.

Scylla and Charybdis (G) two rocks between Italy and Sicily. In one dwelt Scylla, a fearful monster with six barking heads and twelve feet. Under the opposite rock lived Charybdis, who thrice daily swallowed and then regurgitated the waters of the sea. See *Odyssey* XI, 11.85–110, and also **108, 359**.

Scylla daughter of Nisus, **230**.

Scyros 216, 295, 326.

Selene 84, 89.

Semele 26, 119, 126, 244.

Semiramis (G) with her husband Ninus, mythical founder of Ninus or Nineveh.

Seriphos 132, 141, 142.

Servius Tullius (R) legendary king, fifth successor of Romulus. His conception, birth and childhood were marked by supernatural portents. Brought up as a slave in the household of Tarquinius Priscus (q.v.) his succession to the throne was engineered by Tanaquil (q.v.) after her husband's assassination. He built the first wall round Rome and established the cult of Diana on the Aventine Hill, as well as making important constitutional reforms. Servius's mother was Ocresia (q.v.). According to the Emperor Claudius he was originally an Etruscan hero known as the Mastarna (q.v.) and the Etruscans believed him to have been a companion of Caeles Vivenna (Vibenna) (q.v.). See also **447**.

Sibyl, the **413, 417.**

Sicily 56, 112, 414.

Sicyon 118, 382, 383.

Sileni see Satyrs.

Silenus (G) one of the Sileni who brought up Dionysus and was his constant companion. He was a jovial, bald old man usually drunk and riding on an ass. He had the power of prophecy. See also **121**.

Silvius (R) first king of Alba Longa, son or half-brother of its founder Ascanius (q.v.).

Sinis or **Sinnis** (G) a robber living on the Isthmus of Corinth, where he killed travellers by tying them to the top of a fir tree which he tied to the earth and then allowed to spring upright. He was killed in the same way by Theseus. See also **205**.

Sinon (G) **329, 330, 333.**

Sirens (G) sea-nymphs who could allure by their songs all who heard them. When the Argonauts sailed past, Orpheus surpassed them, and Odysseus contrived to hear them unscathed.

Sirius (G) the dog-star.

Sisyphus (G) son of Aeolus, married Merope the Pleiad, who bore him Glaucus. He seduced Anticleia, daughter of Autolycus, and mother of Odysseus, and some said that Sisyphus was really the father to Odysseus. He founded Ephyra, later Corinth, and though he promoted navigation, was a notorious knave (see *Iliad* VI, 153). In the Underworld he was condemned always to roll uphill a huge stone which always toppled back again.

Smintheus a name of Apollo.

Sol see Helios.

Sophocles 197, 259, 260, 266, 322, 323, 391.

Sparta 45, 64, 86, 282, 284, 285, 286, 385.

Sparti or 'Sown Men' 243, 258.

Sphinx 255, 256, 257.

Stentor (G) herald of the Greeks in the Trojan War. His voice was as loud as that of fifty men.

Steropes 1.

Stheneboea also called Anteia, 146.

Sthenelus (G) (i) son of Perseus and Andromeda, and King of Mycenae. His wife Nicippe bore him Alcinoe, Medusa and Eurystheus.

(ii) son of Capaneus and Evadne, 268, 288, 328.

Stheno 134, 138.

Strophius 390.

Stymphalian Birds 178.

Styx 184, 294, 405, 406.

Suppliants, The 267.

Sychaeus 415.

Symplegades 157.

Syrinx see Pan.

Tages (E) sage who is said to have risen from a furrow. His head was grey, but his face that of a child. He revealed to the Etruscans all the arts of divination.

Talaus 261.

Talos (G) (i) Cretan giant, 228.

(ii) nephew of Daedalus, 237.

Tanaquil (R) wife of Tarquinius Priscus (q.v.) and sometimes known as Gaia Caecilia, under which name she is depicted as the traditional domesticated Roman matron, but according to most stories she was a vigorous and domineering woman who engineered her husband's accession to the throne and later arranged for her protégé Servius Tullius to become his heir.

Tantalus 251, 371, 372, 373, 374, 375.

Taphians 165.

Tarchetius, King of Alba Longa 432–434.

Tarchon (R) Etruscan ally of Aeneas in his fight with Turnus (421–427).

Tarquinii p. 111. See also Tarquinians.

Tarquinians, the (Tarquinii) 448–456.

Tarquinius, Arruns 447, 453.

Tarquinius Priscus (R) legendary King of Rome, fourth successor to Romulus. Originally an Etruscan named Lucumo, he later took the name of Lucius Tarquinius Priscus. According to some his father had been a Greek refugee from Corinth named Demaratus. Tarquinius Priscus began the building of the Capitoline temple to Jupiter,

Juno and Minerva, later said to have been completed by Tarquinius Superbus. He was assassinated by the sons of Ancus Marcius (q.v.).

Tarquinius, Sextus 448, 450.

Tarquinius Superbus 446–453.

Tartarus 4, 8, 9, 13, 14, 184, 400.

Tatius, Titus, King of the Sabines 441–444.

Tauris 86, 300, 395, 396.

Tecmessa 306.

Teiresias or **Tiresias** (G) 258, 259, 264, 270, 358, 360, 366. See Tennyson's poem *Tiresias*.

Telamon (G) son of Aeacus, King of Aegina, joined with his brother Peleus in killing their half-brother Phocus and, expelled by his father, he went to Salamis, where he married Glauce, daughter of the king, whom he succeeded. Telamon later married Periboea of Athens, who bore him Great Ajax. He joined in hunting the Calydonian Boar, and some say that he sailed with the Argonauts. See also 188, 189, 275, 276.

Telchines, The (G) variously described. It is said that Rhea entrusted the infant Poseidon to them and that they were artists in metal, making the sickle of Cronos and Poseidon's trident. But they were also said to be destructive beings, interfering with the weather and earning the hostility of Apollo, who assumed a wolf's form to destroy some of them, and of Zeus, who overwhelmed others by flood.

Telegonus 368.

Telemachus 291, 363, 364, 365, 368.

Telephassa 223, 240.

Telephus (G) son of Heracles and Auge the priestess, daughter of Aleus, King of Tegea. He was abandoned as a child, but on reaching manhood questioned the Delphic oracle as to his parentage. He was told to sail to King Teuthras in Mysia, and there found his mother married to the king. He succeeded Teuthras and was said to have married Priam's daughter Laodice. He tried to prevent the Greeks on their way to Troy from landing in Mysia. See also 299.

Telephylos 357.

Tempe (G) a beautiful valley in Thessaly watered by the River Peneus. Apollo here pursued Daphne, daughter of the river-god Peneus. He had also purified himself here after killing the Python.

Tenedos 301, 302, 329.

Tenes (G) son of Apollo, was reputedly the son of Cycnus, King of Colonae in Troas. His stepmother, failing to seduce him, falsely accused him to Cycnus, who put Tenes, with his sister

Hemithea, into a chest and threw it into the sea. The chest was driven to the island Leucophrys, whose inhabitants made Tenes king. The island was then called Tenedos. Cycnus, discovering his error, sailed to Tenedos and was reconciled with his son. When the Greeks landed on Tenedos on their way to Troy, Achilles killed both Tenes and Cycnus.

Terateus 434.

Tereus (G) a son of Ares, was King of the Thracians and lived in Phocian Daulis. He helped Pandion, King of Athens, and was therefore given Pandion's daughter Procne in marriage. She bore him a son, Itys. But Tereus was in love with Procne's sister, Philomela, and hiding Procne among the slaves, he told Philomela that her sister was dead, and so seduced her. He also tore out Procne's tongue, but Procne wove a message for her sister in a robe. Philomela then released Procne, who, to avenge herself on her husband, killed and cooked their son Itys for Tereus to eat. When he realised what he had been eating, he pursued the sisters with an axe, but the gods changed all three into birds, Procne to a swallow, Philomela to a nightingale, and Tereus either to a hoopoe or hawk. Some say that Tereus tore out Philomela's tongue, that he told Procne that Philomela was dead, and that Procne became the nightingale, Philomela the swallow.

Terpsichore (G) the Muse of choral dance and song, carries the lyre and plectrum.

Tethys 1, 25, 432.

Teucer (G) (i) son of Scamander, 274.

(ii) son of Telamon, 189, 292.

Teucri 274.

Teuthras (G) King of Mysia, he married Auge and was succeeded by Telephus, son of Auge by Heracles. See also 306.

Thalia (G) (i) one of the nine Muses, and in later time the Muse of comedy, appearing with a comic mask, a shepherd's staff, or a wreath of ivy.

(ii) one of the three Charities or Graces.

Theano 340.

Thebe 250.

Thebes 240–271.

Thebes, Seven against of Aeschylus 263.

Themis 1, 21, 25.

Theogony of Hesiod p. 108 and 2.

Thersander 269.

Thersites 317.

Theseus 203–218, 260, 267.

Thesmophoria 114.

Thespius 168, 192.

Thessaly 8, 10, 117.

PART 4

Bibliography

AESCHYLUS *Plays,* translated by G. M. Cookson. J. M. Dent & Sons. 1906/56.

*ANDREWES, A. *The Greeks.* Hutchinson. 1962.

APOLONIUS OF RHODES *The Voyage of the Argo,* translated by E. V. Rieu. Penguin Books.

APULEIUS *The Golden Ass,* translated by Robert Graves. Penguin Books. 1950/60.

BARROW, R. H. *The Romans.* Penguin Books. 1949.

*BLAKENEY, E. H. (ed.) *A Smaller Classical Dictionary.* J. M. Dent & Sons. rev. corrected ed. 1931.

CICERO *The Nature of the Gods,* translated by Horace C. P. McGregor. Penguin Books. 1972.

COTTRELL, LEONARD *The Bull of Minos.* Pan Books. 1955.

DUMÉZIL, GEORGES *L'héritage indo-européen à Rome.* Paris: Gallimard. 1949.

—— *L'Idéologie des trois fonctions dans quelques crises de l'histoire romaine. Latomus* 17, 429–446. 1958.

EURIPIDES *Alcestis* and other plays, translated by P. Vellacott. Penguin Books. 1953.

—— *Bacchae* and other plays, translated by P. Vellacott. Penguin Books.

*FERGUSON, JOHN *The Religions of the Roman Empire.* Thames and Hudson. 1970.

FINLEY, M. I. *The World of Odysseus.* Penguin Books. 1962.

*GRANT, MICHAEL *Myths of the Greeks and Romans.* Weidenfeld & Nicolson. 1962.

*—— *Roman Myths.* Weidenfeld & Nicolson. 1971.

*GRANT, MICHAEL and HAZEL, JOHN *Who's Who in Classical Mythology.* Weidenfeld & Nicolson. 1973.

GRAVES, ROBERT *The Greek Myths.* Penguin Books. 2 vols. 1955.

HOMER *The Iliad,* translated by E. V. Rieu. Penguin Books. 1950/58.

—— *The Odyssey,* translated by E. V. Rieu. Penguin Books. 1946/59.

*HUTCHINSON, R. W. *Prehistoric Crete.* Penguin Books. 1962/65.

KERENYI, C. *The Gods of the Greeks.* Thames & Hudson. 1951.

—— *The Heroes of the Greeks.* Thames & Hudson. 1959.

KITTO, H. D. F. *The Greeks.* Penguin Books. rev. ed. 1957.

LLOYD-JONES, J. *The Greeks.* Watts. 1962.

LIVY *The Early History of Rome.* Books I–V of 'The History . . .' translated by Aubrey de Selincourt. Penguin Books. 1960/73.

—— *The War with Hannibal.* Books XXI–XXX of 'The History . . .' translated by Aubrey de Selincourt. Penguin Books. 1965.

LUCAS, F. L. *Greek Drama for Everyman.* J. M. Dent & Sons. 1954.

OGILVIE, R. M. *The Romans and their Gods.* Chatto & Windus. 1969.

OVID *Metamorphoses,* translated by Mary M. Innes. Penguin Books. 1955/71.

*PALLOTTINO, M. *The Etruscans.* Penguin Books. 1955.

PLUTARCH *The Fall of the Roman Republic. Six Lives by Plutarch,* translated by Rex Warner. Penguin Books. rev. ed. 1972.

*ROSE, H. J. *Ancient Roman Religion.* Hutchinson. 1958.

*—— *The Handbook of Greek Mythology.* Methuen. 6th ed. 1958.

SENECA *Four Tragedies and Octavia,* translated by E. F. Watling. Penguin Books. 1966.

SMITH, WILLIAM *Dr. Smith's Classical Dictionary.* John Murray.

SOPHOCLES *Electra* and other plays, translated by E. F. Watling. Penguin Books. 1953/61.

—— *The Theban Plays,* translated by E. F. Watling. Penguin Books. 1947/61.

Two Satyr Plays: Euripides: 'Cyclops', Sophocles: 'Ichneutai', translated by Richard Lancelyn Green. Penguin Books. 1957.

*Books with useful detailed bibliographies.